1/92

OTA
THE PYGMY IN THE ZOO

OTA

THE PYGMY IN THE ZOO

Phillips Verner Bradford &
Harvey Blume

St. Martin's Press
New York

Design by DAWN NILES

Library of Congress Cataloging-in-Publication Data

Bradford, Phillips Verner.
   Ota Benga : the pygmy in the zoo / Phillips Verner Bradford and
Harvey Blume.
     p.   cm.
   ISBN 0-312-08276-2
   1. Benga, Ota. 2. Benga, Ota—Captivity. 3. Pygmies—Zaire—
Biography. 4. Pygmies—United States—Biography. 5. Pygmies—
Zaire—Crimes against. 6. United States—Social life and
customs—20th century. I. Blume, Harvey. II. Title.
DT650.P94B72   1992
967.51'02'092—dc20
[B]   92-22296
                                                    CIP

First Edition: September 1992
10 9 8 7 6 5 4 3 2 1

Some of these men have been talking much to me about savage and civilized man. They say my people savage, but they civilized man. Now, I want to know what is civilized man they so much talk about? . . . If I go back to my people in Africa and do like them will my people think civilized man is good? No; they would run me out of the town. So I say these men, "You stop talking about civilized man and savage before you be civilized."

from "What Is a Civilized Man?"
a speech by Prince Kassongo in 1902
at the Stillman Institute in Alabama.

Dedicated to the memory
of Ota Benga

CONTENTS

ACKNOWLEDGMENTS

The authors would like to thank our agent, Nancy Trichter, for letting the story the book tells—as well as the story of the book—enter so deeply into her life. We thank James Fitzgerald, our editor at St. Martin's Press, for energy and patience in helping to shape the final product. Thanks also to Alex Kuczynski of St. Martin's for her able assistance.

Enid Schildkrout of the American Museum of Natural History (AMNH) guided us through the relevant archives and resources of the great museum and proved, in many ways, a good friend to our project. It may well be there is no greater benefit to researchers than the services of a knowledgeable and sympathetic librarian: It was, in any case, our good fortune to discover Barbara Mathe at the AMNH. Steven P. Johnson opened the archives of the New York Zoological Society to us and gave generously his time and knowledge. Kathleen Boldt helped us access the Bronx Zoo's photographic library.

We wish to acknowledge the help and cooperation of James

Croker, Mary Jo Arnoldi, and Paula Fleming of the Smithsonian Institution; Claire Lamers of the Brooklyn Historical Society; Sarah Hickson of the Jones Memorial Library in Lynchburg, Virginia; Herb Hartsook and Dr. Stokes of the South Caroliniana Library at the University of South Carolina; Martha Clevenger and Kirsten Hammerstrom of the Missouri Historical Society; Mary Lou Hultgren of the Hampton University Museum and Fritz Malval of the Hampton University Archive, Hampton, Virginia.

Recollections of Samuel Phillips Verner shared with us by numerous relatives afforded privileged insight into his character. Verner's niece, Mary Schlaefer and her husband, Dr. Ed Schlaefer, were gracious hosts on our visit to Columbia, South Carolina, where we were joined by Elizabeth "Betty" (Verner) Hamilton and her husband, John Hamilton. The discussion about Verner—hero or black sheep, noted explorer or impractical dreamer, scientist or sinner, depending on one's point of view—had already begun that January evening when we arrived. Our book benefited.

Another of Verner's nieces, Mary Wade (together with her daughter, Ellen, and son, Jerry) entertained us with similar graciousness in St. Louis on several occasions; perspectives on S.P. Verner gleaned from those evenings are likewise included here. Verner's great nephews, David E. James and Phillips "Flip" Jennings, and Verner's great niece, Caroline Claiborne, volunteered time and memory as well.

The late Mrs. Laura Battle (Verner) Bradford was the youngest and last surviving of Verner's four children. As the mother of author Phillips Verner Bradford, she is missed in ways that will not be addressed here; at the same time, as authors, we must acknowledge how much we benefited from her charm, geniality and recollections. Laura's oldest sister, the late Mary (Verner) Allston, demands special recognition of another kind: It was she who scrupulously saved masses of her father's letters, compositions, and memorabilia from the fire. Without her efforts there would have been no Verner collection at the University of South Carolina, and quite possible, no book.

Mary Allston's daughter, Beatrice (Allston Bedford) Ware, and granddaughter, Martha Elizabeth "Lisa" Bedford, have taken interest in this work throughout. Sherrill (Brumfield) Verner, widow of Verner's only son, John, and a longtime resident of Brevard, North Carolina, shared personal memories and described local traditions concerning her father-in-law. Judy Wyer, one of Verner's granddaughters, recalled his character through poetry. All in all some seventeen relatives and in-laws have made notable contributions to the portrait of S. P. Verner that emerges in our book.

We have also benefited from conversations with two longtime students of Verner's African career, Dr. Gordon Gibson (Curator Emeritus of Ethnology of the National Museum of Natural History at the Smithsonian Institution) and Dr. Jack Crawford (Professor of History at Montreat College, Montreat, North Carolina). We wish to thank them for their observations and for availing us of unpublished manuscrips. Similar thanks to Joan Harris for providing us with her unpublished work.

As children, Chauncy Spencer and Hunter Hayes were among Ota Benga's companions. Their memories were indispensable in releasing Ota from obscurity and helped set this book in motion.

Francis X. Stephens introduced us to descendants of Thomas Fortune Ryan, one of the men decisive to Verner's African career. In addition, Frank provided translations of several pertinent French documents, as did Claire Schub.

Drs. Frances and Floyd Horowitz of the University of Kansas, and their son, Dr. Benjamin Horowitz, put us in contact with Nkonko Kamwangalu who provided us with English versions of the letters Verner wrote to Ota Benga in transliterated Tschiluba.

Phillips Verner Bradford would like to thank his energetic wife, Camille, for her consideration and support for time devoted to this project. His sons Phillip and Anthony also are recognized for their attention and patience.

Harvey Blume would like to acknowledge the many friends who listened, encouraged and conversed as the story revealed itself chapter by chapter, level by level, chamber by chamber. Special thanks to Ted Kaptchuk whose support was constant, enthusiastic, timely. And thanks to my daughter Ariel into whose life story the story of Ota Benga has been wound these last four year.

PREFACE

He asked me to remember just one thing: that no one, including me, gets to choose their parents. I was too young then to know what he meant, and it took me a long time to figure it out.

I remember meeting my namesake grandfather, Samuel Phillips Verner, only once, when I was barely three years old. My parents brought me up in Baltimore and our family took the Pullman on the Southern Railway to Asheville for a visit to my grandparents in Brevard in the summer of 1943. Shortly after we arrived, my mother placed me beside him, her father, where he gently held my hand as he rocked slowly back and forth in his rocking chair on the front porch.

He muttered about stale tobacco as he stuffed his musty old pipe in his pocket and drew me closer to look me over and tell me a story by which I might remember him. I did sense his approval of me and his glance of appreciation to my mother that she named me after him. My mother may have been apprehensive about what he might say to me, for he was known to say some strange things now and then. However, she knew that this might be our last meeting, for his heart was fluttering from the ravages of a lifelong struggle with malaria, so she let us have some private time together.

My mother was his youngest child, born in 1912 in Bas Obispo in the Panama Canal Zone but raised in the mountains of the western Carolinas. Like many others in her family, she excelled in school and was the valedictorian of her high school class. Later she went north to Washington, D.C., to earn her R.N. degree. My grandfather told me that I had the best mother that any young man could ever want.

My father was there, too, and my grandfather asked him about things like radar and microwaves. A Radio Engineer, my father knew all about these things and believed they would help us win the war. In my grandfather's eyes, my father was one of those ingenious (damn) Yankees who could take apart his car and put it back together again without any help.

As I grew up, I wondered about what my grandfather meant when he said nobody could choose their parents. Was he apologizing for his faults that I might inherit, or a name that would be cumbersome? Was he asking me to forgive others, less fortunate than I, in the circumstances of their birth? Or was it a way of guarding me against others' expectations of me—that I should assume his views or that his would be identified as mine? Perhaps it was a reminder that I was bonded to him, whether I liked it or not. I wondered if there might be some terrible deep secret about him that would come to embarrass me in later years.

Soon after I learned to read, I found his book, *Pioneering in Central Africa*, which was filled with hair-raising true adventure stories featuring the fabulous African king, Ndombe, with his noble black warriors who vanquished evil slave traders and stood up against the dreaded Force Publique. He included a picture of a big pile of human bones that were alleged to be the remains of a cannibal meal. He visited markets where humans were offered up as meat. He was the prey of leopards, dodged poison arrows, and he fell into a game-pit and felt the injury for his entire life. Death was at his doorstep on every page. While white-water canoeing down the Kasai, he lost his rear canoe to hideous river netmen who captured his crewmen and dismembered them, scattering them through the forest. He brought "ex-cannibals" into New York City and lost them for a while, and he was one of the first white men ever to live for an extended period among a tribe of African pygmies.

My father had the first television set on our block in Baltimore in 1947. He made it himself from spare parts. It had a little round green tube, and the whole neighborhood came over to see National Brand Beer bottles dancing across its screen. They were buzzing with excitement as they all knew that the world was about to be changed forever. Even with the allure of the mighty tube to distract me, I read on about my grandfather Verner and his life with the pygmies, his meetings with kings, cardinals, and clowns over four continents, and wondered how I could have ever come to exist after all his hair-breadth brushes with death.

There were more and more questions about my grandfather as I grew older. He dedicated his book to one now in the "Choir Invisible." He often wrote of the "silent whisper" that guides us all. Had he been hearing things? My mother and my cousins discreetly told me of certain mentally insecure relatives in the extended family. There had been many suicides in past generations, and, were it not for modern medications, some of my relatives in current generations might also be at risk to themselves. Does this explain what he meant by not being able to choose my parents?

Upon enrolling in college as a resident undergraduate at the Johns Hopkins University, I became more aware of a certain complex that my mother seemed to bear about her genetic heritage. Her ancestral lines include many revolutionary war heroes, prominent leaders and well-connected and well-educated men and women in the deep South. My grandfather used to joke that the Hapsburgs of Europe were but a minor branch of the Verner family.

I learned then of the pressure on my grandfather Verner. He was his mother's oldest son, and greatness was expected of him. His mother was a Phillips, whose family name is emblazoned upon the University of North Carolina at Chapel Hill back to its very foundation. His father was a prominent attorney who played a major role in Reconstruction as a leader of the White Supremacy Party, which redeemed [sic] the government of South Carolina. The 1,200-acre plantation on which he was born was torn up by the War of the Rebellion and his family had to settle for a great deal less. He was expected to bring it all back, and do it without slaves. Family history demanded him to be a success, for the sake of his native state and nation. I'm sure he felt he couldn't choose his parents either and wanted me to know that from a very early age.

As I advanced through my academic life, I felt as if my grandfather was watching me at every step. While I couldn't choose him to be my grandfather, I wondered if he chose me to be his grandson.

Perhaps I felt chosen to pursue a doctorate that he always felt he should have had. When I received my Doctorate in Engineering Science at Columbia University amid the Vietnam-related student protests of 1968, I was keenly aware that he was once within a gnat's hair of being in both scenes. But for his financial needs he would have pursued his doctorate at Columbia in Ethnology as he was so invited, and but for his commercial desires he would have been with another famous protest group, concerned with the conditions in the Congo at the turn of the century.

As my own family began to take form, I thought further about the choices that my children would have, and again about what my grandfather Verner would have to say about it. The concept of spousal choices entered my thinking and I began to realize that all of us are the result of what a mathematician might call a binary tree of spousal choices. Although we cannot choose our parents, we can and do choose our mates. Perhaps our essence as beings is not so much a result of our ancestors themselves, but rather of their spousal choices. I began to look not for who my parents and grandparents are or were, but, rather, why they choose each other from the seemingly endless field of opportunity.

Then it dawned on me. My mother, who grew up under some of the same ancestral pressures that my grandfather Verner felt, married my father in large part because he is a genealogical gold mine. Should there be any discussion of the quality or quantity of ancestors, my father, who really is more concerned with other things, could have buried his in-laws with cousinships with no less than 11 U.S. presidents, hundreds of governors and Revolutionary heroes, thousands of prominent persons of all varieties, and at least four Mayflower ancestors, not to mention an extended family estimated to contain about 4 million individuals, possibly the largest in the U.S., with a distributed net worth estimated to be more than $2 trillion.

But remember, please, I had no choice in this situation. My grandfather Verner had the wisdom to assure me of that.

I first learned about Ota Benga while listening to my widowed grandmother tell me stories about her late husband. She was a kind of filter for many things, always preserving the good notions about him. She told me that my grandfather Verner was a man of great integrity, that he always kept his promises, sometimes to a fault. He was a scholar and a scientist, graduated summa cum laude from his college, a reverend, a founder of the American Anthropological Association.

I saw for myself his collections among the exhibits of Africana in the Smithsonian Institution. It was the largest and most treasured African collection of its time. There are mineral specimens of uncut diamonds and unprocessed rubber as well as the anthropological items. There is also the rarest of rare books, the last known copy of which is locked up in a special cabinet in the Smithsonian research library. It is entitled *Mukanda wa Tshiluba*, which he wrote phonetically in a now vanished language, published at his own expense in London, and scattered among the poorest natives, of tribes now extinct, in central Africa in 1905. It was to teach Christian values through animist parables, the Ten Commandments and the Golden Rule.

His collections also reached as far as the Putnam Museum in Davenport, and the Shaw Botanical Gardens in St. Louis. The Verner Collection donated by my Aunt Mary Allston to the Caroliniana Library at the University of South Carolina contains the bulk of his writings, including his unfinished autobiography, which he left to me. There are also unpublished manuscripts, numerous articles, and sensational true stories of his life with Ota Benga in the wilds of Africa.

I found many ominous signs, however, that my grandfather Verner may have had other lives, and may have marched to different tunes. There were the mysterious visits to sanitaria, passed off as curatives for the malarial fever. Was he not employed by agents of King Leopold II? Wasn't his brother-in-law a ranking officer of the Ku Klux Klan? Did he keep a secret family in the Congo? Whatever happened to the diamonds? Why was he so interested in Africa in the first place? There is evidence that he was regarded as mentally off-balance. Some say he became an atheist, others laud his service to God and Christ as a Presbyterian minister. Did he really think that an evolutionary missing link might yet be found in the jungles of Africa? Was he a freak show impresario at heart? Did he really put a pygmy in the zoo? Outrageous!

I learned that he was not always accepted in all circles. He had to struggle for recognition, and it seemed to me that many people took great advantage of him, especially in business matters. He seemed to bear the guilt of generations for the ravages of slavery on the souls of black Americans, and some criticized him for that. Some members of his own family and some of his in-laws distrusted him, not always without cause.

These questions, and others, drove me to retrace his steps. In more recent years, I searched the American Museum of Natural History in New York to track his movements and finally caught up with him.

Just as if he could jump out of his grave to meet me in person, I was greeted by him through a curator in the anthropology department, Dr. Enid Schildkrout. She presented to me an old letter addressed to the museum from my grandfather, which stated that someday a descendant of his would come to the American Museum to set the record straight. There I was, dumbfounded, with his very words in my hand, as if I were right beside his rocking chair once again. His letter was written long before I was born, and before my parents were married. But he knew I would be there someday.

His writings, now scattered over at least ten states, include intentions that he never had time to fulfill. The most outstanding was to write a book about Ota Benga, who also, like everyone else, could not choose his parents.

My affection for my grandfather Verner would most certainly not escape any critical analysis of this work, its veracity, and its technical accuracy. With no apologies, except for my limited capacity to find the words needed to tell this story objectively and properly, I have relied upon my esteemed co-author. Harvey Blume was with me through many of the critical paths of the search for Ota Benga. In South Carolina, in St. Louis, in Lynchburg, at the American Museum, and at the Bronx Zoo, Harvey felt the pains and shared the joys with me and Ota Benga all the way.

This book is a result of all the above. It is to set the record straight. It is to complete the work that my grandfather never finished, to express his conviction in me that I would get it done. Most important, it is a memorial to one of the bravest men of this twentieth century, Ota Benga, the first African forest person to settle in the United States of America.

INTRODUCTION

In most interactions between Westerners and African pygmies, the pygmies are depicted as the hunters. Their eyes pick out paths invisible to big people. They weave noiselessly through the bush, easily negotiating nearly undetectable openings. In a clearing up ahead they turn, waiting patiently for the clumsier, larger, slower Westerner to catch up.

The Westerner is there because he wants to witness and describe their hunt, or he wants to write about how nomads select a new campsite, or he just needs to get from one point to another in the forest and cannot possibly find the way by himself. Only the pygmies can help him. They are his guides.

With Ota Benga, the situation was reversed. In this case it seemed as if we, the authors, were the hunters, his life story the quarry. We were determined to find his path and stay on it wherever it led.

How do Westerners track an African pygmy who has been dead

for roughly seventy-five years? You have to become a passable hunter yourself. You use primary sources, secondary sources, consult the historical record. You learn to evaluate the oral record, the stories passed down from generation to generation in the Verner family and elsewhere. You have to go where the forest dweller has gone, see what traces of him remain. Finally, you have to learn not to reject out of hand hints that arise from other sources—dreams, intuition, and the imagination.

It wasn't necessarily as if Ota was determined to evade us in our research. Quite often it seemed the opposite was true. A dream: We arrive in an apartment in some American city. (Ota came to know many American cities.) There is the remnant of a campfire in an empty room, but Ota himself is gone. It is frustrating; he has eluded us once again. On the other hand, the indoor campfire tells us something; it is, in fact, a perfect symbol for the hybrid existence Ota forged out of African and American elements. Ota, then, is still a nomad; an apartment is no more than a campsite to him. He does not trouble to hide his traces. Perhaps we are not so far behind after all. Perhaps the charred wood was left there to encourage us to keep on going.

Perhaps somewhere up ahead he is turning to face us, waiting patiently for the big muzungus—Westerners, whites—to stop stumbling around and finally catch up. There is something he wants to show us. It only seemed as if we were hunting him. In fact he was serving all along as our guide.

It suggests a novel way of looking at his story: he wanted to leave a record, did everything he could to plant unmistakable evidence of his being. Hence the battles on Plaza St. Louis, the chair whizzing past the ear of Florence Guggenheim, the 1906 *New York Times* headline—BENGA TRIES TO KILL. With such a storm of commotion, how could the future fail to notice the singular passage of a pygmy through turn-of-the-century America?

Yet it did fail to notice. Embarrassment and guilt over the way in which he was treated combined to reinforce amnesia. Ota's story was soon forgotten, though it is hard to conceive a more unusual journey, as strange and dangerous in its own way as better-known trips made by H. M. Stanley and other nineteenth-century explorers. Ota's travels are distinguished from more celebrated voyages not necessarily by rigor or degree of difficulty but because, as an African exploring America, he was going in the opposite direction, against the flow. He left no travelogues behind. Lacking sufficient mastery of written English, he never set down his impressions of a journey extending from the Congo to Virginia.

Nor could he rely on the print media to do the job for him. For the most part newspapers and journals could not write about him without resort to mockery. Even when the writers were scientists trying to resist the impulse to entertain their readers at Ota's expense, intellectual interference set in, blocking the attempt to put the record straight. The facts never seemed to come out right. Distortion was evident at every turn. It was as if the turn-of-the-century mind could not cope with the sheer incongruity of a pygmy, a hunter/gatherer from the heart of Africa, at large in the United States.

Who was Ota Benga? Elf, dwarf, cannibal, wildman, savage loose in the metropolis, beyond ape but not quite human, stunted, retarded, incomplete, someone to gawk at, tease, put in cages, ridicule—these are among the contemporary descriptions of him. Conspicuously absent is the possibility that he was just as evolved as President Roosevelt, say, or Thomas Edison. It was difficult to entertain the proposition that he and his people were as fully and authentically human as J. P. Morgan or Andrew Carnegie. It was nearly inconceivable that Ota might be just as curious about the anthropologists who bedeviled him as they were about him.

The anthropologists wanted to quantify everything about him—his head size, foot size, the distance between heel and toe, nose and forehead, the space between his eyes. It was considered worthy of scientific note to put a baseball in his hand and find out how far he could fling it. All these numbers would then be rubbed together, mumbled and jumbled and chanted over, to determine what a pygmy was.

The scientists, spectators, and journalists were impervious to the fact that their attention was returned. Ota wanted to know with equal intensity and a greater necessity—though without the emphasis on statistics, the need for tape and calipers—what a Westerner was. He dedicated years of his life to finding out.

To others what mattered most of all was the color of his skin. In their eyes he was black, or black enough, and that was decisive. He was just another variety of colored man, shorter than most, foreign born, a peculiar strain of African who had somehow slipped in years after the floodgates closed. That gave him no special dispensation. Like American-born blacks, he would have to adjust to Jim Crow and the back of the bus.

Samuel Phillips Verner, the man who saved his life and brought him to the United States in the first place, described Ota as "an extremely interesting little fellow." At about 4 feet, 8 inches, according to Verner, and weighing in at about a hundred pounds, he was "active as a cat, lithe as a monkey, and extremely strong for his size. His front teeth had been filed to a sharp point in imitation of the crocodile's tooth." Verner might have added that journalists, scientists, showmen, and crowds could not get enough of him.

Verner said he "could write a volume about Ota Benga, and some day . . . may do so." If he had ever gotten around to delivering on this promise, his book would have had to encompass his own origins—his grandfather had been a slaveowner in South Carolina, and his father, after the Civil War, a militant white supremacist. It would have had to devote some pages to late nineteenth-century Africa, a continent barely recovering from the ravages of the slave trade only to suffer the deeper and perhaps still more destructive encroachments of colonialism. Central Africa was once ruled by Arab slave traders based on the island of Zanzibar. After explorations carried out by Stanley and agreement among the European powers it was made over to Leopold II, king of Belgium.

Ota Benga, then, shortly after his birth, came under the authority of a European king. Why should this have mattered to him? Living in the old way within the nearly impregnable forest, why should he care who flattered himself with the empty title, "King of the Congo"? In fact, it did matter. Leopold's rule reached in to where even slave traders dared not go. Soon Ota was confronting massacre, and white men. He was leaving Africa, en route to the United States.

The story would then have to turn to those American institutions that, directly or indirectly, mattered most to him—the St. Louis Fair, for example, the American Museum of Natural History, the Bronx Zoo. Jim Crow has already been mentioned. And the story— the book Verner proposed to write—would have to pause long enough at the triumph of Darwinism to marvel at how a theory that posited such radical equality—all men descended from a common ancestor—could be used widely, soon after its inception, to reinforce every possible division by race, gender, and nationality.

The story of Ota Benga would have to be wide-ranging, dealing with malaria, on the one hand, and electrification, on the other, taking in the importance of elephants to the ivory economy of Africa and the entertainment economy of New York City, and describing characters as disparate as Geronimo and W. E. B. Du Bois, both of whom were acquaintances of Ota's.

S. P. Verner devoted a book, many articles, and numerous stories to his African experiences. Fact and fiction, often not so easy to distinguish from each other, issued from his typewriter, but he never got around to the book about Ota Benga. Perhaps it is just as well.

When writing about Ota Benga he did not rise above the prevalent tendency of the age; the subject of Ota inspired him with a need to improvise. It seemed he could not tell the same story about the pygmy in the same way twice.

This, then, is the long-delayed story of Ota Benga, the forest dweller who spent more than a decade in the United States. Compared to any version Verner might have written it has the advantages of contrast and perspective.

The contrasts abound. Ota's world is a fractured mirror of our own. Technologically, culturally, it is the underpinning of our day, just beyond reach, for the most part, of living memory. And it is perhaps instructive, as the century draws to a close, to consider that when it opened men and women were routinely put on display for the benefit of others. Some called this science, others entertainment. The line between was thin and artificial. The showmen had scientific pretensions; the scientists wanted to popularize their findings. All of it, including the achingly unresolved question of race, came together in the case of the pygmy in the zoo.

This book, then, is the story of an age, stretching from the Congo Free State to St. Louis and New Orleans. It is the story of the friendship between S. P. Verner and Ota Benga, but in the end it is one man's story. Ota's lifeline knits it all together.

1

A GATHERING OF TRIBES

Meet me in St. Louis, Louis,

Meet me at the fair,

Don't tell me lights are shining

Any place but there;

We will dance the Hoochee-Koochee

I will be your tootsie wootsie

If you will meet me in St. Louis,

Louis,

Meet me at the fair.

—Andrew B. Sterling

Forest Park, a rectangular greensward running toward the western boundary of the city of St. Louis, a peaceful terrain of trees and gentle hills, a place for walks, picnics, recreation. So it was before 1904 and so it is today, except for a creek or two has filled in or diverted, a pavilion or a statue standing where none stood before, an art museum, and a justifiably renowned zoo, with bears, pythons, leopards, and monkeys, where, in 1904, there was only a large birdcage.

Another mark of subtle alteration is that many of the trees look as if they haven't aged since the turn of the century—and, in a sense, they haven't. They are second-growth trees, planted to replace the woods that were chopped down. On some days and in some areas of the park there are archaeology students digging and sifting as if they were looking for traces of another Troy or for marks of that vanished culture that flourished along the banks of the Mississippi before whites ever set foot in America.

What they are searching for is of much more recent vintage. With the same attention they might devote to Pompeii, they are excavating for leftovers of the event that transfigured Forest Park and its environs for a brief time in 1904. They are looking for signs of a small city that was constructed in a few short years, existed for a mere seven months, and then disappeared from the face of the earth. They are looking for remnants of the great World's Fair, the Louisiana Purchase Exposition, that glorified the city of St. Louis and put it in on a par for a time with the likes of London, Paris, and New York.

They know in advance that there are limits to what they will discover. Ancient peoples left aspects of their material culture behind them, clues to a meaning to be deciphered by posterity. The situation is the opposite with the Ivory City of the fair. It did not wait around for a gradual burial by the eons. It had no time for time. Its palaces and buildings, built on a scale that could have housed a race of giants, its towers, fountains, and minarets were blown to smithereens after the closing of the fair and carted off in pieces to a landfill in Illinois.

It was in keeping with the spirit of the exhibition—and of the age—that a price of admission was charged to witness the demolition, the speed of which, like so much else at the fair, aimed to set new records.

The meaning of the fair lives on even if most of its body has been, in effect, cremated. It survives in volumes of formal documentation, probably also record-setting for sheer mass, as the organizers of the fair had no doubts about the importance of their work and took care to see that future generations, too, would be informed. It survives as well in the accounts of those who visited the fair, sometimes repeatedly, but it may be that its meaning lives on most of all in the little-told story of those who were assigned the task of living at the fair.

They did not reside in those grand buildings constructed so cunningly as to make plaster of paris and manila fiber appear to all the world like marble. They inhabited humbler dwellings—huts, tepees, treehouses, igloos. These men and women who lived at the fair, in contrast to the vast majority of the white-skinned visitors who came to inspect them, were red, yellow, brown, and black-skinned.

They were the native people of Alaska, the Eskimo; inhabitants of the recently conquered Philippines, some 1,200 in all; the indigenous people of Japan, the Ainu; natives of South America and representatives of fifty tribes of North America; Zulus and Baluba from Africa; and pygmies from the Congo who had been convinced, somehow, to voluntarily leave their forest homes and cross an ocean to an unknown land.

Once they had settled in, these peoples indigenous to tundra, forest, and prairie, became, in effect, the indigenous people of the exposition. Tourists were invited to come and go. Eskimos, Filipinos, Apaches, and pygmies, on the other hand, were invited to stay put. Except for a relatively small number (Zulus mostly) who took it into their heads to disappear into America's heartland, most did stay put, and just by staying put they made their contribution. They allowed St. Louis to carve out a special place for itself in the history of fairs.

America's first World's Fair, the Philadelphia Exposition of 1876, proclaimed that one hundred years after independence the United States had the will and the wherewithal to be treated on equal terms by the European powers. At Philadelphia, technological marvels were housed and demonstrated in one colossal building. On June 25, 1876, for example, the very day, it just so happened, that General Custer met his doom at Little Big Horn, Alexander Graham Bell pronounced the words "to be or not to be" into a telephone transmitter in that building. A little ways down the hall, the effect on the receiving end was overwhelming. Don Pedro II, emperor of Brazil, jumped out of his seat as if shot out of a cannon and cried in astonishment, "I hear, I hear!"

America's next major foray into fairmaking came in Chicago, in 1893, at an exposition called in honor of the four hundredth anniversary of Columbus's arrival in the New World. Marvelous as Philadelphia had seemed at the time, the Columbiana Exposition dwarfed it. Compared to Chicago, Philadelphia was nothing but a one-room country schoolhouse; immense no doubt, the schoolroom of a budding Prometheus perhaps, but a one-room schoolhouse all the same. The Chicago Exposition, on the other hand, with its nearly seven hundred acres and its multitude of buildings, reflected the urbanization of America. It was designed as a perfect city, with no poverty and no bad neighborhoods. Just building the

Columbiana was an advance exercise in transport, architecture, crowd control, and city planning.

St. Louis took after Chicago and hoped to top it, which it did in most respects. St. Louis also proposed something entirely new. In St. Louis man would do more than display his wares and test out his technology; he would also study and display himself. For this a new science was needed, one unavailable to previous fairs, one which the presence of pygmies, Apaches, Eskimos, and the rest made possible for St. Louis. That science was anthropology.

Anthropology was the centerpiece of the St. Louis Fair and distinguished it from its predecessors. Anthropology allowed fair organizers to proudly label their work a "University of Man." Modern, Western man was exempted from the need to be studied in the flesh. The fair itself spoke eloquently for him. His position on the evolutionary scale was guaranteed by the technological and mechanical wonders visible on every side.

The organizers of the fair wanted something more for St. Louis than a glimpse into the coming age of the auto and the dynamo. They wanted a comprehensive look back into the age of stone and before. They wanted to show not only where Western man was and where he was headed but also where he had come from. They wanted to give the twentieth century a vision of the archaic against which it could measure itself. If the tone was sober, the treatment scientific, and if the setting, above all, was authentic, organizers saw nothing amiss in casting their net wide over the globe and submitting the catch to the St. Louis Fair.

Supervising this ingathering of tribes was the job of Dr. W. J. McGee, head of the Anthropology Department of the fair, where he was known simply and informally as Chief. By 1904, Chief McGee was a veteran of anthropology's relatively new old-boy network. In fact, his career in anthropology owed much more to a talent for networking than to any commitment to fieldwork.

St. Louis was an ideal focus for McGee's talents as anthropology booster and promoter. Most sciences need time to legitimize themselves. Only later, once established, can they hope to achieve some degree of popularization. St. Louis put McGee in the enviable position of being able both to establish and to popularize his science on a single, highly visible national platform.

On a more personal note, the Chief had hopes that while he was establishing anthropology he would at the same time be reestablishing his career. He had left the Smithsonian Institute in 1902, reeling under charges of mismanagement, incompetence, and corruption. At St. Louis, he hoped to get out from under the cloud by changing the subject. Getting the public to think about intraspecies variation, racial hierarchy, the descent of man, and other fine points of social Darwinism was a good way to make it forget charges of personal misconduct.

Under Chief McGee's direction, special agents of the fair were dispatched to the four corners of the Earth. Their mission, McGee wrote, was to assemble "representatives of all the world's races, ranging from smallest pygmies to the most gigantic peoples, from the darkest blacks to the dominant whites." Anthropology wanted to start with "the lowest known culture," and work its way up to man's "highest culmination." This "highest culmination" was plainly the culture symbolized by the exposition itself, a culture moving rapidly from the "Age of Metal" into the "Age of Power."

McGee regretted that it was impossible to exhibit examples of "all the world's peoples on the Exposition grounds." The Anthropology Department had to settle for being less definitive than Carl Hagenbeck's Circus, also featured at the fair, with its "largest representation of an animal paradise ever constructed."

Anthropology was a hit nevertheless. People did enjoy seeing Hagenbeck's "wild and domestic beasts roam at large in a vast natural panorama with nothing between them and the spectators." But they loved to see primitive versions of themselves even more. Especially when these primitives lived, like Hagenbeck's animals, in simulations of their own natural habitats.

Authenticity was all. Or at least what the Anthropology Department construed—and enforced—as authenticity. The Eskimos, it boasted, did not need to take off their fur coats even in the stifling heat of St. Louis summer. As for the pygmies, when chill, damp weather arrived in the fall, anthropologists were ready to protect them from their ill-considered impulses to take measures against the cold. "It required constant vigilance and half-cruel constraint to keep the pygmies out of . . . close-fitting clothing," wrote the anthropologists, as

clothing "would have interfered with the functions normal to
... naked skins and brought serious if not fatal results."

Left to their own devices, the pygmies would gladly have
risked any amount of long-term damage to "their naked skins"
by putting something warm over their bark loincloths. They
were not reported to have enjoyed their first encounter with
authentic cold. When October and November rolled around, it
wasn't easy to lure them out of their heated huts, and it could
be dangerous to try. But by then the pygmies had already
established themselves as the most anarchic and unpredictable bunch of primitives at the fair. The only discipline they
seemed to respect was that of keeping their native American
neighbors regularly doubled up in laughter.

In fact there was reason to suspect that the pygmies were
involved in a subtle, ongoing parody of the exposition. But the
authorities were not ready to give the forest dwellers credit for
so much craft. They put their best anthropological minds to
work to come up with a more scientific, less flattering expla-
nation for the pygmy tendency toward mischief.

They noted that the pygmies had brought an assortment of
pets from Africa with them to keep them from becoming too
homesick. Extrapolating from the fact that "pygmies live in
rather close association with parrots and monkeys," the authorities deduced that the pygmies' "erratic behavior showed
the influence of the lower creatures upon their habits of
thought."

Here was an excellent chance for anthropologists to do
some experimentation, in the style of the "hard" sciences. The
anthropologists could have removed the offending parrots and
monkeys whose erratic behavior patterns spread like a conta-
gion to their susceptible hosts. Or they might have left some
pygmies with only parrots, others with only monkeys, while
keeping still other pygmies pet-free to determine which, if
any, of these beasts carried the germ of riot. But perhaps this
would have violated the rule of authenticity. Or perhaps the
anthropologists felt, no matter what its source, the damage to
the pygmies was irreversible.

The authorities did their best to tolerate the pygmies' mer-
curial ways, but in the end were forced to conclude that "the
Pygmies were capricious and troublesome to control; more so
even than the headstrong Patagonian, and infinitely worse
than the peaceful Ainu."

*   *   *

The press, like the public, was fascinated by, or addicted to, the spectacle of primitive man. Anthropology, according to the Fair's aptly named Division of Exploitation, received nearly two fifths of all press notices devoted to the fair, but even without Anthropology, St. Louis's enhancements and innovations kept it indelibly etched in visitors' minds. It could easily be argued that St. Louis was the pinnacle of that series of international expositions that had first appeared in 1851 with London's Crystal Palace and then, like visitations from the future, touched down in New York, Paris, Philadelphia, and Chicago. These fairs, each of them international in character, and with scores of nations contributing exhibits, seemed to point to an age of universal peace and cooperation. At the same time, drawing multitudes to them, they focused a populace on national heritage and destiny with an intensity second only to war.

The international expositions were built to dazzle for a season and be destroyed, to awe and edify. They disdained the buying and selling that were the primary functions of the medieval and renaissance fairs, their distant forerunners. Immediate mercantile reward did not concern them. At first glance they resembled the potlatch culture of Northwest Indians, where prestige accrued not to the taker but to the exhibitor and giver of gifts, more than they resembled the acquisitive culture that spawned them. World's Fairs were extravagant boasts, fleeting monuments to the city, the country, and, above all, the civilization that could afford them. They were proofs that such a civilization was supreme and entitled beyond question to annex and enlighten the rest of the globe.

In an era that was beginning to know and dread the conflict between labor and capital, World's Fairs served as national unifiers. In an age that still subscribed to the idea of infinite progress, they posed as utopias, harbingers of the grand utopia to come. They summed up and extended existing industry and technology. They brought together the universally acclaimed artworks of the west.

If, like St. Louis, most world's fairs left proportionately little behind them in the way of material artifact, their impact on design, technology, and culture was incalculable. Their influence lived on like the memory of a dream in the mind of a dreamer and might manifest itself in the most unlikely ways.

The St. Louis Fair came after much had already been learned about the financing, organizing, and mounting of expositions. And it came well enough before the nightmare of world war that lay at the end of the dream of Fairs—for it was world war more than anything else that negated World's Fairs.

With so much experience behind it, and so much innocence at its disposal, there were hardly any limits to St. Louis's dream of the fair. St. Louis could dream that Thomas Edison himself would be on call as consulting electrician and it would come true; that the largest time piece ever, a floral arrangement 112 feet in diameter, with hands weighing 2,500 pounds would be constructed on exposition grounds. It could, and did, imagine putting a dab of ice cream on a rolled-up waffle in order to invent that revolutionary concoction, the ice cream cone. It commissioned the biggest organ on earth, ten railroad cars of pipes, and had it delivered and played by the world's most famous organists.

George Ferris reproduced the spectacular wheel he had devised for the Chicago Exposition of 1893, explicitly to outdo the Eiffel Tower, itself the remnant of Paris's Exposition Universelle of 1889. Reinforced by tons of steel, the Ferris Wheel was a moving observation tower. Its thirty-six cars held sixty people each. People held wedding receptions in them as they rotated slowly, rocked gently, and looked, with champagne glasses in their hands, down upon the rest of the dream.

St. Louis had Marconi on hand to oversee wireless communication, which progressed measurably while the fair endured, and by the end sent publicity notices all the way to Chicago newspapers. Helen Keller welcomed the mute and the hearing deprived, Max Weber was among the notables to address one of the Fair's many scientific colloquiums, John Phillip Sousa conducted the band on opening day.

On April 30, 1904, David R. Francis, president of the fair, pushed a button alerting President Roosevelt that all lay in readiness, and President Roosevelt in Washington responded by pressing a gold key. Geysers, fountains, lights, rides, and waterfalls turned on. Sousa struck up the band, and the fair came to life. From then on there were parades, special events, and gala occasions scheduled for nearly every day.

The size of the fair was such as to bring on fatigue and cases of heat prostration. In scale the fair mirrored the event it commemorated. Jefferson's purchase of the Louisiana Territory from France in 1804 had more than doubled the land area of the United States. Likewise, the Louisiana Purchase Exposition dwarfed all previous fairs. Spread over 1,272 acres, or nearly two square miles, it took days simply to traverse the agricultural exhibits. It required repeated visits to see all the steam- , gas- , and electricity-driven surface conveyances in the offing for the twentieth century. Meanwhile, telegraph-equipped balloons and dirigibles bobbed and floated overhead where Alexander Graham Bell's new invention, the tetrahedral kite, joined them in the sky.

And this, so far, is but a fraction of the exposition's serious side. St. Louis had another face, a dream of gaiety, giddiness, and release. The Chicago Exposition had already pioneered the integration of mass entertainment into the planning of a fair. P. T. Barnum had been consulted. His advice, not surprisingly, was to make Chicago "the greatest show on earth—greater than my own Great Moral Show if you can."

Mark Twain, Barnum's longtime friend and fellow Connecticut Yankee, chipped in with his own free advice. For years Barnum had been priming Twain with letters from people who claimed their mice had no heads, their chickens had four legs, or their bulls had human hands. Twain cherished what he called a "perfect feast of queer literature," and made his own contribution to it when he suggested that it was Chicago's duty to erect a religious shrine for Christopher Columbus's real or imagined bones.

Europeans envied Americans' ability to mix the serious with the silly, the earnest and the inane. European fairs tried their luck at mass-producing fun. But Europe seemed to lack the touch. European crowds departed from their entertainment areas distinctly unamused.

It remained for America to assert itself further in a field in which it was to remain supreme. So far as fairs were concerned, St. Louis was charged with making the next leap forward. Its organizers knew that for the first time a fair would be judged just as much by developments in entertainment as by advances in education.

A large area just north of the fair was reserved for the art and business of having fun. There were over five hundred separate concessions on the Pike. Many were entertainment laboratories run by the same men who had transformed Coney Island from a sleepy beach resort into the site of the world's greatest amusement parks, designed to make you "cast aside your hampering reason" and become "a plain lunatic."

Some of the startup capital for Coney Island had been a side effect of fairs. When visitors to the Philadelphia Centennial of 1876 traveled further east to catch a glimpse of the sea, one Coney Island entrepreneur sold them boxes full of the sand they were standing on, and bottles full of ocean. In 1904, on the St. Louis Pike, Coney Island's now seasoned entertainment specialists returned the favor, devising rides and special effects and cooking up an atmosphere in which the world hung precariously upside-down.

On the Pike elephants slid down chutes into pools of water. People visited the moon or experienced Dante's Paradise. They could be present for the six days of Creation, or climb the Alps and sip Busch beer in a German beer garden. Major battles and famous floods were reenacted with spellbinding realism. At dusk, after the fair's more edifying exhibits subsided into the glow of a million lights, the spirit of carnival flared up on the Pike.

Pikegoers enjoyed access to a part of their personalities that had been kept in check by genteel codes of behavior and Victorian morality. Yet the boisterous Pike and the sober Anthropology Department, with its fetish for fact and its emphasis on authenticity, were intimately related.

The Ivory City awed (and fatigued) fairgoers with the marvels of modernity.

The Pike was a walk on the wild side, but just a walk, a guided tour. Return tickets to normalcy and decency were always included. The Pike teased and thrilled fairgoers like a drug, and like a look into a crazy mirror, gave them images of freer versions of themselves.

The Anthropology Exhibit, on the other hand, housed men and women who had no choice, no return tickets. Without rollercoaster rides, without artificial stimulus of any kind, these were the permanent wildmen of the world, the races that had been left behind, the stunted, ridiculous, romantic races. Looking at them was like looking straight from civilization into prehistory. Looking at them fairgoers felt a potent mixture of envy and contempt; contempt that Apaches, pygmies, Zulus could never make it in the modern world, and envy that they didn't even have to try.

*   *   *

No wonder then, that seventy-five years afterward, some who had been present at the fair recalled it as clearly as survivors recall war, upheaval, or disaster. For some it was as if the high point of their lives had already elapsed while they were still teenagers, or children clinging happily to the hands of adults who led them safely through the throng.

For some it was as if the lines "Don't tell me lights are shining/Any place but there" from the song "Meet Me in St. Louis, Louis" had proven to be prophetic. Never again would they experience so many lights, hundreds of thousands of them, concentrated to such effect. Never again would mere electricity bear down upon their imaginations like a magical force.

Some of the other words to "Meet Me in St. Louis, Louis" were risqué for their day. It was particularly the promise to "dance the Hoochee-Koochee," and the eagerness to be someone's "tootsie wootsie" that put worried parents on their guard. The Hoochee-Koochee had come to the public's attention when performed sensually and suggestively by the incomparable Fatima at the Chicago Exposition eleven years before. In St. Louis, a Board of Lady Managers had been formed to oversee public morality. And if there was anything the Board of Lady Managers was bound and determined to prevent, it was another outbreak of Hoochee-Koochee.

The century had turned, and the times had changed. The floodgates to "giggling, laughing, having fun," as one ex-fairgoer characterized her visits to the fair, had opened forever. How could the Board of Lady Managers stamp out Hoochee-Koochee when it was advertised so prominently in a song that was on everyone's lips months before the fair even opened? One ex-fairgoer recalled her mother's attempts to get the family to sing, "I'll meet you at the station/We'll have a conversation," and to drop all reference to Hoochee-Koochee or tootsie wootsie. But the child knew the difference.

For another ex-fairgoer, remembering the bananas and macaroons she always carried to the fair was enough to raise up Pike and Ivory City like sunken treasure from the sea. "I can smell macaroons and bananas now and I'm right down at the World's Fair," she said. As at the end of the movie *Meet Me in St. Louis*, to enter the charmed circle of the fair was to leave one's problems far behind.

Naturally, those sequestered within the Anthropology Department (not shown in the movie) might not take away such poignant memories as visitors who came and went from Pike to Ivory City until they had their fill and retreated home to rest up for another day. In fact, some of the human exhibits, the peoples arrayed and catalogued like entries in an encyclopedia, indicated they would have liked the end to come well before the appointed hour. For them, too, the fair took on the character of a dream or hallucination, but not necessarily one they cherished. And when they got back home, which most of them did, they were faced with a double challenge to their powers of narration. They had to explain not only what they saw, which was difficult enough, but also how they themselves were seen in the city of St. Louis.

No two men represented the opposite poles of experience in St. Louis better than Henry Adams and Geronimo, both of whom left written impressions of the fair; Geronimo's dictated after applying for government consent. Adams had come to record his thoughts in his autobiographical work-in-progress, his *Education*. Geronimo was there by special dispensation of the War Department. Billed, among other things, as a "Human Tyger," he was on view regularly on the grounds of Anthropology.

Adams dutifully if condescendingly saluted the sheer daring of the enterprise. "One saw here a third-rate town of half-a-million people," he wrote, a town "without history, education, unity, or art, and with little capital—without even an element of natural interest except the river which it studiously ignored—but doing what London, Paris, or New York would have shrunk from attempting."

A gentleman, Adams knew how to pay tribute to a cause lost in advance, castles built only to be destroyed, a "thirty or forty million dollar . . . pageant as ephemeral as a stage flat."

He surrendered to the rapture of electricity and illumination deployed for other than purely utilitarian purposes. "The world had never witnessed so marvellous a phantasm," he wrote. "By night Arabia's crimson sands had never returned a glow half so astonishing as one wandered among long lines of white palaces, exquisitely lighted by thousands on thousands of electric candles; soft, rich, shadowy, palpable in their sensuous depths."

He liked the fair so much it seems he would have preferred to have been able to take it home with him, where he could have enjoyed this electric world, "bathed in the pure light of the setting suns," in solitude, like a painting by an Old Master framed on a Beacon Hill wall. "Had there been . . . no visitors," he admitted, "one would have enjoyed it only the more."

Adams registered his truest estimate of the fair by leaving it at the earliest possible convenience. He was in haste to be in France, among works raised up centuries ago in homage to the Virgin, who dazzled him, "her lover, as though she were Aphrodite herself, worth all else that man ever dreamed." In France he lingered long among the imperishable cathedrals of Chartres, Rouen, and Amiens, yielding himself utterly to these testaments to the Virgin's "mental and physical energy of creation." Adams called the French cathedrals "World's Fairs of thirteenth-century force," and wrote that by comparison, they "turned Chicago and St. Louis pale."

He made no mention of the Anthropology Exhibit and therefore had no words to spare for Geronimo.

Geronimo's steps were not fettered by a ball and chain at St. Louis, but he was dogged by an armed guard, his constant attendant, and a reminder that his status was that of prisoner of war. If he had been able to enjoy Henry Adams's freedom of movement, he too would have sped to a holy place, one older still than Chartres, Rouen, or Amiens. He would have disappeared into the hills and mesas of the Southwest and northern Mexico, the sacred grounds of the Apache, from which they had been expelled and to which they were forbidden to return.

Once, Geronimo had done battle with the likes of William Tecumseh Sherman. He had frustrated posses led by the Earp brothers. Then, as an old man retiring for the last time from the warpath, he had said with finality, "I give myself up to you. Do with me what you please. I surrender. Once I moved about like the wind. Now I surrender to you and that is all."

At the very moment of surrender, as his enemies in the Southwest clamored for his blood, promoters elsewhere in the country bid top dollar for the rights to display him. The whites who didn't want him dead tended to look at him as if he were a two-legged department store. Geronimo learned quickly that "White Eyes" was willing to pay good money for bits and pieces of him, as if by owning his photo, autograph, or the buttons from his coat, they could somehow own his power. By the time of St. Louis, Geronimo was an experienced merchant of his notoriety.

His warriors had relied upon his gift of second sight. They counted on his ability to know from afar the position of his enemies, to summon animals from a distance, and on one night, it was said, to sing the sun into putting off rising until his men could finish a retreat.

As a young man, he had returned to his camp to find his mother, his wife, and his three small children dead, slain by Mexicans. Geronimo had turned aside and stood by the river, for how long he could not say. Finally, without weapon or even, at that point, the will to fight, he followed the "soft noise of the feet of the retreating Apache."

Three nights later, for the first time since the slaughter, he took some food with the other Apache. They too, he said, "had lost in the massacre," but none had lost as he had. He alone had lost all.

During his three-day fast a voice had called him by his private name. Four times, the sacred number, it called to him. The voice promised that he did not need to fear dying from a bullet wound and that his arrows would be guided home. He woke from dazed grief and consecrated himself to a life of revenge.

Nearly eighty years of age at the St. Louis Fair, Geronimo stayed for the most part in a private booth, making and selling bows and arrows while the press by turns applauded and disparaged him: Was he a fraud, a mere "pill pusher"—that is to say, a medicine man and not a warrior at all? A demon who should have been hanged long ago instead of lingering on to profit from the fair? An old man in whom the painful lesson of resignation had been carved as deeply as the "million wrinkles" time had embroidered on his skin?

Henry Adams looked upon the fair as an outsider. Here, on the other hand, is Geronimo slowly coming to terms with the Ferris wheel:

One time the guards took me into a little house that had four windows. When we were seated the little house started to move along the ground. . . . Finally they told me to look out, and when I did so I was scared, for our little house had gone high up in the air, and the people down in the Fair Grounds looked no larger than ants.

Geronimo also recorded his curiosity about the many "strange people" among whom he was shown, and noted his respect for some of them—Turks welding scimitars on the Pike, for example—as warriors. He was more careful than Adams about being openly critical. Geronimo had learned from his keepers at Fort Sill, who liked to call him Gerry, that White Eyes preferred a show of humility and gratitude from defeated peoples and took criticism poorly.

Geronimo had once wound his way on moonless nights through the gorges and rocks of the Southwest. He could get hopelessly lost by daylight in a cornfield. However resigned and congenial he appeared to be at St. Louis, however preoccupied with getting a nickel for a button, or a few dollars for a bow, he never gave up hope that one day he would lead his dwindling people back from the forts of Oklahoma and the malarial swamps of Florida to their ancestral home.

His autobiography does not mention those times when he was treated to beer or whiskey at St. Louis, and chanted vision songs to a doorpost, a stranger, or the moon.

> O, ha le
> O, ha le
> Through the air
> I fly upon a cloud
> O, ha le
> O, ha le
> There to find the
> holy place
> Ah, now the
> change comes
> o'er me!

And it does not make explicit mention of the race of small Africans next to whom the Indians were lodged.

But seeing that he took an interest in "strange people," it is probable that he mused over the many similarities between Apache and pygmy culture. The pygmies believed they were not merely from, but of, the forest, as the Apache were of the hills. And, by listening, Geronimo learned that the forest dwellers shared the Apache's affection for night-long chanting. He also, when occasions for healing arose, would have seen that the pygmies had an Apache-like respect for herbal remedies and a disdain for witchcraft.

On a more disturbing note, there was a widespread belief among Apaches, as there was among Africans, that White Eyes secretly liked nothing better than to dine on human flesh. Geronimo knew, for instance, that after being killed, the head of one Apache chieftain had been severed from the body and boiled down to the skull. (Believing skull size to be an index of intelligence, scientists were amazed this skull was larger than that which had belonged to the statesman Daniel Webster.) The belief that White Eyes was a cannibal was furthered among the Apaches by the fact that cans of meat given out by the cavalry were often decorated by pictures of human beings.

Geronimo, like other native Americans, was glad for the entertainment provided by the pranks of his pygmy neighbors, but he could turn the tables. Through an interpreter, the serious old Apache warned the pygmies that they would do well to keep close watch on the crowds of White Eyes. When the pygmies asked why, he replied in a whisper that in addition to being rude, some White eyes appeared to be hungry.

And Geronimo became aware that one pygmy in particular had, for a short time, elbowed him out of his accustomed place in the headlines. This forest dweller came from a different tribe than the others. The event that brought him to St. Louis was a disaster not unlike the one that had endowed Geronimo with a spirit ally and transformed him into a warrior.

The pygmy was referred to in the papers first as Artiba, then Autobank. His name was Ota Benga.

It is said that one day, no doubt followed by his guard, Geronimo, chanting softly to himself, approached the pygmy huts and put a stone arrowhead into Ota Benga's hand.

Rarely did the Human Tyger part with such an item free of charge. Then he turned and shuffled back to the Indian School which White Eyes had built to demonstrate that with the proper handling, even the likes of the Sioux and the Apache were not incorrigible.

Geronimo's gift of an arrowhead has never turned up in the archaeological digs in Forest Park in the city of St. Louis. Neither did it survive the rest of Ota Benga's journey.

2

DANCERS OF GOD

I came into the clearing and
asked, jokingly, why he was dancing
alone. He stopped, turned slowly
around and looked at me as though
. . . surprised by my stupidity.
"But I'm not dancing alone," he
said. "I am dancing with the forest,
dancing with the moon."

—Colin Turnbull,
The Forest People

pygmy, a stone arrowhead in his hands, looks at the back of the Apache warrior who gave it to him. It is an unprecedented event. It could never have happened before.

The link between Geronimo and Ota Benga opens up the possibility that many unusual connections were being forged among the residents of the Anthropology Department, any number of conspiracies and affinities of which the authorities were unaware. Eskimo and pygmies, for instance, expert hunters both, could have had wonderful conversations, with the help of interpreters, about the very different animals they stalked and their ways of stalking them. In fact, to many of the peoples of the fair, White Eyes, the fair's host, the one responsible for bringing them all together, was perhaps, despite his Ferris wheel and his combustion engines, the least interesting of all.

St. Louis was not the first place a pygmy had appeared abroad for purposes of display. The historical record shows that pygmies had been heavily in demand since time immemorial. The first known written reference to Africa's forest dwellers is in fact an invitation for them to appear, to perform, and presumably to otherwise conduct themselves authentically, as at St. Louis, before an alien audience. That invitation was issued some 4,500 years previous to the Louisiana Purchase Exposition.

Well before Moses led the Hebrews across the Red Sea, well before a blind Greek chanted epic poems about the siege of Troy, an Egyptian pharaoh had already pointed south, past the borders of his kingdom, and asked that a pygmy be brought to him. Pharaoh Neferkare expressed this interest in pygmies in a letter to his Governor of the South, Herkhuf, sent, approximately, in 2500 B.C.

The pharaoh was already aware of the pygmies' reputation as marvelous dancers who captured leafwork and forest shadow in their movements. It seems that even earlier such a "Dancer of God" had been brought to Egypt "from the Land of Trees and from the Land of Spirits" and had performed before one of the pharaoh's forefathers. Now Neferkare longed to see dances said to "gladden the heart." The pygmy, he wrote, is "the one who rejoices the heart of Pharaoh," the one that the divine "King Neferkare, who lives eternally, sighs for."

Herkhuf had to take every precaution to assure the pygmy a safe and comfortable journey. It was assumed that a resident of the Land of Trees would not be on familiar terms with boats and rivers. Herkhuf was to post men on all sides of the ship so that the pygmy would not leave his forest only to accidentally drop into the Nile. Even when the pygmy slept, Herkhuf was to see to it that "stout men sleep alongside him," and Herkhuf was to communicate the pharaoh's words of greeting: "Hail to the Dancer of God," wrote King Neferkare.

The pharaoh's request for a pygmy was significant enough for Herkhuf to have the letter inscribed on his tomb. Unfortunately, no further information is forthcoming about the success or failure of his mission. We do not know if the dancer from the from the Land of Trees and from the Land of Spirits arrived in Egypt, and if he did, how Neferkare's hospitality might be compared to that of Chief McGee. We can only wonder how the career of a pygmy in the ancient land of Egypt might differ from Ota Benga's in the United States.

There is evidence that, if not on this then on other occasions, pygmies did turn up in Egypt and, by their dancing, gladdened the hearts of many a pharaoh. To the Egyptians, they were exalted, sacred entertainers. Not so for the Greeks, who next wrote about the forest dwellers. The Egyptians knew real pygmies in the flesh. The Greeks seemed content to work with rumors.

Homer, for example, embroidered a scenario that would have done a nineteenth-century publicist like P. T. Barnum proud. Homer liked to award the Greeks larger-than-life opponents—Trojans, Centaurs, Amazons. In the *Iliad*, the pygmies drew a more humble and definitely more Hitchcockian nemesis; the half-men had to contend with birds.

The pygmies meet their match in a sidelight to a passage describing a nearly irresistible Trojan charge. Homer compares the battle cry of the Trojans to the crying of wildfowl. It is like the clamor of the flocks of migrating cranes escaping "winter time" and "rains unceasing" as they prepare to rain down at dawn upon hapless, half-sized "Pygmaian men." Before this "baleful battle" is even joined, the pygmies are shattered by the awful racket of the birds' approach.

The Greeks, on the other hand, are not so easily dismayed. They advance "silently, breathing valour," into the din of the Trojan charge. They close ranks, "stubbornly minded each in his heart to stand by the others."

This contrast between brave Greeks and nervous pygmies makes for an effective setpiece. And if we subtract the birds, it is not without a kernel of knowledge, or correct intuition, concerning the Pygmaian race. It holds true to the pygmies' aversion to "noise."

"Noise" to them is more than an acoustical quality. It has aesthetic and ethical dimensions. It is a term applied critically and in disgust to anything thought to be devoid of sense, meaning, humor, harmony. Noise is discord and discontent within a hunting band. It is lies, pretense, misinformation. There is no more profound opposition than between "noise" and "quiet." "Quiet" is accord—not silence—among the forest dwellers, and it is natural order in the forest—monkey chatter, birdsong, and insect buzz included.

In the centuries after Homer, even less fact and more noise

grew up around the pygmies. They were thought to be not only half-sized but half human, a false start on the day of Creation. They existed on the periphery of European consciousness, entries in its bestiary, bright eyes staring in from the shadows at civilization's campfire.

In the seventeenth century, science tried to put the problem of the pygmy to rest. In 1699, Edward Tyson, a noted English physician, published a treatise that promised to resolve this question and other outstanding issues left over from antiquity, such as the anatomical status of satyrs. Tyson's conclusions about satyrs does not concern us here. But it is worth noting that he did not get science off to a very good start so far as pygmies were concerned.

After studying a skeleton presumed to belong to a pygmy, Tyson concluded that "an ape is an ape, tho' finely clad," by which he meant that no matter what Homer or Herodotus had to say, the Pygmaian race was a race of apes. Tyson contributed an illustration of what he called "our Pygmie," who is depicted as a crouching imp with a furry mane, a tail, and an unnerving grin.

Tyson's confusion of ape and impish pygmy was to prove pernicious and not so easy to dispel from popular thought. Even after Darwin, some two hundred years later, showed that all humans descended from apes, the suspicion remained that some races had descended further than others. According to this way of thinking, some races, namely the white ones, had left the ape far behind, while other races, pygmies especially, had hardly matured at all.

Tyson can't be blamed for late nineteenth and early twentieth-century racism, and the reason for his confusion of ape with pygmy was innocent enough. The skeleton upon which he based his conclusions belonged, as it turned out, to a chimpanzee.

At about the same time Tyson was working with falsely labeled bones, European explorers of Africa were getting closer to the real thing. Portuguese slave traders reported seeing small, manlike creatures with tails. These forest dwellers seemed to possess a magical talent for becoming invisible at will. No doubt they had to call on this talent often when performing the other feat the Portuguese reported of them, that of bringing down elephants singlehandedly despite the vast discrepancy in size.

The tails the Portuguese saw were bark loincloths, and a pygmy hunter was and is, just as the Portuguese said, capable of subduing an elephant alone. Some 4,200 years after the Egyptians, authentic as opposed to imaginary pygmies were reappearing in literature.

By the late nineteenth-century, close encounters between Europeans and pygmies were becoming more frequent. There was no longer any question of pygmies being a variety of chimpanzee. They had been heard to speak. They were known to possess implements, notably sharp spears and bows and arrows which they were adept at using. Thousands of years of living in proximity to elephants had taught them every way a wooden weapon could surprise the huge animal and pierce its armored hide. It took the forest dwellers less time, after confronting gunfire, to find that becoming invisible while being shot at, then rushing in to spear a rifleman in the act of reloading was an excellent way to counter "bang medicine."

It turned out, contrary to Homer, that pygmies were very good at defending their terrain. But at the very moment when, nursing their wounds, explorers avowed that pygmies were human, they were so impressed by the small people that their descriptions nearly reinstated them back into myth.

The traveler Sidney Hinde, for instance, had many encounters with the Batwa, "the interesting little people of the forest," during his years in central Africa, and in *The Fall of The Congo Arabs*, published in 1897, he wrote that though they were short, often less than four feet, they made up for it by being "both sturdy and independent." Hinde also observed that the pygmies were nomadic hunters and followed "game in small parties, changing their locality with the migration of the game."

Their maddening power to become invisible was no less impressive when understood to result from size, skin pigment, and stealth rather than magic. Not witchcraft, but mastery of the "science of woodcraft" made it as difficult for the average person to find a pygmy in the forest as it was, wrote Hinde, "for a town-bred person . . . to discover mice in a cornfield."

Hinde reported that slave-raiding and ivory-hunting expeditions entering the forest had often "suffered to such an extent at the hands of these small demons, that few, and sometimes none, have returned to tell the tale of how they died, without even seeing who smote them." He too, while traveling in the forest, had the uncanny experience of seeing "gnome-like beings" springing up on all sides without any warning. The Batwa's ability to appear and disappear impressed Hinde so deeply that he came to "almost doubt their being human."

If only because he was the most widely read, it is Henry Morton Stanley more than any other explorer who must be credited with alerting the general public to the reality and the humanity of pygmies. Between 1870 and 1889 Stanley made four trips to central Africa. It was on his last journey, during which he and his caravan came close to starving to death in the Ituri Forest of what was then known as the Congo Free State, that the explorer's eyes were drawn to his "first specimen of the tribe of dwarfs."

It was a seventeen-year-old woman, less than four feet tall, who impressed the explorer immediately with her "glistening and smooth sleekness of body." Stanley found her face "very prepossessing," and her eyes struck him as "magnificent . . . almost as large as that of a young gazelle; full, protruding, and extremely lustrous." The pygmy woman was effortlessly casting a spell on the explorer and doing it, so it seemed, just to cheer him up. "Absolutely nude," wrote this normally hard-bitten man, "the little demoiselle was quite possessed, as though she were accustomed to be admired, and really enjoyed inspection."

As a rule, H. M. Stanley was considerably less easy to charm. He was known in Africa under the name of Bula Mutadi, which means Smasher of Rocks, and he had not come by this title by stopping often to utter gentle, admiring words about the continent's natives. He became Smasher of Rocks by blasting away at anything, people included, that retarded his progress. Bula Mutadi liked to give "a belly full of lead" to tribes that resisted the incursion of his always armed and usually hungry men.

The pygmies would seem to have earned the full treatment, the standard Bula Mutadi dose of a belly full of lead. On this journey, which had started in Zanzibar and was meant to end up in the Sudan, Stanley's men were already suffering from hunger, disease, and a gnawing doubt that they would ever get out of the forest alive. The pygmies who made the forest their home were casually hurrying this process of demoralization along by now and again shooting poison-tipped arrows into the ailing troop. And yet Bula Mutadi never lost his admiration for the "tribe of dwarfs." Even as they made his life miserable, he noted with pleasure the footprints left by the forest dwellers, admired their "high delicate insteps," and compared their small feet with the feet of "young English misses of eight years old."

Stanley daydreamed about the "ancient ancestry and aristocratic descent" of the diminutive forest dwellers and mused about Herodotus, who had called the pygmies "a nation of wizards." Meanwhile his companion, Dr. Thomas Parke, acquired a pygmy handmaiden whose skill in foraging kept him alive.

Europeans like Stanley and Dr. Parke saw the forest as a vast, trackless, arboreal desert. Devoid of comfort and sustenance, it seemed to actively thwart their passage, suffocate and depress them, rob them of hope. Stanley himself could conceive of "no more gloomy spot," nor imagine anything more dreary than "those dark woods, which rose in tier upon tier from the river's edge."

To Dr. Parke's pygmy handmaiden the forest was a friendly place, bursting with good things to eat. Dr. Parke wrote that her greatest difficulty was not in finding food but in keeping it hidden from the "ravenous men" waiting to rob her. She would wander off in the forest by day and try to sneak what she gathered to him after dark, neatly "wrapped in a plantain leaf."

The forest provided her with ample food and protection from the African sunlight. It was only when the caravan finally left its shadows, and everyone else began to feel better, that she herself fell ill. Dr. Parke left her behind to convalesce. She had been "a universal favorite in the caravan," he wrote, and:

> our parting with her was a very pathetic one . . . this little dwarf always maintained an exalted dignity and superior position among the other women of the caravan . . . her last act at parting was to give me the ivory bangles which she wore in the forest, but which now dropped from her attenuated arms and ankles.

By piecing together the accounts of explorers like Hinde, Stanley, and Parke, the nineteenth-century reader arrived at a portrait of African pygmies that was fragmentary, but accurate so far as it went. The pygmies were expert hunters. They lived apart from other Africans, surviving with privileged ease in an environment nearly everyone else preferred to avoid. They tended to give as good as they got in their relations with outsiders: if attacked they defended themselves like "small demons"; if treated with respect, they could, like Dr. Parke's handmaiden, be loyal, resourceful friends.

In *The Land of the Pigmies*, Guy Burrows, another late-nineteenth-century traveler to central Africa, added another detail to the composite portrait. Burrows found the pygmies to be experts at mimicry. He was astounded by their ability to reproduce from memory, down to "the most insignificant details," the actions of Europeans, himself included, whom they hadn't seen for years. The pygmies Burrows met were entertaining, crowd-pleasing, show-stealing visitors to campsites or settled communities. One pygmy's gift for mimicry, and his "comical ways and quick, nimble movements," wrote Burrows, made the "little fellow the clown of our society."

Burrows knew and appreciated this gift of mimicry purely for its entertainment value. He did not see that for the pygmy it was a survival skill. At bottom it was a hunter's art, the outgrowth of intimate, sympathetic knowledge of the prey. Acting out an animal's habits was a hunter's way of becoming the hunted, of knowing, as if from inside, the moods and movements of the animal he stalked—while all the time he himself remained unseen.

Burrows had stumbled upon a secret of the forest dwellers' coexistence with outsiders. *Muzungus*—the African version of Geronimo's White Eyes—were new targets, and pygmies like the one who became the clown of Burrows' campsite must have relished the opportunity to imitate their movements down to the last detail. For generations pygmies had been practicing mimicry upon the varied groups of Africans that had migrated to the periphery of the forests and had become, in effect, the pygmies' neighbors.

Mimicry confers a kind of invisibility upon the mimic. Again, this makes it a hunter's art, a form of disguise. It allowed the pygmies to seem as if they were taking on the manners and mores of neighboring cultures while all the time they were peering out from behind their masks, giving no indication of what they really thought, and keeping their own belief systems safe from inspection.

The strategy worked. The ways of the village were transparent to the pygmy but the ways of the forest were hidden from the villager. This was so in a physical sense as well. The pygmy could appear at any time in the village, but villagers rarely went into the forest. To the villagers, the forest was constantly threatening to swallow their painstakingly cultivated lands. It was the hiding place of demons, and the place where the restless spirits of the dead gathered and made trouble.

It was in the pygmies' interest to keep it that way. Anything they could do to encourage the villagers in their superstitions worked to keep the forest safe from village noise. Which was why, when the pygmies brought already rotting bits of game to the village, they would make sure to accompany the gift with tales of all the malevolent spirits they had met and vanquished on their way. It was understood, of course, that in return the pygmies could take their fill of yams, stuff themselves on bananas, and recover from their terrible ordeal by downing vast amounts of palm wine.

Like the anthropologists at St. Louis, who concluded that parrots and monkeys had a debilitating effect on the pygmies' mental faculties, the villagers believed the hunters could not live for months on end in close quarters with ghosts and demons without showing some ill effects. That went a long way to explaining why the pygmies were unable to grow anything for themselves, except for those cannabis plants whose spindly stalks were the one horticultural adornment of forest campsites. It explained as well why the pygmies were unreliable; why, after promising to help out in the fields, they might, when the time came, be nowhere to be seen, having retired back into the forest as silently as they had emerged from it.

"Manners, beastly/Religion, none," was how an Englishman expressed his opinion of Africans—exactly what many Africans felt about pygmies. If Africa was a word for the barbaric and the benighted, then the Englishman had his Africa, and the villagers theirs. And just as the newly arriving muzungu felt it was his duty to boost the cultural level of Africans, so did the villagers assume the burden of educating pygmies.

They could try to instill a respect for witchcraft, for example, and to initiate pygmy boys into manhood so that at least the forest dwellers didn't go stupidly scampering through the woods unaware of the distinction between adults and children. In reality, these lessons didn't make much of an impression. If the village was school, then the forest dwellers, when they weren't truant, were usually only pretending to pay attention.

The pygmies preferred to do without witchcraft. In times of misfortune, they didn't, like the villagers, trouble to probe deeply into the hearts of men to uncover the evil thought that was responsible. If natural remedies failed to cure their illnesses, they mourned, sometimes violently, but without casting blame.

Then they would seek the privacy of the forest to perform a ceremony known as the *molimo*, which is also the name of the trumpet used in that ceremony. Once out of sight of the village, the forest dwellers would summon the *molimo* trumpet from the treetop where it was said to sleep and begin the ritual that could go on all night for weeks, if not months. The rhythmically accompanied call and response between song and trumpet focused their attention on the forest and, implicitly, the forest's attention on them.

The *molimo* was the high point of the pygmy's romance with the forest. When there was pain, failure, or grief that simply had to be borne, it was the rite of acceptance and reconciliation. It gathered the encampment into a kind of rapture that brought them still deeper into the forest's embrace. While the *molimo* dashed around the outskirts of the camp, now hidden, now open to view, ranging through all the sounds of the forest, from the growling and snarling of animals to the sheer loveliness of the forest's own voice, the people would respond energetically with refrains as simple as "The forest is good," and the dancers would move in and out of the campfire without being harmed.

The hunters had no use for the poison oracle, or any of the other techniques indispensable for tracking down a witch and testing his or her guilt through an ordeal to the death. The pygmies didn't even know enough to treat their own religious objects with respect. They might even retire the *molimo* to a creek, where it could get choked with mud or carried off downstream. The forest dwellers knew no better than to find such a calamity hilarious.

The villagers had dread and solemnity to spare. They would have loaned these ingredients out to help upgrade the forest dwellers' silliness into a real religion. But the pygmies were forever stuck at the level of actually enjoying their religion.

In private, that is. In the village, on the other hand, their skill at mimicry allowed them to pass themselves off as somewhat retarded mini-villagers. This is how the first professional anthropologists—men like Paul Schebesta, whose *Among Congo Pygmies* appeared in 1903—tended to think of them. Living with the villagers, they saw the pygmies through village eyes and accepted the view that the pygmies owed their culture to the influence of the village. That was the prevailing view until the 1950s, when Colin Turnbull reversed the roles.

By traveling with the nomadic forest dwellers, Turnbull became the first anthropologist to see the village through the eyes of the pygmies. It is from Turnbull's writings, in particular *The Forest People*, that we know that though villager and pygmy do sometimes have the same name for their rituals, the rituals are alike in name only. Where, for example, a coming-of-age ceremony in the village might be defined by fear and a need to propitiate all the relevant spirits, a ritual by the same name in the forest would be a joyous occasion, performed, the pygmies say, to "rejoice" the forest.

There are reasons why the two rituals are mirror images of each other, the one informed by dread, the other by joy. The pygmies have a rare if not unique relationship to their environment. No one is thought to have proceeded them into the forests of central Africa. They love and trust this environment and draw their confidence from it. The villagers, on the other hand, are latecomers by comparison, still ill at ease with both the forest and the forest dwellers.

It is also from Turnbull that we know that pygmies have their own purposes in lending themselves for brief periods to village customs. Turnbull was with the pygmies when they entered villages and played to the hilt their roles as delinquent villagers. He was also with them when they reentered the forest and laughed at village ways as so much noise and superstition, utterly "null and void," as they put it, within the real world, the world of the hunt.

Turnbull confirmed the observation made by Burrows that the pygmies are marvelous mimics, but deepened it. When hunting an elephant, for example, a pygmy might chose to imitate its smell by rubbing himself liberally with elephant droppings—a technique that led one Western observer to say, "You might say you could *never* understand someone who voluntarily smears himself with elephant dung, but 'civilized' people sometimes go to even greater lengths to earn a living."

When "hunting" people, on the other hand, mimicry stands for the pygmy's freedom to maneuver within an alien culture without being assimilated by it.

It is 1904. A pygmy holds an arrowhead in his hands as the warrior who gave it to him for reasons of his own turns and walks away.

There is probably no place on earth more distant from the pygmy's home than St. Louis has become that summer. And yet the pygmy is not without resources. What is this fair, this city, this entire land of the *muzungu* but a village magnified and multiplied? The pygmy has a lifetime of experience dealing with villages, insinuating himself into them, getting what he wants, and leaving when he wants to.

This *muzungu* village is bigger, more dangerous and ridiculous, noisier, even more null and void than the villages he has seen—more interesting and tempting, but a village nonetheless.

Of course, the key to this pygmy's confidence in his ability to survive a village is that he can leave. He can pass himself off as anything, play any role, assume any disguise, provided his people, his hunting band, his family still exist and he can return to them.

A pygmy can hunt even so large a creature as the St. Louis Fair, as the entire land of the *muzungu*, if his home still exists and if he knows he can still get there.

3

"GHOSTS! GHOSTS!"

It was in 1868 when nine years
old or thereabouts, that while looking at a map of Africa of the time and
putting my finger on the blank space
then representing the unsolved mystery of that continent, I said to myself with absolute assurance and an
amazing audacity which are no
longer in my character now: 'When I
grow up I shall go there.'

—Joseph Conrad

Who was, who wasn't human?
It was a big question in turn-of-the-century
Europe and America and a big question in turn-
of-the-century Africa. The Europeans arriving
there in increasing numbers were asking and answering it
about pygmies, for example. The form their query took was
often influenced by the current interpretations of Darwinism,
so it was not simply who was *human*, but who was *more*
human, and finally, who was *most* human, that concerned
them. And just as Europeans were measuring the humanity of
Africans, Africans were forced into making similar judgments
about Europeans; the difference was that it was the Westerners
who were turning up on African doorsteps uninvited and
unannounced.

(The pygmies' response—to hide, or to shoot arrows at
caravans that strayed too near their campsites, or to use the

29

odd *muzungu* as a stalking horse for the perfection of their mimicry—was fine so far as it went. But it was not meant to serve as a philosophical response. It did not get to the root of the perplexing question—what was a *muzungu*?)

Muzungus had been talked about in central Africa for a long time. It was known they had something to do with mass disappearances during the height of the slave trade. And their existence was often associated with water in some way—they lived in or came from over a great water. But who were they? Why were they turning up in the flesh (if whiteness indeed was flesh and not its remarkable absence)? What were they coming for? There was no one answer. As in the West, there was room for diverse opinion.

One commonly held belief was that the *muzungus* were refugees from the land of the dead. A missionary was informed that "the white men are dead people who have once lived in our villages, but when they died, they came to the place where the dead are to be found, and there, they shed their skins (just as some snakes), after which they had white bodies." Occasionally, Africans crying "Ghosts! Ghosts!" fled in terror at their approach.

In general, it was not regarded as a good sign that these *muzungus* were appearing where they had never been sighted before. If they were white because they had no skin, that was likely to be painful. Perhaps that was why they covered their bodies with so many clothes. Or perhaps they were envious of those with skin, which was why they so often insisted that Africans cover themselves with clothes as well. Perhaps they wore the clothes to disguise who and what they really were, and where they came from. Or it could be they were simply ashamed.

More alarming still was the rumor that the *muzungus* were man-eaters. They had been starved in the land of the dead. Now they were returning to the land of the living with a huge appetite, which, it was feared, could only be satisfied by human flesh. Cannibals or not, the consensus was that they were agents of destruction. "The white man belongs to the most feared of all idols, which chain and kill people," was what one missionary heard. And he recorded a discussion between an escaped slave and some chiefs on the nature of the *muzungu*. The chiefs wanted to know what the whites were. "They are human," the ex-slave told them.

"Yes, but in which way?" asked the chiefs.

"They are white and they have soft and flexible bodies."

"But don't they eat people?"

"I don't know, but I almost fear that that is the case, as death follows them where they go."

"May they stay where they are," intoned the chiefs.

They didn't stay where they were. In the last decades of the nineteenth century they kept on coming, for a variety of motives, some of which disguised the others, some of which they had to hide even from themselves.

Nineteenth-century Africa was the moon, and an explorer like Stanley, in effect, the chief moonwalker of his day.

The odds in favor of their surviving had increased to the point where they could come. Quinine was the difference. Even before the links between human host, mosquito carrier, and malarial spore were spelled out near the end of the century, it was noticed that quinine, isolated from the cinchona bark imported from South America by Jesuits, worked against the disease.

Before quinine, a sailor's ditty about the effects of malaria ("Beware, beware the Bight of Benin, For few come out, though many go in") described the situation well, and Europeans had to conduct their business with Africa—the slave trade—from shipboard or from coastal ports of call. After about 1850, quinine opened the way to the interior.

They came because of maps, because science abhorred ignorance, and when geographers left large portions of the map of Africa blank that was equivalent to posting a challenge. Where did the great rivers—the Congo, the Niger, the Nile—begin? What truth was there to the rumors of enormous, heretofore unseen lakes and hidden mountains?

Missionaries came to spread the gospel: to rid the Africans of their superstitions, their pagan love for dance, and their sinful comfort with their bodies. The missionaries wanted to replace the thousands of specialized African charms and talismans with a single all-purpose amulet—the cross.

David Livingstone, before being saved by Stanley, was already known as an African geographer and evangelist. He was also a vehement opponent of the slave trade. "Besides those actually captured," he wrote in 1868, "thousands are killed, or die of their wounds and famine, driven from their homes by the slave-raider. Thousands perish in internecine wars, waged for slaves with their own clansmen or neighbors; slain by the lust for gain which is stimulated by the slave-purchasers."

Livingstone was not inveighing against the slave trade on a soapbox from afar. Again and again he had seen the grisly consequences up close. "The many skeletons," he wrote, "amongst the rocks and woods, by the pools, and along the paths of the wilderness, all testify to the awful sacrifice of human life which must be attributed directly or indirectly to this trade of hell."

Livingstone's writings were clarion calls. Westerners heard him and came to Africa to save it from the continuing ravages of the slave trade. So far as East and central Africa were concerned, that meant opposing the Arabs, based on the island of Zanzibar.

The irony of Europe taking a position of militant abolitionism was not lost upon the Arabs. It was not so long before that Europe had been the leading customer for their wares, and that the foundations of European might were being laid by the labor of black bodies on plantations in the Americas and the Indies. In those days it was understood that an East African slave who had survived the added passage around the Cape of Africa to the Americas had already given the best possible proof of durability.

Why, then, had Europe changed its mind? Why was slavery wrong in 1885 when it had been so very right one hundred years before? And what gave Europe the authority to impose its change of mind by force of arms on its old trading partners?

Tippu Tip, the leading Arab slave trader of the day, named, it was said, for the "tip tip tip tip" of his guns, could never be persuaded that slave trade was wrong or even that Europeans truly thought it wrong, although a man like David Livingstone might think so. Tippu Tip had saved Livingstone in 1867, four years before Stanley found him. It was of course peculiar that Livingstone wound up in the care of the greatest slaver of them all. Or perhaps it was simply inevitable that anyone blundering around in search of the mysterious sources of the Congo or the Nile would sooner or later run across Tippu Tip. The Arab coddled Livingstone, fed him, and supplied him, as charmed by the evangelizing *muzungu* as Stanley was by pygmies. He even put up with the old man's endless scolding about the evils of slavery, occasionally eluding him to see to the requirements of his trade.

But Livingstone was an oddity, bumbling around the interior without any apparent purpose, and quoting from his holy book as if that alone could put an end to the age-old traffic in human bodies. Livingstone was not to be mistaken for the typical Westerner. When the typical Westerner spoke of human rights, justice, progress, and so on, those words were pure pretext, so far as Tippu Tip was concerned. Behind them he heard Europe's raging greed for Arab lands. Behind them he heard guns.

"And who is to be my judge?" he once challenged a Westerner to whom he was extending hospitality.

"Europe," came the answer.

"Aha! Now you speak the truth," he said. "Do not let us talk of justice; people are only just when it pays. The white man is stronger than I am; they eat my possessions as I ate those of the pagans."

Tippu Tip did not wait around for violent dispossession by the muzungu. He had visited the permanent white settlements of South Africa and come to an estimate of the kind of power they represented. And when he witnessed Europe's new repeating rifles, this man named for the sound of gunfire drew the only possible conclusion. As his fellow slave traders perished one by one in futile acts of resistance to Western force of arms, Tippu Tip withdrew to the island of Zanzibar, where, with concubines, slaves, children, and grandchildren, he lived in luxurious retirement until his death in 1905.

But he left behind two curses for the whites who "ate" his possessions, the first a prophecy: "Justice will be done. The Europeans are throwing the Arabs out now, but they will be thrown out in turn." The second curse took human form. It was the legacy of tribes without land or roots, tribes thoroughly corrupted by their years of mercenary service to the slave trader and eager, with their Arab masters gone, to attach themselves to Europeans.

Europeans came, then, to deliver Africans from Tippu Tip and to gather around the flag of Leopold II, the Belgian king who succeeded the Arabs in the interior. In 1885, the Berlin Conference, chaired by Otto von Bismarck, made Leopold the ruler of the newly created Congo Free State, a territory within cen-

tral Africa roughly eighty times the size of Belgium. By award-
ing this territory to Leopold, the European powers achieved a
number of aims at once.

They satisfied Leopold II's colonial ambitions at no cost
and a good deal of benefit to themselves. The lust for colonies
ran in the family. Leopold I had once attempted to buy Texas.
His son, even before becoming king in 1865, had made the
acquisition of a colony the central goal of his career. Giving the
Congo to Leopold II—as if it was theirs to give—was convenient to all the major powers. It allowed Germany to thwart
France, France to thwart Germany, and England to forestall
them both. It was true that Portugal could present a claim to
central Africa dating back to the fifteenth century, when it had
introduced Christianity to the King of the Congo and then stole
his population out from under him. But Portugal could safely
be ignored. What was important was that the major powers
keep each other out of central Africa. Neutralization of interests was preferable to war. Leopold, then, ruler of a small,
utterly vulnerable country, was perfectly positioned to emerge
as a deliverer.

And it was Leopold personally, rather than the Belgian
nation, who was put in charge of the Congo Free State, as the
Belgian parliament and people wanted to stay clear of colonies, great power politics, and the shifting sands of ententes,
alliances, and accords. This unusual arrangement made him
the greatest single landholder on the face of the earth. The only
checks on his power were expressed in the agreements reached
at Berlin.

The Berlin Act bound Leopold "to watch over the preser-
vation of the native tribes, and to care for the improvement of
the conditions of their moral and material well-being, and to
help in suppressing slavery, and especially the Slave Trade."
He was also to lend special cooperation to "Christian missionaries, scientists, and explorers" who might assist in "instructing the natives and bringing home to them the blessings of
civilization."

The rest of the agreement laid out, at greater length and in
finer detail, Leopold's responsibilities to England, France, Germany, and the ten other signatories of the Berlin Act. The king
was to put no obstacles in the way of free trade with inhabitants of his colony; all the signatory powers were to have the
same rights of access as he himself enjoyed.

The Berlin and the subsequent Brussels Conference may have taxed delegates with the "hard work," as one complained, of "dinners, receptions and balls," but the dancing, dining, and feasting was toward a worthy cause. The conferences had, in one fell swoop, kept the great powers from each other's throats, satisfied the dictates of conscience, and opened a vast new area to commercial exploitation. In the long run, of course, it all depended on King Leopold being as good as his word, which, in 1885, there was no reason to doubt.

He was, it seemed, a perfect sovereign of the Congo. He was an amateur geographer in his own right who had convened conferences of geographers. In 1879, at his own expense, he had contracted with H. M. Stanley for the explorer to chart central Africa and lay the foundations for his colony.

Stanley's journey on behalf of Leopold did more than open new paths and decrease the sum total of white space on the map of central Africa. It left Leopold's regime with a name. All members of the Free State, from the king himself down to his armies, his tax collectors, and his merchants, were known in the Congo as if they were part of a single entity, or members of a tribe. This tribe was called, after Stanley, the Bula Mutadi, the Smashers of Rocks.

It was almost as if Europe had never played the crucial role in shrinking African commerce to reliance on the export of a single cash crop—its population. Now, when Westerners came to Africa they came to colonize, to conquer where necessary, and to civilize. These were considered roughly equivalent, completely justified activities. Africans needed saving not only from the likes of Tippu Tip but from a more fundamental enemy, themselves. As the historian David Lewis put it, "Whether participant or spectator, virtually every European embraced the dogma that the scramble for territory beginning in the last quarter of the nineteenth century was as beneficial for Africans as it was beyond the power of Africans to resist."

There were other reasons for muzungus turning up in greater numbers in the African interior. Africa was not just Europe's geographical but also its psychological frontier, and going to Africa was a way of filling in the unknowns, the psychological white spaces, on the map of the self. Africa conferred the priceless gift of metamorphosis on Westerners. The white man in Africa stood a good chance of shortening his life through battle, mishap, or disease. The reason for going in spite of the danger was that he also stood a good chance of becoming the man Europe or America never suspected he could be.

And the Africans knew. Once they overcame the initial shock of seeing their first *muzungu*, they displayed an uncanny gift for renaming him after the qualities of the man within. In the end it might seem as if there were two men, one visible only to Africans, the other only to Europeans. Stanley, for instance, had one face for David Livingstone when he rescued him, and another for the porters who got him there.

Stanley had been sent after Livingstone, missing for nearly four years, by James Gordon Bennett Jr., the owner of the New York *Herald*. In 1869, Bennett, who was to newsprint roughly what P.T. Barnum was to showmanship, sent Stanley off with the rousing mandate: "Draw a thousand pounds now; and when you have gone through that, draw another thousand, and when that is spent, draw another thousand, and when you have finished that, draw another thousand, and so on; but FIND LIVINGSTONE."

Stanley complied. He drew his thousands and two years later, after completing the grueling trek from Zanzibar, pronounced those famous words, "Dr. Livingstone, I presume?" to the old man dying slowly on the shores of Lake Tanganyika. Livingstone welcomed Stanley but declined to return to Europe with him, choosing instead to remain in Africa, where he died eighteen months later, still in pursuit of the mysterious source of the Nile. But Stanley's own character was softened, his temper cooled, by the several months he spent in the company of Livingstone.

"My dear Doctor," he wrote back shortly after leaving him, "very few amongst men have I found I so much got to love as yourself." The stifling syntax of this message reveals better than the words how unaccustomed Stanley was to the emotion Livingstone had aroused. But it was almost immediately after sending this letter that Stanley disappeared and Bula Mutadi emerged in his place.

Stanley's caravan was fording a flooded stream. A porter balancing a box of Livingstone's writings on his head fell into a hole while crossing, with the water rising to his chin. Stanley waved a pistol in the direction of the struggling porter and bellowed in Swahili, "Look out! Drop that box and I'll shoot you."

The transition had been made from the man known to Europeans to the man known to Africans, from Henry Morton Stanley to Smasher of Rocks, in a matter of minutes.

Conquest, colonization, conscience, gain, and the possibility of expanding or, in the case of Bula Mutadi, exploding into the identity opened by a new name—these were reasons why most *muzungus* appeared in central Africa near the end of the last century. They don't adequately describe what a man like William Henry Sheppard was doing in the Congo Free State in 1890.

In many of the pictures taken of him in Africa, Sheppard wears a white explorer's outfit and a pith helmet. He tends to stand toward the front of the groups of Africans with whom he is photographed. The Africans lean on their spears. Sheppard leans on his rifle. His relaxed posture and the big smile on his face say more eloquently than his letters home that he is glad to be where he is.

Sheppard's first appearance among Africans raised more questions than it put to rest about the nature of the *muzungu*. Sheppard spoke like a *muzungu*, dressed like one, but had not shed his skin like other *muzungus*. Was he or wasn't he, then, like other *muzungus*, conceivably a new arrival from the land of the dead?

William Henry Sheppard was an ordained Presbyterian minister from Virginia, and he was black.

4

CHURCH AND STATE

I could cut off everything else,
but not their hands. What else but
their hands do I really need in the
Congo?

—Leopold II

Reverend Sheppard had long nurtured the dream of preaching in Africa. He thought of Africa as the land of his "forefathers." He spoke of Africans as "his people."

This was the positive side to his appearing in the Congo with the good book and the black skin, the pith helmet and the rifle. Sheppard had, for his day, an unusual pride and interest in his roots. In Africa, he relied on the Bible and preached the story of Christ. On his return trips to the United States, he relied on African artifacts and stories of his adventures to fill halls with his black countrymen. He brought them news that Africans, too, had culture, laws, government, and highly developed art.

The negative reason for Sheppard's being in the Congo was simple: the alternative was being in America. In America, especially in the South, where Sheppard was born in 1865, one month after Lee's surrender to Grant ended the Civil War, a black might no longer be a slave but neither could he be called free. Both Sheppard's parents had been slaves; and as he matured in Virginia and went to school in Alabama, Sheppard saw the return of the old racism in new forms.

Jim Crow was the name given to the postbellum system of disenfranchisement and segregation by skin color. It was legal, which is to say it was passed into law by all-white legislatures and eventually seconded by an all-white Supreme Court; it had the force of the police behind it; and where daytime enforcement did not suffice there were lynchings and the Ku Klux Klan.

Not long after being ordained at Stillman College, a white-run, Presbyterian religious school for blacks, Sheppard filed with the Southern Presbyterian Mission Board for a transfer to its proposed mission in the Congo. The church didn't think a black man could, or should, be at the head of the Congo mission. No matter how often, how respectfully, or how well Sheppard argued his case, the missionary board kept him waiting. Because he was black, it was thought he would never be accorded the same treatment from Free State officials that a white man could expect, and that he would never learn the languages necessary for preaching in the Congo.

On this second point, especially, Sheppard was to prove his superiors dramatically wrong. His quick grasp of African languages was no small part of why his career in Africa was so notable. Sheppard made two trips in the Congo that together frame the history of the Congo Free State. The first trip brought his name to the attention of an elite audience of geographers, anthropologists, and explorers. The second trip made him quotable by Mark Twain and Arthur Conan Doyle. In the end, the patience and persistence he had developed in trying to get to Africa turned out to be best possible training for him. Once in the Congo, this soft but steady pounding at barred and bolted gates got him into places no foreigner, white or black, had ever seen before.

In 1890, a man with an eagerness to preach in the Congo that matched Sheppard's own appeared before the missionary board. In every other respect this man, Samuel Lapsley, was Sheppard's opposite. He was white, wellborn, and equipped with social connections that even King Leopold II was bound to respect. This was the man Sheppard and the mission board had been waiting for. Without Lapsley, or someone like him, Sheppard might have spent a lifetime applying to go to Africa and being told to wait. With Lapsley, Sheppard became co-founder of the American Presbyterian Congo Mission (A.P.C.M.).

Lapsley was connected through his father, a prominent judge, to Senator John Morgan of Alabama, who had prompted the United States to recognize Leopold's Congo Free State. Leopold, therefore, was in his debt. If there were any problems about the Congo being open to "Christian missionaries" and others who might assist in "instructing the natives and bringing home to them the blessings of civilization," as per the Berlin Act, the senator's name could make all the difference.

Senator Morgan wasn't interested in Congo colonies or Christian missionaries in and of themselves. But he was deeply interested in resolving the unstable racial situation left by the Civil War, and he was willing to manipulate everyone from kings to missionaries toward that end. Morgan sent missionary after missionary off to Africa with his personal blessing because he saw missions as leading to one of a very limited number of ways out of the racial impasse.

Of course, blacks could simply have been given the same rights as whites. Although this approach had simplicity and ease of implementation—not to mention justice—on its side, there were very few white people in the southern states after 1876 willing to espouse it. It was regarded as the most bizarre and improbable approach of all. Senator Morgan never considered it, preferring Jim Crow. Jim Crow, however, made no allowance for the final removal of that source of annoyance, the black race, which, after slavery had been abolished, continued, when there was no more need for it, to linger on in the United States.

In two last solutions, this graceless lingering of the ex-slaves and their descendants on American soil was addressed directly. The first of these was by natural selection. Darwin was understood to have shown that when left to itself, natural selection would accomplish extinction. Without slavery to embrace and protect them, or so it was thought, blacks would have to compete with Caucasians for survival. Whites' greater fitness for this contest was beyond dispute. The disappearance of blacks as a race, then, would only be a matter of time.

One problem with the solution by extinction had to do

with evidence. The censuses taken after the end of slavery were eagerly inspected. Sometimes it seemed as if blacks were, as predicted, on their way out; other times, contra Darwin, the black population showed no signs of failing, and might even be on the rise. Further, how long could whites be expected to wait for extinction to take effect?

In the last approach to ridding the United States of the blacks, Senator Morgan's activism played a role. Not content to wait for natural selection to grind out the answer, he hoped that blacks could be made to see that America no longer had any use for them. There was nothing to keep them from leaving and much to encourage them to go. Morgan wanted them to pack up and go back to Africa. He viewed the American missions to that continent as scouting expeditions, advance parties sent to pave the way.

Morgan's hope for a black return to Africa was a revival of a colonization scheme in circulation decades before Abraham Lincoln, in a speech made in 1852, called it a "glorious consummation" to send back "a captive people to their long-lost father-land." Lincoln thought the expatriation of blacks preferable to the "dangerous presence of slavery." Senator Morgan, on the other hand, did not go on record as being particularly troubled by slavery; it was the mass of free blacks that worried him.

Did Lapsley and Sheppard know what a great geopolitical burden had been placed on their shoulders as the two of them set out to found a mission? They may have. When they met with King Leopold in 1890 on their way to Africa, the king told them it was fine with him if masses of black Americans came to his Free State. Apparently they been briefed about Senator Morgan's grand ideas for a Congo mission.

They had left New York harbor two weeks before, with Lapsley's mother putting her son into Sheppard's safekeeping. "Sheppard, take care of Sam," were the last words heard from shore.

During their meeting with Leopold, the king was characteristically humorless, but not yet grim. He was heavy but not yet enormous. And he had not yet surrendered to his terror of germs to the extent of wrapping his long, full beard to seal it off from bacteria.

Himself a Catholic, Leopold promised the Protestant missionaries that he cared much less about doctrinal differences than about the welfare of the Congolese. He was earnest and persuasive. He had convinced the world of his good intentions and gave Sheppard and Lapsley no reason to disbelieve him. They left for Africa assured of his support.

In the United States, William Sheppard and Samuel Lapsley would have lived in mutually exclusive worlds. They would have gone to different churches, prayed with different prayer books, and read from different Bibles. Africa integrated them. The ease they discovered in each other's company was a trait necessary for survival. There was no one else to look after them as they struggled through repeated bouts of fever and disease. They were each other's best and only nurses as they wound their way ever further into the interior, until they reached the Kasai region of the Congo, 1,200 miles inland from the Atlantic coast and virgin territory for proselytization. They adopted a monkey as their pet and called it Tippu Tip, in humorous reference to the deposed slave trader.

Lapsley's heartfelt sermons in the wilderness frequently prompted Sheppard to shed a tear, but tended to have less effect on the natives. "Why, Mr. Lapsley," one woman exclaimed after listening to him preach, "if we had known God loved us we would have been singing to Him." Lapsley hardly needed words to attract an audience. His skin color was enough. The Africans had an irrepressible curiosity about the parts of him tucked away and hidden by clothes. Could his private parts be as unbelievably white as the rest of him? Reverend Lapsley could gather a considerable throng almost any time he wanted simply by taking off his shoes and socks and wriggling his toes.

While Lapsley preached, but made nary a convert, Sheppard took note of native religious beliefs. "The itching of the hand, the twitching of the eye, a crow flying across one's house, an owl hooting in the jungle, a snake crossing your trail," were all regarded as bad signs, he recorded. The universe of the Africans he met did not tolerate luck or random events. It was held together by that skein of human intention known as witchcraft: "The capsizing of a canoe, the falling out of a palm tree, a hunter or traveler killed by elephant or leopard—these are caused by some enemy."

The missionaries had some countervailing magic of their own—guns and books. When the Congolese were shown their first book, wrote Sheppard, they "excitedly crowded and jostled each other, eager to see and to touch it. How strange it was. They turned and counted every leaf." When they were done counting, they held the book "upside down, for they saw as much in it upside down as they did right side up." It was nothing short of a miracle to them "that you could mark down your thoughts and they would stay there."

The missionaries had come to baptize and to christen, but the Africans, as usual, were swift at renaming and slow to be renamed. Lapsley soon was called the Pathfinder, because, said Sheppard, he had found his way into "their homes, their language, and into their hearts." What impressed the Congolese most about the white man was the fact of his simply being there.

Because of his accuracy with a rifle, Sheppard became the Hunter, or the Great Sheppard, dividing hippopotamus steaks among the Congolese. On one occasion, against native advice, he swam out to retrieve a hippo and was saved from death only because a very large crocodile preferred dead hippo to live missionary. Sheppard's response was typical of his healthy respect for the Congolese and willingness to learn from them: It was just asking for trouble, he concluded, for foreigners go about central Africa "disregarding the advice of natives."

The meeting between Christianity and witchcraft, mu-zungu and African, was entirely peaceful except for some disquieting encounters with a tribe known as the Zappo-Zap that had once worked for Tippu Tip and were now about to be installed in Leopold's Congolese constabulary, the Force Publique. But the pace of conversion was slow, conditions hard, and disease recurrent. The missionaries, who had hoped to set up a string of bases, were forced to settle for one station, established at Luebo.

It was at Luebo that they heard their first rumors of a Forbidden Land, and of its king who claimed all this territory as his own. They met occasional travelers from that land and remarked on their "apparent superiority in physique, manners, dress and dialect." The missionaries were curious to know if the sophisticated Kuba would be more receptive to the Gospel. They considered traveling to the fabled "red halls of the Lukenga," the Kuba's king, which no outsider had ever seen.

It was a journey Sheppard was destined to make alone.

Lapsley never returned from a conference to which he was called by Belgian officials. Sheppard, anxiously awaiting the steamer he hoped would be carrying his friend back, was instead handed a note which dazed him and nearly made him fall. When he recovered his footing he cried to the Congolese who had gathered with him at the landing, "Ntomanjela wa kafu." The Pathfinder was dead. Lapsley had died of fever.

Sheppard grieved that there would "no more kneeling together in prayer," no more "planning together future work." He anguished over not having been at Lapsley's side one last time to nurse him.

It was a crucial moment not only for Sheppard personally but for the Congo mission. It was almost as if by surviving, he had disregarded orders. He was alone now and in charge in the field, the very situation the mission board had been determined to avoid. There was talk of closing the mission and recalling him. But it was easier to send Sheppard to Africa than it was to get him back. He had no desire to wait indefinitely for another Lapsley, another white permission slip for going where he knew he had to be.

He never really found the words to adequately explain his next move, or its conclusion. Perhaps Protestant orthodoxy would have frowned on the real reasons for his decision. About Africa, Sheppard often spoke of being happy and feeling at home. But now it was as if he was going to his home within that home. At the very moment when he might have been expected to flounder for a while, Sheppard, as if answering a private call, fled directly toward a source of danger. He prepared to travel to the Forbidden Land, defying his superiors' expectations in another way than by surviving.

In casual conversation with Kuba traders he had quickly mastered their tongue, displaying a facility with language blacks were thought to lack. Without this advantage, his attempt to penetrate the Forbidden Land would have had nothing to justify it except an unspoken assumption that it was meant to be. Now, with what companions he could rally from Luebo by invoking Lapsley's name, and by saying this was what the Pathfinder wanted, he began the journey.

The Bakuba sealed off their realm by a simple expedient, which, until Sheppard, had kept it inviolate. The "Lukenga," wrote Sheppard, "sent out word through all his kingdom: 'The Bakuba who shows a stranger the road will be beheaded.' "

Since no one who knew the way dared point it out, Sheppard had to advance on the capital obliquely and by small steps.

At every village where he stopped he would ask to buy eggs. It was an innocent request, hard to deny to this black foreigner who inexplicably spoke the language. Once the village's own supply of eggs was exhausted, Sheppard would request permission to send one of his men farther on to buy some more. Permission granted, he would then secretly follow his man to the next town.

By this means he drew steadily closer to his destination, until finally his hosts promised him eggs beyond number, a mountain of eggs, if only he would go back the way he came. He was not of the Kuba, and when his presence in their village became known to the king, all heads would be forfeit.

Feeling the weight of his responsibility, he retreated to the woods to ask guidance of his "Master" in coming to a decision. But it was too late, even if he decided to retreat: The Lukenga had been alerted.

The king had already "called for his sons; called for his forty fighting men, who use bows six feet high, and can send an arrow through a buffalo." He had given "his spear and knife to his son . . . and said: Go down . . . and bring back the chief, the foreigners, the villagers—all—and I will behead them."

In the morning, as Sheppard lazed about, looking through a two-year-old newspaper, he was interrupted by the squad of warriors led by the king's son. Something about Sheppard puzzled the prince. He paused for a moment to interrogate the stranger, if stranger he was, before carrying out his father's decree.

He said, "You are a foreigner, yet you speak our language."

"Yes," answered Sheppard.

"But did you know all these paths many years ago?"

"No."

"This is the first time you have been here, and you had no guide, yet you are a foreigner?"

"Yes, that is true."

"Well that is very strange," the prince concluded.

Turning on his heels, he told Sheppard he would be back in three days' time to announce the king's verdict.

"If ever I prayed," wrote the missionary, "I prayed most earnestly then." When the prince returned, he pulled his father's knife, the emblem of royalty, out of his belt and announced there was no more need for subterfuge or disguise. He knew now why Sheppard had seemed familiar.

"You need not try to hide it longer from us. You know our paths, and we," he assured Sheppard, "know who you are."

"I said to my father," continued the prince, " 'The stranger has no guides, our people try to turn him back. He knows our roads, he speaks our language.' "

The king had called the wise men together and asked: "Who is this stranger? He knows our roads without a guide, yet he is a foreigner. He speaks our language, yet he is a foreigner."

"The wise men studied this mystery, and they told my father: 'This stranger is no stranger, but Bope Mekabe, of your own family, who has returned to earth.' "

"Then my father was glad, and said to me: 'Son, go and tell our people that Bope has returned to us.' "

At that very moment, according to the prince, the people were rejoicing. Bope Mekabe, a.k.a. William Henry Sheppard, had reigned before the current Lukenga. He was the prince's grandfather. After he died his spirit had refreshed itself in the land of the dead, and had then been reborn. And, announced the prince with finality, "You are that spirit."

Reverend Sheppard was escorted to the Kuba capital in state. To some who saw it later, the splendor of that capital called forth comparisons with imperial Rome. Sheppard himself, when presented to the Lukenga with his seven hundred wives, and his courtiers who clapped at the end of his every sentence and laughed when he laughed, coughed when he coughed, compared the red halls of the king to the courts of the pharaohs. He thought the Kuba civilization could only be a remnant of ancient Egypt.

He spent months in the markets and the royal halls. He observed and recorded the customs, myths, and complex laws by which the Kuba were governed. He was impressed by the fact that art adorned life at every level of society, and began his own celebrated collection of Kuba art with a knife, seven generations old, handed to him by the king.

He was permitted to preach as much as he wished, although, to the Kuba, the story of Christ seemed like a fable he picked up in the land of the dead. "It was wonderful," marveled Sheppard of the response to one of his best sermons, "they did not understand it."

Finally, perhaps because he tired of being treated as a reincarnation none of whose current opinions made the slightest impact, he asked permission to leave. It was granted on condition that he promise to return, and gave his word.

On none of his frequent return trips to the Kuba did he come close to convincing them that he was nothing more than William Sheppard, born of ex-slaves in a place called Virginia. The Kuba, equally, never got him to admit that he was truly that royal ghost come back from the dead, Bope Mekabe. But he and the Kuba remained inextricably bound up with each other for the rest of his African career.

From the Kuba side of things, Sheppard, as royalty incarnate and reincarnate, was implicated in all questions of succession, and nearly murdered once on suspicion of trying to take back the throne. From the Western side of things, Sheppard served as a crucial link between the Kuba and the outside world. He spoke up for the kingdom against those who later came close to destroying it.

The Kuba saw through his attire and religion and recognized the soul of a king. In the West he gained recognition as an explorer. On the strength of the egg-eating path blazed into the Forbidden Land, Reverend Sheppard became a Fellow of Britain's Royal Geographical Society.

In the seven years after this first journey to the Kuba in 1892, the Presbyterian mission at Luebo survived and grew, with Sheppard as a mainstay. He made journeys to the United States, marrying, bringing back his wife and fresh recruits when the mission lacked manpower. His recruits were always black. The missionary board still had its problems finding whites.

During these years the first doubts about Leopold's rule of the Congo were heard. As required, Leopold had put an end to the slave trade. The evil presided over by Tippu Tip was no more. The doubts had to do with what had been put in its place. There were rumors that the king had devised something still more inhumane than what David Livingstone had denounced as a "trade of hell."

In 1899 Reverend William Henry Sheppard made another journey, one which he resisted and feared to the same degree he had earlier been drawn, against all odds, to his meeting with the Kuba.

First the natives had come to him on their own, telling

him of atrocities, bringing him presents, hoping to prevail upon him to accompany them. Sheppard refused. The natives came again, begging, reminding him that he had once said he loved them, telling him that now they were in need, that there was no one but him to turn to, and would he not come? Dread filled him, and was stronger than his feelings of obligation. There was an Africa to which he was utterly open, and which he would risk anything to know. He was now being asked to visit another Africa. He knew without going what was waiting for him there.

He had come to Africa in part to avoid the plague of racism in the United States. The nightmare had caught up with him. It was as if he had escaped burning crosses only to confront, so many thousand miles away, a magnification of the same horror. Lynchings were obviously on his mind when he answered, "It is just as if I were to take a rope and go out behind the house and hang myself to that tree. Go back and tell your friends I can not come. There is no use in exposing myself in that way . . ."

Finally a note came from his superiors. "Dear Brother Sheppard," it read, "we hear of atrocities being committed in the Pianga country by the Zappo-Zaps. We commission you immediately on receipt of this letter to go over and stop the raid." He called an assembly. He announced the mission at hand and gave his followers a choice: "You who are willing to go, stand in line. You who are not willing, go to your homes."

He looked away for a moment, to give them a chance to decide. When he looked up again he found "everybody had gone!" "And to tell the truth," he admitted, "I also wanted to join them, for I did not want to go to Pianga at all." But he did not join them. Instead, with the eleven men he finally mustered, he began a trek into a dream of carnage.

He and his men passed through village after deserted village. At night they entered into call-and-response, with human voices wailing and crying from the forest in the dark—voices of men and women too terrified to return to their homes. One day, from a distance, they beheld what at first seemed a welcome instance of normalcy, a sign, perhaps, that the hell they were entering had not swallowed everything. They saw a lone woman leaning against a doorpost, as if relaxing after daily chores. When they drew closer it was obvious she was dead, with portions of her flesh carved off.

As Sheppard and his party left the forest for the plain of the Zappo-Zaps, eighteen armed men sprang toward them. Sheppard screamed out his name and was recognized. He had saved the life of one of these men some years before and now the favor was returned. As he moved on toward their main encampment, he noticed the village behind him had burst into flames.

He exchanged ceremonial greetings with the Zappo-Zap chieftain. There was a short, absurd but necessary show of ritual deference at the entrance to the stockade. Sheppard declined to enter first. The Zappo-Zap was the greater chief.

He spent two days in that chieftain's company, tabulating carnage. He made note of three hundred human skeletons, the flesh of many of them having been prepared as food. He saw a spear sticking out of the blackened heart of a man who had once been a friend. He counted eighty-one right hands—hacked from the living and the dead—from the arms of adults and children, which were to be put in a basket and delivered to Bula Mutadi.

The Zappo-Zaps were unashamed. They held back nothing. Were they not the Force Publique, trained and corrupted first by the slave trade and now selling their skills to Leopold, who demanded they bring back either tribute or proof of corporal punishment? Was it not the case that the peoples of the Congo were either to spend their days in the forests collecting wild rubber while their farms went to ruin and they starved, or to have their hands sliced off and put in baskets?

The Zappo-Zaps were merely following orders. As to whose orders they were, Sheppard wrote, "We saw a flag flying [in] the center of the stockade. You would be surprised to know what civilized nation's flag it was." It was Belgium's insignia raised over Africa—the flag of Leopold II.

Sheppard's report went through missionary channels to a journalist turned crusader named Edmund Morel in England. Morel had gradually become convinced that scenes like those witnessed by Sheppard were not the exception but the rule, the standard means by which the Congo was plundered, "tax" collected, and a Belgian king made fabulously wealthy. Morel became the fulcrum of an international movement that aimed at divesting Leopold of his prize colony. "Rubber is death," was a Congolese proverb coined in honor of Leopold's rubber-gathering system. Morel took the saying and hurled it in fury at the ruler of the Free State.

Through Morel, Arthur Conan Doyle became involved in the Congo Reform Movement. Author of the Sherlock Holmes mysteries, Doyle also indulged his passion for prize fighting in less renowned stories about gambling aristocrats, stalwart iron smiths, and fierce Jewish fighters from the lower depths of London society. When Jim Jeffries emerged from retirement to assume the mantle of The Great White Hope in his challenge to Jack Johnson, the first black champion, and some thought the future of white supremacy if not civilization itself hung upon that forty-round fight in Nevada, A. C. Doyle was invited to referee.

He declined. The priority was to remain in England to finish *The Crime of the Congo*, an exposé of what he called "the greatest crime in all history, the greater for having been carried out under an odious pretence of philanthropy." In that book, Doyle spoke of Sheppard and another American missionary as making, in the Congo, finer Statues "of Liberty than Bartholdi's in New York Harbour."

In the United States, an old and ailing Mark Twain devoted some of his last literary energies to the cause of Congo reform. In an effective twenty-five-cent pamphlet entitled *King Leopold's Soliloquy*, published in 1906, he drew on Sheppard's conversation with the Zappo-Zap chieftain, quoting the latter as saying, "I ordered the fence to be closed so they couldn't run away; then we killed them here inside the fence."

"We killed plenty," this man boasted to Sheppard, "will you see some of them?"

In 1904, Roger Casement, a British consul sent to the Congo to investigate the charges against Leopold, cut short his visit in disgust. A few months of traveling confirmed everything Sheppard saw, and damned Leopold. The Casement report was the beginning of the end of the king's private hold on the colony. But Casement himself could not forgive the British Foreign Office for being, to his mind, slow to condemn atrocities and lukewarm when it finally did. The Congo Report was Casement's first step on a path of disenchantment with England that ended with him on the opposing side during World War I, and soon thereafter, on the gallows.

Leopold defended himself against the accusations. If Edmund Morel can be credited with leading the twentieth century's first international protest movement, then King Leopold should be acknowledged for assembling its first modern public relations apparatus, with a secret payroll and branch offices in most Western countries.

According to Leopold's public relations squadron, the camera didn't lie, but the men, women, and children captured on film with arms ending in stumps instead of hands were victims of sudden, inexplicable attacks by wild boars. (Mark Twain's pamphlet had an illustration of a bloated Leopold being chased by a little camera, an "incorruptible kodak," which the king liked even less than "busy-body American missionaries." Doyle dismissed the story of mutilation by boars as beneath contempt.)

According to Leopold, any sharp decline in the population of the Free State was either a fiction concocted by his enemies or the result of one of those strange tropical ailments to which white men were mercifully immune. (Morel documented torture: "Floggings! Agony of lacerated bodies cut to ribbons with penetrating lash of hippo-hide thick as a man's thumb," and tribes "thoroughly broken." But what he was trying to describe in all his works had not yet found expression in that single word, genocide.)

Leopold believed that harsh measures were required in an environment where cannibalism was a fact of life. (Cannibalism, countered Morel, was not the cause of Leopold's brutality, but all too often a result. How, he asked, could cannibalism decrease when forced labor created mass starvation, and when the most depraved tribes were enlisted into the Force Publique, which armed them and gave them license to treat all others as fair game?)

In a sense it had all been seen, stripped of polemics and reduced to grotesque essence, by a man who knew both Casement and Morel but regarded himself as unqualified for political debate.

In 1890, as Reverend Sheppard was nearing Africa and H.M. Stanley was leaving it for the last time, this man made his way to the Free State as a lowly employee of a Belgian trading company bucking for a promotion. A Pole who took the English name Joseph Conrad, his Congo journey helped him conclude that literature, not commerce, was his true vocation.

In his novel *Heart of Darkness*, published twelve years

later, he evoked an Africa that was a primal stew of life but could become, with the additional element of Western greed, the opposite, a poison. He fashioned his impressions of Belgian rule into words that, before the rubber boom, were fit to hang above the entire enterprise:

> The word "ivory" rang in the air, was whispered, was sighed. You would think they were praying to it. A taint of imbecile rapacity blew through it all, like a whiff from some corpse. By Jove! I've never seen anything so unreal in my life. And outside, the silent wilderness surrounding this cleared speck on the earth struck me as something great and invincible, like evil or truth, waiting patiently for the passing away of this fantastic invasion.

In the character of Kurtz, Conrad posted a warning sign. A renegade trader, Kurtz had stepped far beyond the reaches of even extraordinary avarice. He had crossed into a territory of corruption from which there was no return, making a sacrifice of his own humanity in exchange for complete power over a native population. In the end, his bloated form and vast power were reduced to a voice and a monologue of pointless, persuasive eloquence.

All efforts to identify Kurtz with individuals Conrad met in Africa have been futile. And no one at the time suggested that Kurtz was modeled upon the character of King Leopold. Leopold, after all, never even set foot in his prized colony. The closest he came to the Free State were the legitimately purchased villas in the south of France, where he went regularly on vacation.

Yet in Brussels, in 1890, Reverend Sheppard had been reassured by a large persuasive man. Nine years later Sheppard saw what horror lay behind the king's words. That act of witnessing transformed the American Presbyterian Mission. Instead of serving as a vehicle for the expatriation of American blacks, as Senator Morgan had planned, it became thoroughly engaged in the cause of Congo reform. Sheppard, who had fled the racial politics of the United States, found himself engrossed in the deadly politics of colonial Africa.

5

FATHER ELEPHANT

A great silence around and
above. Perhaps on some quiet night
the tremor of far-off drums, sinking,
swelling, a tremor vast, faint; a sound
weird, appealing, suggestive, and
wild—and perhaps with as profound
a meaning as the sound of bells in a
Christian country.

—Joseph Conrad,
Heart of Darkness

Some things were the same: The forest, the subtle change of season, the season of honey gathering, the dances in which women were the bees and men the gatherers, the honey songs and honey drunkenness. Even the induction of young men into hunting, the initiation of girls, their attack on the boys they singled out for lovemaking, their learning to sew circular huts out of leaves and saplings, the frequent change of campsites, the scattering of bangi (cannabis, or marijuana seeds), the sharing out of game, the settling of conflicts by means other than violence: These things did not change.

Leaves and trees made a marvelous cushion against the outside. They were a medium in which time and change traveled more slowly. What was plotted in Brussels, debated in London, and implemented via Leopoldville by the Bula Mutadi might expire well before it reached so far.

Ota Benga was born in the forest in approximately 1883. By the turn of the century he had had his night of lovemaking in the ceremonial hut of a girl-become-woman in whose eyes he found favor. Older women beat him up, punched, pinched, and laughed at him as he fought his way through the human tunnel they made to her door. Not long thereafter he presented her parents with the gift of an antelope slain in proof of his ability to provide. The gift was accepted. As a very young man he was already a husband, and not long thereafter an expectant father.

Lithe, strong, skilled in the woodcraft known to his people, he was a formidable hunter of all varieties of game but especially the forest elephant, most prized and dangerous of all, capable of scattering a campsite, trampling a leopard, crushing a hunter with its great nose.

A great nose as long and full of sound as the pygmy's own trumpet, the *molimo*, so that Ota saw something of himself in those intelligent animals, those roving camps of elephants endowed with *molimo*-like noses, trunks like the trumpets the pygmies played for the forest when there was death and sorrow.

Once, perhaps—it was amusing to think, it was a story to tell or to dream while smoking *bangi*—the elephant and the forest dwellers were the same until they fought for sole possession of the *molimo*. The *molimo* came apart. The elephants pulled away with flexible nose trumpets, huge ears, tusks, and small eyes; the pygmies with hands and trumpets made of wood, and then they were opposites, the elephants enormous and quick to anger, quick to take insult, easily swollen with wrath at the very thought of being hunted; the forest people small, stealthy, silent—their hunters.

Ota thought of the hunting song:

> The spirits are wandering.
> Elephant-hunter, take your bow!
> *Elephant-hunter, take your bow!*
>
> In the forest lashed by the great rain,
> Father elephant walks heavily,
> *baou, baou,*
> Careless, without fear, sure of his
>   strength,

Father elephant, whom no one can
    vanquish;
Among the trees which he breaks he
    stops and starts again
He eats, roars, overturns trees and
    seeks his mate.
Father elephant, you have been
    heard from afar.
Elephant-hunter, take your bow!
Elephant-hunter, take your bow!

Father elephant, *baou, baou.*
The pygmy mused at the ill-humor into which it would throw elephants if they ever suspected that some thought of them as "meat which walks like a hill."

But even in the forest where much was unchanged, some things were different. Dreams and things not talked about.

When Ota and his hunting band had last descended on the village which they regarded as especially abundant in fruits, yams, and gourds of wine, they found it barren. There were no bananas left to pick on the stalks, nothing growing in the fields.

Usually the villagers greeted them with a familiar irritability. The forest dwellers would offer meat which the villagers would predictably scowl at, sniff, and pretend only reluctantly to accept. The chiding would continue as part of the setpiece by which farmers and hunters said hello. But if it was evening and the drums were out in the village square the drummers would get up and ask the forest dwellers to sit in their place.

Now at last it was the pygmies' turn to hurl recriminations. How could they be expected to play when they were thirsty, and when thirst made their hands dry as dead wood? Would the villagers like to see arms break on the drums like boughs in the wind?

A look of errant affection might cross the faces of the women who served them their wine. They would play for hours to a village that settled back to a grandfatherly pride in the rhythmic skills of "their" pygmies. And then came food.

But the last time the pygmies came there was a smell of burning and no one came out to greet them. When they reached the town square the looks that greeted them were

charged with misery and fear. The villagers spoke of men
with no hearts, men with sticks that could burst into flame
and kill. These men had come that very day, demanding
ivory from the villagers, who had none. They said that next
time they came they would expect to take away large gourds
of wild rubber.

Wherever these strangers went they left death behind
them. Before leaving, their chief had opened a pouch he wore
around his waist. In it were human hands, some the hands of
children, which had been smoked over a fire. This chief threw
small hands on the ground for all to see, and then, with a look
of murder in his eyes, pointed to first one and then another of
the village small ones.

To Ota these strangers were worse than animals, worse
than leopards who devoured men. What animal would kill the
bees and leave the honey? What crazy animal would kill the
elephant for the sake of its tusks and leave the meat to become
a nest for beetles? What crazy, wounded, worse-than-animal
would carry off the hand of a man as a trophy?

At the end of telling their story the villagers stared at the
forest dwellers.

"Where will the famed elephant hunters be when the
strangers come back for tusks?" an old woman asked.

"Will you help us when those men came back?"

"Will you bring tusks? Will you bring rubber? Or stay
hidden in the trees?"

There was no exchange of food or thought of drumming
on that occasion. The villagers stared hard until the pygmies
felt a resentment strong enough to turn them back to the
woods. Afterward, there was new tension in the forest. Some
laughter, but less. An unspoken assumption it was best to stay
away from the village. And bad dreams.

One morning Ota remembered a dream that began with a
vision of flies walking along the folds of wrinkled, grey rock.
The rock moved, the flies flew off. Ota found he was looking
up at the ear of an elephant that was turning to face him. The
animal's head was twisting with the effort it took to balance its
uneven tusks, one enormous and one that was only a small
nub, red as the coal of a fire. The animal rose on its hind legs
and Ota felt fear when he saw it was a man with the ears, nose,
and tusks of an elephant.

The monster pulled off its tusks with its hands. It blew

on the small tusk until a flame licked out. It held the other tusk like one of the fire sticks the strangers used in the village.

Before the creature could point the stick at him, Ota rushed in to spear it in the stomach and then darted back into the trees. The monster spun about wildly, cursing through its trunk, pointing the fire stick everywhere but finding nothing. Then its stomach burst as an elephant's intestines, full of gas, explode when cut through, splattering blood and undigested bits of food. Ota woke.

6

COPELAND'S GRAVE

> He asked me what reasons more
> than a mere wandering inclination I
> had for leaving my father's house,
> and my native country . . .
>
> —*Robinson Crusoe*

Miss Amanda liked to use her whip. She liked the way the sapling felt in her hand, the whistling of it through the air, the crisp landings on exposed, delinquent child flesh. She was equally good at the sidestroke to the back of the knee, the overhand to the knuckles, and the stinging uppercut to the obediently waiting backside. She raised welts, drew blood, left splinters. Children routinely hobbled home as if from war, not grade school.

One of her pupils recalled the atmosphere of that classroom as being "charged with fear more than half the time." That student, Samuel Phillips Verner (called Phillips by most), tried to keep his mind on his spelling book while his teacher toured the class and tanned the students. He had a good mind, but was subject to distractions.

He never had to pay the price for common violations of tardiness, laziness, or excess stupidity. But Miss Amanda kept an eye out for the rarer infractions; she was no more forgiving toward excess intelligence than toward its opposite. This is how the boy ran afoul of her. Knowledge came to him just a little too easily.

Not only that, his particular brand of intelligence disposed him to see many sides of a question. If his teacher was guaranteed the last word on most subjects then it was only fair he got his two cents in on others. Or so it seemed to him, despite numerous splintery lessons to the contrary.

Was Miss Amanda making a point about some battle in the revolutionary war? Well, unfortunately, she had got the year wrong. That battle was family history. One of his great-grandfathers had been wounded in it, and the boy had heard about it often enough for the date to be fixed firmly in memory.

Was the subject now the Civil War, concluded some eighteen years ago?

The boy raises his hand. Miss Amanda ignores it. He holds it high and steady, a flag hoisted to the top of a pole. He waves it around a bit, a flag fluttering in breeze. In this tiny grade school in sleepy Walhalla, South Carolina, in ruined South Carolina after the war, always having something extra to say is not interpreted as good form. Verner continues to be ignored.

Eventually, he rises, standing straight and tall as if General Lee on his white charger were due to inspect him. Life goes on all around him. The subject at hand, for instance, is no longer history but one even thicker with chalk dust and canings—sums. Finally, Miss Amanda, as if only now noticing him, says, "Just what, Samuel Phillips Verner, are you waiting to tell us about three thousand two hundred forty-seven plus one hundred fifty?"

The boy has nothing pressing to say about 3,247 plus 150, but is dying to tell the class what his Grandpa Charles did during the Civil War, his Grandpa Charles Phillips who single-handedly turned aside a column of Sherman's cavalry on its slash-and-burn journey to the sea. A giant of a man, Grandpa Charles stepped out from the trees as the troop rode toward Chapel Hill to raze the university. Horses reared as, dressed in black and holding a heavy Bible over his head, Grandpa Charles demanded the Yankees scour the fields and fire the plantations if they must but let the school be. They did. That's why the University of North Carolina is still standing to this day.

That, roughly, is what Phillips is waiting to say, and, in the defiant spirit of Grandpa Charles, he says it. And when he is done, Miss Amanda drawls, "Very interesting, Phillips. And a fine man your grandfather was and is up there in Chapel Hill. He, however, wasn't in question. Can anyone tell Phillips here what the question was?"

The odds against anyone else remembering were long, so Verner provides the question and the answer, too.

"Three thousand two hundred forty-seven plus one hundred fifty equals three thousand three hundred ninety-seven, ma'am."

"Too late for numbers. Arrogance again, Phillips. Dreaming on your feet, child. Talking in your sleep. Step up here and take your medicine. Or better yet, I'll bring it around."

Whistle, crack, and Grandpa Charles's grandson knows the cane.

Good old Miss Amanda. If there were a competition for whipping at the county fair, her ox-driver's arm would make her a good bet to win. Verner would wince for a while, take the pressure off the tender parts, but sooner or later rise to argue once again. Especially when the subject was slavery and the Civil War.

There had been a small-scale civil war in his own family, a test of wills between matriarchs, on the question of slavery. Northern-born Great-Grandma Rebecca opposed slavery, and if she had her way, "would have freed the plantation from that blight." Grandma Emily strove to acquire slaves faster than Rebecca could ever hope to set them free. In the end it came down to economics. The way "the Africans multiplied, the number of bales of cotton, the way they multiplied also the hands available for planting and picking, and the way they enabled grandfather to broaden out his mercantile interest" gave pro-slavery Emily the victory over her abolitionist rival.

There had been internal division as well when, led by his home state, the South seceded and war came. The "tribe," recalled Verner, "stood for peace under the Union until it became a question of choosing between their neighbors and their more remote countrymen." Then, like many others, "they went into battle with sore hearts." And when it was all over and the last battle fought, the grandfather who once owned a plantation had no other way to make a living than by asking an ex-slave to teach him blacksmithing.

There had been room for misgivings about slavery, a heavy heart about the Civil War. But there were no second thoughts about what came after. The Verners saw Reconstruction not as the era of equal rights for blacks but as the advent of black rule. And if it was to come to a choice between black supremacy and white supremacy, race would unite the clan as nothing else did.

In 1876, South Carolina had two legislatures, one of them militantly white. This was the one to which Verner's father, an impoverished lawyer, was elected. In that same year, the North abandoned its effort to reconstruct the South. Yankee troops were withdrawn, and Phillips, at the age of three, was taken to demonstrations celebrating the return of white rule.

Miss Amanda was privy to most of this story. She had learned some directly from the boy himself; more came from conversations she had about the bright, worrisome child with his parents. And then there was local lore, in which the Verners figured prominently.

The family's pride had not been shattered along with its fortune. If anything, it had grown stronger to compensate. And Verner's mother, especially, laid enormous expectations on the eldest of her six children. It was Phillips, she was sure, who was born to restore the clan to its proper estate. No wonder, then, that the boy saw himself as a knight, a chevalier, only temporarily in homespun.

Miss Amanda knew that various members of this large, old, aristocratic family were given to odd behavior. Some were high-strung and eccentric, others completely mad, and there were suicides now and again. What about young Phillips? Mad or sane? Well, certainly not completely crazy. But it was far from a sure thing he'd turn out completely sane. He spent a lot of time fluctuating, as if trying to work out which state was more comfortable.

And she knew the boy's nearly morbid fascination with questions of right and wrong by how disturbed he had become over the Copeland affair. Joe Copeland, a black man, had killed a white in fury a few years back. Some, without defending the deed, said Copeland had been sorely provoked; the usual bunch called for lynching. In the end, it was the legal system that took charge of Copeland. And it was Verner's own father who prosecuted the case to its foregone conclusion.

On the day Copeland was hanged, Miss Amanda had

fairly worn out her right arm whipping down her class's buzz and blabber. It wasn't every day in Walhalla that a man was hanged. Only Phillips was abnormally quiet. And for days after, there were no unsolicited stories of Uncle This or Grandpa That. No daring of his teacher. No braving the cane with a toss of flaxen hair like a romantic hero facing the firing squad.

Over time the influence of the hanging subsided, but it could never be completely erased from the boy's awareness. Copeland's grave, a haunting memorial to good and evil, rebellion and justice, skin color and death, lay just off the path Verner had to take to and from school each day.

This high level of detail about her prize pupil came in handy to Miss Amanda that day at recess when he struck down Fatty, a bully in the older grades who delighted in tormenting his juniors. One afternoon, during a game of baseball, he stepped between Verner's bat and an incoming pitch. Verner couldn't see the ball, but he had an excellent view of Fatty's head. He swung.

Down went the bully, out came the teacher. In the hushed silence, as Fatty struggled groggily back to his feet, others were assigned to tend to him. To Miss Amanda's mind the real emergency was elsewhere. Verner was invited to follow her into the classroom.

He got into step, feeling all eyes of the younger grades upon him, their hero, who had struck a blow for the long-suffering, the skinny, and the undersized. When he was not mentally inscribing his moral home run into the history of Walhalla he was wondering how to compare the lump that would sprout on Fatty's head with the experience of being flayed alive which he himself was about to undergo. Which parts of his body were about to become acquainted with grief? Or was the question, this time, which parts weren't?

But Miss Amanda had no intention of resorting to customary punishment. Caning, she knew, would never strike deep enough. When she caned Verner it was just to keep up appearances. There had to be a better way to correct his course. So she had devised a personalized object lesson out of the ingredients of his ancestry, his chances of salvation, southern race relations, and the route it just so happened he took to school each day.

She sat the boy down and talked to him in a low tone he

had never known her to use before, asking if he remembered his ancestors who'd fought in the revolutionary war.

"Yes ma'am," he started proudly, "there was Colonel John and Great-grandpa . . . "

"Thank you, that will do just fine. Now Phillips, do you honor your father?"

This line of questioning, and the absence, so far, of physical pain, was beginning to unnerve him. When was he going to get thumped? A child has a right to a certain regularity.

"Why, of course, Miss Amanda, but what's he got to do with . . ."

"I'm coming to that Phillips, as you will soon see."

"What about the saints," she asked next, "can you remember them?"

He managed, reluctantly, to mumble the names of a few. Saints, under any circumstances, were a less than favorite subject. Miss Amanda helped him along by naming some others. This, then, she proposed, was part of the list of the good and the saved.

She propounded another and somewhat lengthier list, a roll call of the damned, fattened, as he later recalled, by "all the murderers she could cull from sacred and profane history." She called his attention to one particular entry on the scroll of the damned, a local entry with whom she believed he was well acquainted. She was referring, of course, to that black devil Copeland who had been hanged for his crime.

"Copeland lashed out at a white man. It doesn't matter whether that man had done him wrong, Phillips. He killed the man. And he was justly punished."

Punished. The event, washed a thousand times in his imagination, came back with full force. A black man swaying from a rope. A neck snapped in midair. A heavy tongue lolling out of a mouth. A grave in which the body rotted. Black skin, dark earth, weeds. Every time he passed that place he tried to keep himself from walking faster, from breaking into a run, but he failed.

"And wasn't he caught and punished by your very own father?"

His father. His father who patted his head every day, including that day, when he left the house. His noble, hardworking, good father. There were no gaping holes, no hell-deep graves on his father's way.

The stage was set. Now Fatty could be introduced, and the braining at recess. What it came down to was this. Phillips could be remembered along with his dad, his revolutionary forebears, and the numbered saints. He had the right. He was of that lineage. Or he could go on braining the Fatties of the world and in the end be counted with the black assassin. There was plenty room where Copeland lay for a full-grown Samuel Phillips Verner or two.

She knew where she'd put the boy. It was the same as on the very day of the hanging. She let him linger for a while in Copeland's company in the unthinkable coffin by the side of the road. Then she lifted him out.

"Phillips, you're young. I know God and also your mother love you. How you end up is entirely your choice. But I'd like to help. Join me in remembering John's useful words on this very subject from the last chapter of Revelation."

At the moment, nothing particularly useful from that or any other chapter of Revelation occurred to him. Miss Amanda provided the text.

"John said, 'The grace of the Lord Jesus be with all the saints.' Amen, Phillips."

"Amen, ma'am."

She sent him out to play and think.

On behalf of the younger grades, and in defense of an inalienable right to a turn at bat, he had struck down Fatty. But to strike down Fatty was to be allied with Copeland. To give in to anger against a terrible bully was to disown a line of saints and good men ending, it just so happened, with his very own father. Maybe he hadn't hit a moral home run. Maybe he'd struck out.

If it came down, like she said, to being buried with Copeland or sticking with his father, it wasn't much choice.

That day, on his way home, as he neared the site of Copeland's grave, he stopped and threw down his satchel. He cried and prayed and whined a little. The whole business of good and bad was much worse than it appeared. Until it brightened up a little, and with deep apologies to the fearsome Copeland and maybe even one for old Fatty, Verner begged only to be counted with his Colonel John and the others who had died for their country.

Miss Amanda had merely sought a means, where corporal punishment failed, to exert some measure of control over the boy. But once released, she had no way of measuring how far her words would go. Verner had always been susceptible to the many sides of a question. Now he was vulnerable to the many sides of what might at first appear to be an obvious case of right and wrong.

He retained his instinctive feeling for the injured and the oppressed, casting himself in the role of deliverer. But this sympathy was now stymied by awe before the powers that be, and immense longing to be instated among them. And though his long life took him far from Walhalla it was as if S. P. Verner never strayed far from the mixed message of Copeland's grave.

Besides Miss Amanda there was another long-lasting influence dating from elementary school days. It came from a vaguer, shadier character, identified only as TweedleDee in the autobiographical fragments in which the elder Verner recalled, and often bewailed, his youth.

"Who has oversight of children to and from school?" he asked. "Who effectively controls them during recesses? What can be done to stop the fatal whisper?" The answers to these questions are no one and nothing. Before school, after school, and recess belong to the likes of TweedleDee. Not TweedleDee the individual, TweedleDee the type; low-born, cynical, knowing TweedleDee.

"What goes on when the little darlings are told to run out and play while the grown folks talk about the Sunday School lesson?" The answer is that this moment, too, is owned by TweedleDee. TweedleDee takes Verner aside. The things he whispers to him are the unforgettable, nasty, but enticing, schoolyard things—foulmouthed, lowdown sexual things.

Miss Amanda rode like a hawk on the thermals of rectitude, sharp-eyed and ready to swoop down on any infraction. Verner's mother was attentive, devoted, and his father the epitome of southern honor. But what, nevertheless, were the little darlings doing? According to old Verner, "war had levelled conditions . . . poverty had destroyed the safe-guards of earlier times." Therefore, bluntly, "the little pigs rooted in the mud."

The very moment when his mother and Miss Amanda were "piously conferring" would be the one TweedleDee chose to make some well-turned, lewd remark. The result was "tar on the aristocracy." Bad thoughts, bad habits. The "fatal whisper" took firm hold of Verner's imagination. It flourished alongside his loftier fantasies. It competed for attention with his romantic dreams.

Childhood was, for this child at least, a most dangerous

place to linger, what with Copeland being eaten by worms on the path to school and TweedleDee, with his disgusting but contagious view of things, lurking in the playground. But at least, rising above it all, like a spire above the town itself, there was church; heavy, foursquare, Presbyterian church, where the boy could turn himself in for a thorough soul cleaning. Except that for Verner, church was a catastrophe—guilt associated with TweedleDee and Copeland plus the interest accrued by the boy's imagination.

School came to him effortlessly. No amount of effort could make him feel like anything but an imposter in church. He went at it with the best of wills, hoping for a breakthrough. In Sunday School, he sawed away at stanzas like:

> Je - sus, Thou art stand - ing
> Out - side the fast closed door,
> In low - ly pa - tience wait - ing
> To pass the thresh - old o'er:
> Shame on us, Chris - tian broth - ers,
> His Name and sign who bear,
> O shame, thrice shame up - on us,
> To keep Him stand - ing there!

To no avail. The hymnal brought neither peace nor pardon to this "heart oppressed." Verner shifted. He fidgeted. He writhed silently in his Sunday best. He hoped services would be over before some sharp-eyed old Presbyter looked into his prematurely tainted soul.

Once out of church, the boy fled to the woodlands around town. He smelled the wildflowers, wound his way through the nut trees, tossed himself down in the clearings to gaze at the squirrel and the mockingbird and admire the "eagle straying down from the mountains." In the woods he abandoned the judgmental spirits of Christianity in favor of friendlier creatures drawn from African-American folklore. In "shady dells" where, to his mind, " 'Br'er Possum,' 'Br'er Coon' and 'Br'er Fox' held concourse," he, too, could be at peace.

Books on travel, exploration, rebirth through adventure were another source of comfort. From early on, he was especially fond of the works of David Livingstone. Livingstone had died in 1873, the year of his own birth. This date suggested a secret connection, a shared mission. Livingstone's passionate

denunciations of slavery left a deep impression. Stories like the
one in which the evangelist came across a column of slaves
yoked to each other by the neck were not lost on a grandchild
of slaveowners. The slaves were laughing and singing, which
confused Livingstone until he drew close enough to understand the song:

> "Yes, we are going away to manga" (abroad or white
> man's land) "with yokes on our necks, but we shall have
> no yokes in death and we shall return and haunt and kill
> you." The chorus then struck in was the name of the man
> who had sold each of them and then followed the general
> laugh in which at first I saw no bitterness.
>
> In accordance with African belief they had no doubt
> of being soon able by ghost-power to kill. Their refrain
> was as if, "Oh, oh, oh, bird o' freedom, oh! You sold me,
> oh, oh, oh! I shall haunt you, oh, oh, oh!" The laughter
> told not of mirth but of . . . tears.

Livingstone's books were followed by Stanley's, whose
adventure stories were the standard boys' reading of the day.
With Stanley, Verner met Tippu Tip, the slave trader; became
Smasher of Rocks; encountered the fabled pygmies; and rescued Dr. Livingstone in darkest Africa. But neither Stanley nor
Livingstone's first-person accounts came close to having the
same impact on Verner as a work of fiction published more
than a century and a half before.

Written when the European image of the non-European
world was still in embryo, *Robinson Crusoe* was Verner's first
book and remained his favorite. His mother gave him Defoe's
classic as a birthday present shortly after he learned to read.
Little could she have known, he reminisced, that her gift was
"destined to put seas and continents" between them. Travel,
loss, risk; a man who leaves his homeland penniless, discovers
heroic inner resources and is rewarded for his ordeal by untold wealth—it is not surprising that such a story gripped the
boy by his "very inmost fibres."

There was also the romance of Crusoe and Friday. Crusoe
saves the aborigine from cannibals and Friday, in gratitude,
becomes his faithful retainer. Crusoe respects Friday's native
ways. When he tries to make a Christian of him, he finds the
man is already well aware that, "the sea, the ground we walked

on, and the hills and woods" owe their existence to one still older than "the moon or the stars." When Crusoe demands to know why, then, this creator is not worshipped, he is reduced to silence when, "with a perfect look of innocence," Friday answers: "All things do say 'O' to him."

At last, Crusoe tries to send Friday home, only to find his man will not hear of separation. He will stay with the extraordinary white man even if it means never again seeing his own people. "What you send Friday away for?" he demands, with tears in his eyes. "Kill Friday, no send Friday away." This was an eye-opener to young Verner. Friday's devotion conferred a blessing on Crusoe that wealth alone couldn't. It certified him as good man.

Verner returned to *Robinson Crusoe* many times as a boy. It was his gateway "into a delectable kingdom." It filled him with "the glamor of the great unknown parts of the earth." What the "blank space" on a map of Africa did for Conrad, this book did for him. It destined, or predestined him. It meant, as with Conrad, "When I grow up I shall go there."

By the early 1880s, Verner had set Defoe aside to study Shakespeare. He was attending the University of South Carolina, where his intelligence could expand to its full measure without running afoul of a teacher's whip. But as his life assumed greater scope, so did its divisions. The issue of race continued to run like a fault-line through his thoughts.

On a visit to the University of North Carolina, saved from the torch by Grandpa Charles, something lured him away from the upstanding relatives he had come to see, and called to him from the other side of the tracks, from the porches, kitchens, and bedrooms of the blacks who derived no benefit at all from Uncle Charles having cut off Sherman at the pass.

What did it mean, he asked, that there "under the very shadow of the citadel of culture . . . was the same eternal and ever-present Problem?" or that he was so drawn to the other side that he rejected the "glories of the campus" to seek out the company of "outcasts"?

Familiarity with Shakespeare helped him give definitive expression to his confusion. From college on, he recollected, hardly a day of his life went by without his suffering "the full force of Hamlet's meditation."

He poured his thoughts into an award-winning essay on

the theme of character. Character, as described in this essay, was everything that Verner, at the moment, notably lacked. It was a magnet; all things came naturally to the man who possessed it. He would be drafted to "direct the industries, to guide the counsels, to rule the governments, and to lead the armies of the world."

Character was the fallen aristocrat restored to his estate. "He walks upon the street and his very air names him an uncrowned king." It was insulation against all the Tweedle-Dees of this world, with all their rude remarks: "Fewer and fewer faults injure it. Rarely and more rarely do temptations overcome it." Character was mastery over oneself and leadership over others.

This was how Verner wanted, and perhaps imagined, himself to be. He was, at this point, a brilliant student who threw himself into his work both because he wanted to excel and because he wanted to forget himself. He was deeply unsettled by all aspects of the question of race, and no less ill at ease with his sexuality. The indications are that, like many men of his class, he looked across the racial divide for sexual gratification.

According to prevailing stereotypes, white women were angelic, untouchable, and in need of protection from carnal desire; black women were better targets for insinuations like those of TweedleDee. At the point where race and sex collided, down came the avalanche of Presbyterian guilt.

Verner compiled an academic record unprecedented at the University of South Carolina, and in 1892, only nineteen years of age, graduated first in his class. It should have been the moment for rejoicing, with the eldest son more than satisfying the family's high expectations and able to chose from any number of possible careers. Instead, stress, strain, and spiritual woe came into the open. Verner suffered his first, long-deferred mental collapse.

He lingered for a while in the vicinity of the down side, the "not to be," of Hamlet's meditation; he raved. There were some moments when he tried to convince others he was the Hapsburg Emperor. Then the storm subsided. Gradually he began to knit himself back together. Of course, any plans for a brilliant career had to be indefinitely postponed. He began his convalescence in the carpentry shop of the Southern Railway in Columbia, South Carolina.

The cornerstone of J. P. Morgan's railroad empire, the

Southern Railway was responsible for what little financial recovery the state knew in those days. Working for it brought a measure of personal recovery to S. P. Verner. He was promoted nine times in nine months, raising himself to a supervisory position. More important, he resumed intellectual life, looking to books now not just for knowledge but direction.

He turned again to David Livingstone. In empty freight cars, when he could steal the time, he read and reread Livingstone until "Africa became as familiar" as "his own blue hills of the Piedmont." When he came to Livingstone's dying words: "May the blessing of Almighty God rest upon all—American, English or Turk—who will come to heal this open sore of the world," he could hear, so he said, "nothing else but this appeal." Livingstone stirred him as he always had done, and directed him to Africa.

He also familiarized himself with the works of Charles Darwin. *The Origin of Species* and *The Descent of Man* engaged Verner on an intellectual level, as the theory of evolution promised to give scientific precison to racial questions that had long disturbed him. According to Darwin the fact that "all the races agree in so many . . . details of structure," could only be accounted for "by inheritance from a common progenitor." For Darwin, it was "more probable that our early progenitors lived on the African continent than elsewhere."

For most men, the moral resolve of an evangelist like Livingstone and the naturalism of a Darwin canceled each other out. To Verner, there was no contradiction. So far as their central messages went, the writers complemented each other. Together, they strongly disposed him to seek knowledge, fortune, and the performance of good deeds on the continent of Africa.

In 1894, he drew a step closer to this goal. Relatives secured him a post teaching and managing at the Stillman Institute in Tuscaloosa, Alabama, the small Presbyterian school Reverend Sheppard had attended. There Verner established a delicate truce with Presbyterianism. The church was powerful medicine. Taken in the right amounts, it helped him feel better. The wrong dosage brought on side effects he knew only too well—guilt, remorse, and self-disgust, the ills that had laid him low. He had to keep something in reserve, and not confuse the church as a temporary haven, or even as a career, with the church as a calling.

He drew up a ten-point proposal in which he declared that Africa had outgrown exploration and was ready for development. Only "Caucasian power" and the twin blessings of commerce and Christianity could save it from becoming a "cesspool of Asiatic vice and corruption." American civilization, which had evolved beyond that of Europe, had a special role to play. Verner hoped he was one of the more evolved Americans.

In 1893 at the Stillman Institute, Reverend Sheppard had personally made an appeal, which was still in effect, for fresh recruits. Attrition by disease guaranteed that the Congo Mission at Luebo was in constant need of manpower. Verner's interests and the interests of the church seemed to coincide. He decided to answer the church's call—which was at once Darwin's, Livingstone's, and Robinson Crusoe's—and to ship out as a missionary.

Like Crusoe before him, he first had to shrug aside family objections. Crusoe's father, trying to dissuade the boy from leaving, herded him toward the "middle station of life," the one prone to "fewest disasters," the road that took men "silently and smoothly through the world, and comfortably out of it." Objections to Verner's leaving, on the other hand, took the form of delicately worded inquiries into whether nervous exhaustion might recur.

The youth thanked his relatives kindly for their expressions of concern, assured them he had never felt better in his life, and was certain his destiny lay abroad. Like Crusoe, he preferred anything, including the risks of shipwreck, warfare, and disease, to the routine comforts of life's "middle station."

The second obstacle was the three-year course of study required of all missionaries. Here the Congo Mission's pressing need for white personnel—and Verner's relatives in high places in the church—came to his rescue. An "extraordinary clause" was invoked. He could skip the schooling, so long as he passed the test. It was a simple thing for him to brush up on subjects like theology, church history, Latin, and Greek. Hebrew, however, stood in his way. He was exempted from having to pass in Hebrew only when he gave his solemn word to learn the language someday.

In the record-breaking time of a single day, he became an ordained minister. Reverend S. P. Verner, the African mission-

ary, was born. In view of the year in railroading he had spent
recovering from his brief stint as a Hapsburg emperor, his
initial assignment as missionary was to improve the supply
line between Luebo and the coast.

With what qualities and credentials then, was this twenty-
two-year-old equipped when he took ship to west Africa by
way of New York, England, and Belgium, in 1895?
    He was, first of all, armed with a letter of introduction
from Senator Morgan. Morgan continued to hope that missionaries were "the pioneers of a great outflow of Afro-Americans
to their fatherland." This "outflow" Morgan continued, was to
be:

> the most important movement of population that has ever
> originated in the United States. Even more important and
> useful to us than it is to the negroes in our midst. So I
> welcome the labors of these missionaries as being the har-
> binger of a great blessing.

In addition, Verner had a good grasp of rhetoric and classical languages; considerable amounts of Shakespeare committed to memory; a mind equally drawn to evangelism and
evolutionism, Livingstone and Darwin; ambition to be a leader
(to "direct the industries, to guide the counsels") of at least a
part of the world; a ten-point manifesto for African development; first-hand knowledge of railroading; the arrogance of a
lord; the racial attitudes of the day riddled deep within his
soul; and a sympathy for the oppressed matched only by respect for their oppressors.
    A photograph survives of Reverend Verner and Reverend
Phipps, another who had answered Sheppard's call, shortly
before their embarking. Phipps, a black man who believed his
grandfather was Congolese, is standing. Verner, seated, com-
municates a hauteur that makes him look enthroned.
    During a brief stop in London, Verner visited Westminster
Abbey to do homage at the tomb of David Livingstone. Then,
on November 27, he boarded the R.M.S. Roquelle out of Liverpool and bore down on the humble missionary station at
Luebo less like a duly minted reverend than a Presbyterian
Napoleon.

7

FWELA

Look at his hat! Look out, he's
going to jump! Oh, my, look at those
clothes! Where did he come from?
Out of the water? No, out of the sky.
Oh, look at his eyes! How white he
is . . .

—S. P. Verner

It had been an interesting sea voyage, featuring impromptu boxing matches between Ashanti warriors and British seamen and theology matches between Reverend S. P. Verner and agnostic British merchants. The outcome of the boxing matches varied, whereas sharp young Verner emerged undefeated from his debates. He might have succeeded in converting an Englishman or two before ever trying to convert an African.

Even before arriving in Matadi, at the mouth of the Congo River, in January of 1896, things began to rub him the wrong way. Reverend Phipps was seasick. "Oh, the helplessness of that race is appalling!" Verner wrote. "One of my hardest works is that of acting as booby-nurse to my negro companion." His letters to his family and the missionary board during his six months at Matadi display mounting feelings of outrage.

It galled Verner that black missionaries received the same

pay as whites. Scanning through the scriptures on this " 'absolute social equality' idea," he mounted lofty arguments against it. Heaven itself was a system of "ranks and ordinations." Why should Earth be any different? He thought black missionaries were fine, but only in their place. They were good preachers whose simple, homespun sermons were ideal for African tastes, but they should never be allowed to assume parity with, or authority over, whites.

Verner had even less flattering first impressions of white missionaries. Blacks, at least, could be excused on grounds of race, and because a regime of misguided equality brought out the worst in them. The only reason he could find for the average white missionary being such a "poor specimen" was that the church "unloaded all her idiots on the Mission field," much as England dumped her convicts on Australia. A certain missionary refused to administer quinine on the Sabbath. The reason could only be "insufferable" idiocy. Many missionaries rejected medicine and relied entirely on prayer when they became ill. The result was a shockingly high death rate.

These deaths infuriated Verner not because he was especially sorry to lose the missionaries—he thought most of them were either as petty as "young debutantes," or as gossipy as "old fishwives"—but because the refusal of medicine indicated a narrow definition of religion, and a huge gulf between religion and science. Verner did not want to make such sharp distinctions. Science, religion, and personal ambition blended together peculiarly well in his mind. He was in Africa to evangelize, as per his ordination, as well as to satisfy his curiosity firsthand about questions of natural history and human evolution and, with any luck, to lay the foundations of his fortune. ("I know my life depends on the next few years," he wrote a few months after arriving, "God help me get through them.")

He liked to speak to his superiors of Christ the carpenter rather than Christ the savior: Christ "was a Carpenter thirty years before He was a preacher." He argued that a little more practicality—and its own river steamer—was exactly what the church needed to succeed in the Congo. The church met Reverend Verner's fiery urgency with blandness, e.g. "Africa cannot be evangelized in a day." His family urged him to moderate his language and curb his temper. They feared another outbreak of the Hapsburg emperor syndrome in darkest Africa.

What really impressed Verner and gave him his first experience of humility in Africa was neither church nor family but disease. The mosquitoes found him after a few months and inducted him into the complicated life cycle of malaria. His first reaction was helpless admiration. Here, at last, was a force to be reckoned with. As he put it in June 1896, "I have just shaken hands—also feet, & everything else, too, by the way— with the Demon of the Country, King Fever." It was, he added, "a really old fashioned country-school teacher shake, such as to scare all you ever learned out of you." After this introductory infection, the agents of the disease never left his bloodstream. They might be inactive for a while only to burst out with fresh hunger for red corpuscles, setting off a new cycle of sweats, fever, and the shakes.

Verner's second humbling experience was the journey from Matadi, near the coast, to Luebo, 1,200 miles inland. Not long after recuperating from the initial attack of malaria, he took the Congo Railway for the two-hundred-mile rollercoaster ride along the gorges of the Crystal Mountains. Next came a march by foot of more than a week to Stanley Pool, where he caught the steamer *Archduchess Stephanie*.

The black crew, supervised by a Bangala giant wielding the *chicotte*, or hippopotamus hide whip, were crowded, along with armed members of the Force Publique, into quarters below. Verner traveled on the upper deck with white officers and Belgian traders. A month later the steamer pulled into Makima, at the intersection of the Kasai and the Lulua rivers.

"Here was old Africa again," mused Verner, as he began the last leg of the journey, "mysterious, silent, awe-inspiring." With just a day or so of walking to go, he pulled up lame. A hammock arrived from Luebo, along with eighty porters and, to his delight, a fresh-baked loaf of bread. Verner was carried the rest of the way. After passing a peanut field and a naked boy parading under an American flag, the crowd of porters cried out, "Sheppati!" A large black man came into view across the grass, drew close, and greeted Verner in the familiar accents of the South.

Verner had just met Reverend Sheppard, fellow of the Royal Geographical Society, traveler to the Forbidden Land, and co-founder of what was at the moment, with the single exception of Verner himself, an all black mission. Verner judged the welcome he received from Sheppard to be "all that heart could desire." And from that moment on a change can be dated in Reverend Verner's character and writings. There were no more letters home calling for an end to fully integrated missions, no more strident demands that black missionaries be demoted. Verner, as an advocate of Jim Crow, ceased to exist. He went away quietly, without fanfare, as if he never had been. Verner had given it his best, but the thousands of miles from America to the Congo, plus the extra twelve hundred or so to Luebo, were too long to stay faithful to a prejudice.

Added to the affection everyone in the district seemed to feel for Sheppard, there was Verner's own respect for the man. Sheppard and Lapsley's founding trip to the Kasai had become the stuff of church legend. Verner had read about Sheppard's journey to the Kuba people, who, instead of beheading him as promised, hailed him as a king come back from the land of the dead. Now Verner had a chance to hear the whole story over again in person, and to ask questions.

Why eggs? What inspired Reverend Sheppard to use egg-eating as a way to get from village to village? What were the most eggs Sheppard downed in any one sitting? Was there any truth to the rumor currently circulating in the church that one way to get William Henry Sheppard really riled at you was to offer him an omelet? The king of the Kuba having seven hundred wives inspired a few humorous remarks, Sheppard agreeing that Kot aMbweeky, now deceased, had been robust for his age.

Eggs and wives were the amusing side to Sheppard's journey. But the business of being taken for a king by absolute strangers had all sorts of serious implications for S. P. Verner, who only a few years earlier had written longingly of the man with character that "He walks upon the street and his very air names him an uncrowned king. Respect and admiration meet him wherever he goes . . ." Verner wanted to know what would have happened if Sheppard had been white. Was there still a chance the Kuba would have accepted him as a king? What was it like to be hailed as royalty in Africa?

Sheppard responded to these questions with one of his own: Had Reverend Verner come to found a dynasty or to help out with the church?

The church at Luebo was a mud-walled, whitewashed, one room building. On Sundays, five hundred converts honored the Sabbath by wearing something special to services, perhaps a cast-off winter coat, wrong by many sizes, or a pair of pants rolled up to the knees. The less fortunate would make do with a pair of shoes or a hat. Even an umbrella would suffice for ornament. Everyone wore something. The rule, as generally applied, was better too much than too little. The flock was motley, but it could sing. Verner was astounded at the harmonics that rose from the devotees.

Verner hadn't done very much preaching yet in Africa or elsewhere. He had not yet learned any languages that would allow him to be widely understood in Luebo. For two months he listened to Sheppard's sermons and to the songs, and studied Tshiluba, the tongue of the numerous Baluba people which served as a common language for hundreds of miles around. Tshikuba, the language Sheppard had used among the Kuba people, was another possibility. But the Kuba tended to stay away from Luebo, and from church.

Two months after he had begun his studies the flock at Luebo was treated to Reverend S. P. Verner's maiden sermon in Tshiluba. Afterwards the singing washed over him as forcefully as ever. Either his words had been well received or he hadn't yet learned the language well enough to do the proceedings any harm. He continued to improve rapidly.

By March 1897, when Prime Minister Joka arrived in Luebo with a message from his lord and master, King Ndombe, Verner had no trouble understanding what was being said to him. Joka was a big man—"a very Falstaff of an African," Verner noted admiringly—and very dark—"a whole hogshead of darkness"—whose name meant elephant. "Behold now this elephantine Joka," wrote Verner, and took a liking to the man at once. Joka announced that King Ndombe wanted a white missionary to pay a visit and explain the meaning of his religion. The point was clear: Ndombe, who ruled a territory about the size of New Jersey and had well over one hundred thousand subjects, wanted to see Verner.

Ndombe's village was only some sixty miles to the southeast, a few days' march, but distance was no measure of the difficulty Verner had just getting out of Luebo. The locals didn't like the idea of losing their resident to another town. Verner's value at Luebo shot up the minute Ndombe expressed an interest in him. There was also resistance from Luebo's merchants, who had become accustomed to being middlemen in all transactions between Ndombe's kingdom and the mission. Verner's friends at Luebo gathered around him to pour discouragement on his plans to go away. Some were even concerned about his safety.

"Do you not know what a terrible man Ndombe is?" they asked. "Have you not heard how he killed his people by witchcraft, and how all the people tremble before him?" When Verner still refused to stay, they issued the most dreadful warning of all: "If you go, you will be eaten, and your friends will look upon your face no more." When they saw that he was still determined to be gone, they threw up their hands, saying, "Was it not always this way with these young men? Let him go, and let him accept the results." Sixty of them defected to his side, agreeing to carry chickens, goats, peanuts, and palm wine on their heads.

Among these were two boys, Kondola and Kassongo. Out of the large stock of orphaned, lost, or abandoned children cared for by the mission, they had attached themselves to Verner from the first. Kassongo was fearless, proud, and beautiful. When squabbles broke out among the mission children he intervened. Kassongo was obviously a warrior, born and bred. Verner discovered he was a young prince of the Batatele people, one of the tribes that had been most preyed upon by the Arab slave traders.

When King Leopold first raised the flag of the Congo Free State, the Batatele took that as a signal to fall upon the Arabs with a fury that left little for the Belgian armies to do but mop up. The Batatele shortly concluded that supplying rubber to Leopold was no better and in some ways worse than supplying bodies to Tippu Tip. They rose again, this time against the white men, and were smashed by Belgian guns.

To Kondola and Kassongo, who lost their people in that war, the mission was a foster parent. About ten years old by the time Verner came to know them, the boys were Christians and learning how to read. Verner quickly worked out that the one mark of royalty left to Kassongo was the friendship of Kondola, homely, loyal, dependable Kondola, marvelous with animals, and gifted, some said, with second sight. Between them Kassongo was ever the prince and Kondola his chief minister, at the ready with advice.

Added together, they gave Verner twice the usual complement of Fridays.

*   *   *

"White man, is it something you ate?"

This was the sort of question Verner fielded regularly on his journey to Ndombe's. The natives wanted to know if it was eating, drinking, falling from the sky, or jumping out of the water every morning that accounted for his paleness. They were just as curious about why he wore a hat and what he was hiding under so many clothes. They did not like to speak too openly of the land of the dead (or perhaps were just being polite), and so did not press him for particulars of his hours spent there shedding his skin.

About twenty miles from the capital a small army of Ndombe's porters and retainers intercepted Verner's troop, sweeping him off his feet, installing him in a hammock and carrying him the rest of the way. He felt morally invigorated by the warmth of welcome. It wasn't so very long ago, he mused, that the ancestors of these men and women were being introduced to Southern plantation life. Now they were bearing a grandchild of slaveowners boisterously along as if none of it had happened. This was better treatment for chronic guilt than mere forgiveness; this was transcendent forgetfulness, as if there were "no race issue, no color line, no question of skin or ancestry," only "African nobility delighted at the chance to exhibit its best qualities."

The porters deposited Verner in the courtyard of Prime Minister Joka. From there he looked up to see an enormous figure dressed in a pleated red loincloth and handsome red robe with brass rings ornamenting his elbows, ankles, and wrists. The man had "broad square shoulders, Herculean limbs," and, most striking of all, "restless and searching" eyes that "seemed to take in the whole horizon at a glance." Verner saw him as "a marked man in a thousand," whose "every movement and feature proclaimed him a king." In comparison to King Ndombe, all other specimens of royalty appeared to be accidental. Only in the person of this African did it seem that nature had troubled to shape a monarch carefully, by hand.

Ndombe extended a hand to Verner and uttered the salutation, *"Mukelenge, Moiyo!"* Reverend Verner returned the greeting, "Oh king, Life!" Leading him into a private chamber, the king told his guest, "I wish especially to hear about the question of God."

Verner spoke for an hour on Christ, man, missionaries,

truth, superstition, Africa, and the Good Book. He pleased
Ndombe by adding he was not Belgian, and bore no close-kin
relation to the Bula Mutadi. He was also not anti-Belgian, and
would not encourage Ndombe to come to blows with Bula
Mutadi.

The king, in any case, had already decided that the coming of the Belgians, if unfortunate, was irreversible. He hoped
that something useful might be gleaned from a people who
made guns that killed from afar and sounded like bad weather,
and who rode steamers that stank and hooted and traveled
upstream. As for Verner himself, Ndombe announced that
when he first heard a stranger from the Land Beyond the Water
had arrived his fears were greatly aroused. (Apparently Reverend Sheppard did not alarm him in the same way. Perhaps,
like the Kuba, he could never bring himself to think of Sheppard as truly a stranger.)

After listening to his words, Ndombe knew Verner was a
friend whose heart was white—devoid of malice. Now the
king's heart, too, was white and purged of fear. He pored
through the pages of the Bible, which Verner had promoted as
if it were a charm that caused all who touched it to tell the
truth, and exclaimed he was glad to have such an item in his
realm, as his subjects were given to the telling of outrageous
lies.

As the first of their "palavers of God" drew to a close,
Ndombe commanded that a house be brought to Reverend
Verner. While Verner watched, a palm-leaf and bamboo structure was carried shoulder-high to a place he picked out just
beyond town. Before leaving his guest to relax in his newly
delivered home, Ndombe turned toward him to swear an oath
of blood brotherhood.

"The heart of the chief is as your own heart," he vowed,
"He that fights Fwela must fight Ndombe also; and when Fwela
dies then will Ndombe die also."

S. P. Verner had surely found a friend and a place to stay
in Africa. Simultaneously, he had been given his inner name.
Fwela means leader. Kondola and Kassongo called Verner by
that name, but they were only boys. It took Ndombe to pull the
name and the identity out of embryo and into the world. The
name was like a summons to an alter ego. If S. P. Verner
faltered or proved insufficient to the day, there was always
Fwela to contend with, rounding the bend with reinforce-

ments. Verner might be defeated, Fwela hardly ever. Verner was riddled with traumas, high standards, and Presbyterianism. Fwela had a lot more freedom to maneuver.

During Verner's first days at Ndombe's, "the plain was thick with throngs of curious Africans, watching my every movement, making various comments and ejaculations; and scurrying away in great alarm whenever I made any quick movement toward them." Normally Verner did not bristle at being the center of attention, devoting a good deal of his energies in life toward securing that position. Nevertheless, it was disconcerting to be unable to take his hat off or to use his pen without creating a stir. At times he saw himself as Africans saw him; he was a white-skinned, blond, manlike creature, an almost-human. He was reminded of the man-monkeys, the pseudo-wildmen, and the unclassifiable "What-is-its?" of P. T. Barnum's shows. In the end, as in London or New York, boredom won out, and the crowds began to thin.

One day, while growing used to domesticity in his portable house, Fwela looked closely at the child from whom he usually got his meat. He thought to ask a townsman why the boy was so wizened and muscular and spoke so gruffly. Was he the victim of some tropical disease? Verner was told that the boy was a man. He learned, furthermore, that this "man" he had been exchanging salt for meat with on a regular basis, was one of that shy and privileged breed: the Batwa.

Fwela had read enough to know that Batwa meant pygmy. And what was an African career that had not been anointed by a brush with pygmies?

Like Stanley in pursuit of Livingstone or either of them in search of the Nile, he determined to follow this Batwa to his source. He hadn't far to go. The Batwa, willing to be stalked, led Fwela to a forest clearing festooned with small, round, beehive huts, and bangi plants, the unmistakable markers of pygmy presence. This group of Batwa had struck a fairly permanent campsite in Ndombe's territory, where they remained as ignorant of agriculture as ever and served as Ndombe's official hunters.

Verner was elated. These were "none others than the Pygmies of Herodotus, the fabled dwarfs of Ethiopia in reality and truth," and hardly a stone's throw from his own front door. Under these conditions, the evangelist had to make room for the evolutionist. For the two years he lived in their vicinity, Verner "prosecuted" a full scientific and psychological study. Many questions suggested themselves for close attention. Were the Batwa human? Had they devolved from a larger and superior race? Were there any signs that they were evolving into creatures of more normal size?

Over time, Verner established that pygmies knew "the difference between a lie and the truth" and had the language to "express both ideas." He observed, furthermore, that they were capable of "love, hatred, fear, self-respect, vanity . . . all the passions and affections" and had perfectly adequate rational powers. It was undeniable that "they were men," perhaps of "the lowest type"—illiterate, short, and nonwhite—but men nonetheless. They were, after all was said and done, and the study prosecuted to its end, a race apart, whose cleverness and sociability Verner came to enjoy.

He divulged his guiding principle, the theory of evolution, to his forest neighbors, informing the Batwa that according to the most advanced notions of his own people, they had all descended from apes. The pygmies did not take to Darwinism with all the relish for which he might have hoped. Instead, it seemed to them that the salt-rich muzungu was making nasty comments about their grandparents.

To "prosecute" their own in-depth study of Fwela, the Batwa released a white-faced chimpanzee of the Soko variety into Verner's care. The Soko was followed in short order by a gray-haired Batwa elder who pretended he merely wanted to know how Fwela liked his new pet. After some moments spent observing the antics of the ape, the Batwa noted that both "Saxon and Soko alike were strikingly white." Verner found nothing to disagree with in that. Pointing back and forth from Fwela to ape, the pygmy then demanded loudly, "If we black Batwa come from the black monkeys in the forest, who then comes from that Soko there!?"

The Gospels had even less impact than the theory of evolution on the "fabled dwarfs of Ethiopia." The pygmies declined to join Verner in singing Presbyterian hymns transcribed into the native tongue. Yet Verner hoped to found a new mission at Ndombe's, far from the nuisances of central authority. He dreamed about establishing a center of trade in ivory, rubber, and palm oil, and he wanted to go on studying pygmies even if they had begun studying him back.

Ndombe's was his very own Forbidden Land, his base of operations, the focus of all his schemes for African development. With the cooperation of the church, the permission of the Belgians, and a little luck, he would have stayed there indefinitely, preparing for the next stage of his African career, a triumphant return to the Congo on behalf of American investors.

Verner was to get his chance to play with millionaires, but not yet, and not while working within the church.

In 1897, Leopold was in no mood to grant further concessions to Presbyterians. Sheppard had not yet made his decisive report on atrocities, but tension had been increasing between the American mission and the state. The church, for its part, wanted Verner back at Luebo while Verner persisted in staying at Ndombe's.

In September, his superiors wrote that they were "pained at the spirit of insubordination . . . pained when our counsel to you is so lightly esteemed." A month later his father turned down Verner's request for a loan of a thousand dollars to be used in setting up shop on his own, writing that his son's language was "intemperate" and his threat to leave his post "madness."

Then came a visit from the Force Publique.

The Force Publique coming to demand tribute—that is, to loot Ndombe's—was a large, unruly, but well-armed bunch. In the woods surrounding the town, Ndombe's warriors were massed by the thousands, waiting. At a word, by sheer force of numbers and despite lack of guns, they would have annihilated Leopold's undisciplined minions and their camp-scavenging followers. But to win this battle would be to lose a war. Bula Mutadi would return in strength, and Ndombe's proud kingdom, like many before it, would be laid to waste. Shielding King Ndombe without giving offense to the agents of Belgian rule seemed impossible to accomplish by conventional means.

Nearly single-handedly Fwela enforced the peace. He gathered the soldiers of the Force Publique into a tent where he put on a magic lantern show depicting the death of Jesus. Entranced by slides projected on a screen, the soldiers stomped and shouted for repeated viewings. At daybreak, he asked if they too would crucify the Lord as they had just seen the Romans do. Stumbling out of the tent into blinkering African sunlight, they swore it could never enter their heads to do such a thing.

Later, intercepting a soldier who had just kidnapped a woman from the town, Fwela brought down his walking stick upon a "rascal's pate in proper evangelical Presbyterian style." The would-be kidnapper went down like a log.

Lastly, and perhaps most demoralizing of all for the Force Publique, Fwela subjected as many of them as he could assemble to a recitation of "Swannee Ribber [sic]" and "What a Friend I Have in Jesus," rendered in the native tongue. Leopold's troops, in all their wide and varied experience of depredation, had never before encountered quite such an adversary as this mad muzungu. Disoriented, their hopes for quick booty dashed, they marched off in search of a less fiercely guarded realm.

It was probably Verner's finest hour as a missionary, but the manic lengths to which he had been forced to go saddened Ndombe. Was this the best that could be expected of white rule?

Through Verner, the king dictated an appeal to Leopold, informing him that "the heart of Ndombe is white" and that he "had always been the good friend of the white stranger." In return he asked only that Leopold not send men "to kill, and plunder, and burn, to destroy the towns and make desolate the country." To men with "good hearts to help the black people, to teach them, to keep the peace with them, and to be their friends," Ndombe swore his lands would be forever open.

Verner thought Ndombe's appeal a sound idea. He kept himself apart from other missionaries' criticisms of the Belgian king, remarking that you needn't "leave Virginia to find Negroes abused." He wanted to believe that Leopold was unaware of and not responsible for the misbehavior of his underlings, and he wanted to do nothing that would keep him out of the king's good graces. It would take many shocks and disappointments before S. P. Verner could let go the notion that Leopold's heart was fundamentally white toward his Congolese subjects.

He knew, as Ndombe was dictating his appeal, that his own first trip to Africa was drawing to a close. He had sustained a serious injury to his leg.

Late in 1897, while climbing a peak to map an area between Luebo and Ndombe, he had been overwhelmed by the beauty of a scene known only to the veteran African traveler. There were hawks and flocks of parrots wheeling over the flowery plains, and hippopotami and elephants bellowing at the mountain's base as they launched into a river. Verner put down his instruments to attend more closely. Such music of the natural world "holds still the beating heart," he mused, "and lifts up the soul to God and higher things."

It was such a moment as recalls fine minds to poetry. Verner prepared to add his own voice to that of hawk, parrot, hippopotamus, and elephant with a stanza from Heine concerning the longing that a northern Pine tree—"lone upon a wintry night"—feels for a Southern Palm—"midst heaps of burning sand"—when all of a sudden the ground gave way and he tumbled into a game-pit.

Verner finished the recitation with a calm-shattering curse upon his goddamned stinking luck. He had been skewered by a stake seasoned with deadly poison and heaven had turned to hell in an instant.

He managed to disimpale his thigh and climb back out, where he lay without shade in the unmitigated heat of the hottest season of the year. Kassongo ran quickly to his aid but was too young and small to carry Fwela down the mountain. During the two hours it took the boy to return with help Verner baked and thirsted and finally became delirious. He prepared to "lift up the soul to God" in another way than first intended.

He was glad, at least, that what were surely last thoughts did not pertain to evil deeds, but were of Christ and of Africa, which he regretted leaving in such haste. But before the poison could complete its work, Kassongo came racing back with rescue in the form of Wembo, "our Hercules."

Wembo could row a canoe against the current for an entire day without tiring, and enjoyed wrestling matches with wild boars and full-grown buffaloes. He was altogether "the most savage and pugnacious" man Verner had ever known. But now he carried Verner down the mountain as easily as one might a child.

At the nearest village Kassongo sucked the poison out of Verner's wound, and Fwela scrawled a note for the Reverend Phipps to come, the same Phipps whose brush with illness three years earlier had prompted Verner to complain, "Oh, the helplessness of that race is appalling!" This time his hyperbole was reserved for the quality of care he received at the hands of Phipps and another black minister. Now he incurred a lifelong indebtedness to "that race" for "the most faithful and remarkable fight against disease" he had ever seen, heard, or read about anywhere in the "annals of African history."

As they worked to save his life, he renewed a vow "to work for them, to secure their happiness, to be their real friend in all the evil which threatens their race to-day." "May God forget me and mine," he concluded, "when I forget them and theirs."

The Mission Committee seized on the bad leg as an excuse to pull Verner out of Africa. He was ready to go. Leaving on grounds of ill-health was better than being court-martialed Presbyterian-style for disobeying orders. In June of 1898, while working on a Tshiluba booklet, *Mukanda wa Tshiluba* ("Book of the Fear and Palavar Affair of the High God"), he received final word that the committee thought it wrong to keep him in the field. He began to retrace his steps. There were goodbyes to King Ndombe, Prime Minister Joka, and Reverend Sheppard as he worked his way back to Luebo and from Luebo to the coast.

When he left America at the age of twenty-two, it was with high hopes and the prediction that mixing S. P. Verner with Africa would have incalculable results. But what had he actually accomplished in his three years abroad? What is the inventory of differences between the untried, ambitious youth and the soon-to-be ex-missionary?

In Africa, the parasites of malaria had stowed away in his blood, to be assimilated into his character. Afterwards it could be hard to tell, when he fell to raving, whether the cause was mental breakdown or malarial fits. The paroxysms of malaria masked those of madness, and vice versa. The unexpected emergence of such a character as the Hapsburg Emperor could be attributed to either.

On the positive side, he had his new name, Fwela, although that might not prove quite as much an asset at home as it had been in Africa. He had met and found favor with King Ndombe. This gave him a place to return to in the Congo with or without church sponsorship. He had put in long hours in the company of the Batwa, and this qualified him as an expert in an area of anthropology in which there were few to contradict him.

Perhaps most important for the course of his career, he had succeeded, by feats of prodigious fence-sitting, and nearly alone among Presbyterian missionaries, in not making an enemy of the king of Belgium.

So far as physical cargo was concerned, Verner was toting one of the largest, most varied assortments ever to leave Africa in one bundle, excluding the slave ships. Reverend Sheppard had set a precedent with regard to art and artifacts, exporting quantities of Kuba art to Hampton College in Virginia. Verner's collection, like Sheppard's, was part of an art and artifact drain imposed on Africa. Verner also brought along mineral specimens and living things—plants, seeds, parrots, two monkeys, and a wildcat.

Kondola and Kassongo were also coming with him. They had become distraught when Fwela packed and prepared to leave. All their teachers at Luebo had come from America, the land of the *muzungu*, the fairyland across the water. And if Fwela would only take them with him they could see it, smell it, walk its roads. Kassongo was too proud to beg, but his face betrayed his feelings. And Kondola pled for both of them.

Verner was moved that they wanted to travel with him. Let them complete their studies in America, then return to Africa to help educate their people. No matter that they were unschooled in English and had seen barely twenty white men in their lives. They would be his responsibility. There was a precedent in his favorite book; Crusoe's trip had been crowned by a return with Friday.

It was unusual if not unique, as the century drew to a close, to be taking humans out of Africa. Boys required more paperwork than art or animals. The Belgian official who signed for Kondola and Kassongo asked Verner if it had not become more difficult for a gentleman from South Carolina to acquire Africans than it had been not so long ago.

Verner, Kondola and Kassongo, parrots, monkeys, cat, chameleons, seeds, battle-axes, and other collectibles shipped out of Boma at the end of 1898 on the Belgian steamer *The Leopoldville*. At sea, one of the monkeys drank enough salt water to kill him. He had been their favorite, and the boys mourned. When they passed through Antwerp its spires and churches caused Kassongo to ask if this was not the fabled city of Jerusalem as foretold in Sunday school. In Brussels, Verner deposited Ndombe's appeal to Leopold, and, as the first tangible benefit for being a friendly missionary, received permission to open a concession at Ndombe's.

In London, the presence of Kondola and Kassongo, and some off-the-cuff banter in Tshiluba, helped Verner solidify his reputation as an Africanist. His articles on the pygmies, penned aboard ship and published in such periodicals as the *Spectator*, brought him into contact with members of the Geographical Society. Indulging his passion for genealogy, he discovered that an uncle many times removed had served with distinction at Waterloo.

In February 1899, while still in London, a chimney crashing through a skylight flattened a chair from which he had just arisen, and Verner, as if rudely awakened from a dream, began the last phase of his journey home.

8

SPECIAL AGENT

Let no man despise the secret
hints and notices of danger, which
sometimes are given him . . . they are
certain discoveries of an invisible
world, and a converse of spirits . . .
and . . . why should we not suppose
they are . . . given for our good?

—*Robinson Crusoe*

A week later the *Southwark* carrying Verner and friends pulled into New York harbor. Like the European immigrants coming in the thousands, Fwela, Kondola, and Kassongo crowded on deck to catch a glimpse of the Statue of Liberty holding up her beacon in the early morning fog.

"Multitudinous trumpetings," scribbled Verner of the great metropolis and gateway to America. He wanted to gallantly trumpet back—"Queen City of the Occident. Wonderful New York!"—but his voice was weak. He wasn't feeling very well. In the form of a million tiny enemies, Africa was still in his blood. "Fevers, labors, anxiety" had worn him down to little more than a hundred pounds. Now East Coast influenza was threatening to fight it out with tropical fever for the little that remained.

After a cursory glance at his cargo, customs officials

passed on a more detailed inspection. The parrots, the surviving monkey, and the seasick wildcat were left in the ship's
hold to keep from freezing. Kondola and Kassongo were temporarily removed for processing. Verner on a New York pier
felt more alone and lonely than he ever had in Africa. He
thought of Wembo carrying him down the mountain, Reverend Phipps nursing him back to health.

Addlement and infection. Fever, blizzards, and a buckling
leg. He was the only person on the pier softly humming a
Tshiluba rowing song to keep up his courage. It was with sheer
disgust that he thought he heard a Southern accent. He was
hundreds of miles from Dixie and in need of no hallucina-
tions. He turned away toward the seagulls and the brine.

A hand tapped him on the shoulder. Verner had half a
mind to bring his walking stick down on the head of this
unruly figment of his imagination. He heard his name and an
apologetic, "Excuse me sir, I thought for a moment you were
my old friend, Samuel." Verner turned and howled in delight.
Here was a college chum from the University of South Carolina. They had corresponded occasionally and the man, now
living in Manhattan, had come to meet the ship.

Verner started to tell his friend the story of the game-pit
and the poisoned stake, how he had been rescued in Africa
and how he was just as pleased to be rescued in New York.
The man suggested they cut short conversation in the frigid
gloom and repair to his apartment where he would enjoy introducing Verner to his wife, born in Kentucky.

They were well on their way before Verner, who had been
talking faster than he could think, pulled up suddenly, saying,
"Damn!! I forgot my Africans."

"Africans? Forgot your Africans? Why, Samuel, you probably forgot them in Africa, which is as it should be. Besides,
that sort of thing was outlawed some time ago, as I seem to
recall."

Verner described how it was with Kondola and Kassongo,
and his friend went back to claim them from Customs while
he, in the company of his friend's wife, gave himself over to
warm liquids and hospitality. "New York is the grandfather of
all cities," said Kassongo when he arrived. "It is a forest of
houses and people," said Kondola.

Perhaps, but Verner wanted to leave multitudinous New
York as soon as he could, the next day if at all possible. There

were people to meet in Washington, D.C., and artifacts to be sold to the Smithsonian. While making preparations for travel he deposited the boys in a boardinghouse.

When he came back for them some hours later they were no longer there. Through a chained door, he demanded to know where they were. The landlord didn't admit he had seen any such things as Africans. But as for the two niggers he found on the premises when he came back, he had put them out.

"The night was deepening," Verner wrote, "it was bitter cold and the wind howled over the snowy streets." Two boys were lost in the labyrinthine yards and alleyways of New York City; Kassongo, who had sucked poison from Verner's wounded thigh, and Kondola who awakened one night in their camp with the indispensable information that a leopard was only yards away.

Verner walked up and down the city streets with a "raging tempest" in his breast and "a rocked and harrowed brain." The image of Ndombe rose up accusingly before him. Old words came back to haunt him. Was this the way to repay hospitality that had known "no race issue, no color line, no question of skin or ancestry?" Was this how to honor the oath: "May God forget me and mine, when I forget them and theirs?"

Forgotten them he had. He had put his own affairs first. If Kondola and Kassongo were never heard from again, if they were lying robbed or frozen on some side street, and if there were still such a thing as responsibility, whose was it but his own? He had agreed to take them to America.

The boys, meanwhile, were cold but safe. They were waiting quietly, not far away, sure in their hearts that Fwela would find them. New York, grandfather of cities, forest of houses and people, bore minimal resemblance to the world they had known. They selected one of those rare points of similarity as if through it they could be saved. Bananas were food in both worlds. Kondola and Kassongo wound up hugging each other for warmth in front of a bunch of bananas visible through a grocery store window.

They had understood only a fraction of the landlord's words, but it was evident his heart was far from white toward them. It was the worst muzungu they had ever known who opened the door and pushed them into the terrible cold. Kassongo, over thirteen now, and growing tall and strong, was curious about what made the white man sure they wouldn't rather turn and fight. Kondola, who had once told Verner that he liked Christianity because it saved lives, thought the landlord must be of some other religion.

Once out on the street, everything was unfamiliar, except for the bananas. And then, who should turn the corner blowing steam, limping rapidly, and chattering to himself but Fwela, as they knew he would. Verner and two Africans in a shivering huddle made a strange sight even for a New York City street. Kassongo told the story of the white man with the bad heart, the ugly landlord who hated them.

After finding lodgings for the boys in another part of town, Verner rode the elevateds until dawn, staring out at the great expanse of city, wondering how and why he had come so near to losing Kondola and Kassongo. Nowhere in his favorite book, he knew, did Crusoe do so poorly by his Friday.

In early 1899, the vast, long-awaited New York Zoological Gardens in the Bronx was still some months away from completion. Verner left the monkey and the wildcat behind bars in the more tenement-like conditions of the Central Park Zoo. The fate of the majority of parrots is unknown, but one of them, born in the Portuguese colony of Angola, became property of the Verner clan and lived to a ripe old age in Chapel Hill, North Carolina, where it is alleged to have spoken English to white people, a Bantu tongue to blacks, and Portuguese when it wasn't sure.

En route to Tuscaloosa, Alabama, where he intended to enroll the boys in school, Verner stopped in the nation's capital. The Smithsonian Institution accepted one thousand cubic feet of African objects, offering two hundred dollars for the collection on condition that Verner catalogue the material first. Verner later received the money, though the catalogue was never done.

The animals were now on view in New York; the battle-axes, masks, and such ready for mounting in a museum. It occurred to Verner that a public use might be found for the boys. He offered to rent Kondola and Kassongo to the Smithsonian as models, to "illustrate photographically some of the arts and industries of their people," but the offer was refused.

Verner held private consultations with Baron Moncheur, the Belgian ambassador and head of Leopold's Congo Lobby, an organization that operated in secret because the king did not want it known he was actively engaged in manipulating American public opinion. The lobby offered full and part-time employment opportunities, with payment in kind—such as rights to a concession at Ndombe's—for a job well done. Through other representatives, the lobby was attempting to intercept Booker T. Washington as the black leader became critical of Leopold and moved toward alliance with Mark Twain.

Ex-missionaries and reverends were especially in demand. A Verner or two on Leopold's side would be just the thing to raise doubts about charges of atrocity by the likes of Reverend William Henry Sheppard. Verner remained on cordial terms with the Baron for years.

Kondola and Kassongo adopted quickly to life at the Stillman Institute in Tuscaloosa. Without forgetting their African origins, they were able to find ample areas of identity with American blacks—the eviction from the boardinghouse served as a quick study in certain aspects of American history. They learned plowing, gardening, and, within months, enough writing to post intelligible letters.

With the placement of the boys, only one component of the African cargo remained on the loose, namely Verner himself. He entered a Baltimore sanatorium. Something diagnosed as brain fever, like a biological synthesis of all his other ills, physical and mental, had assailed him in the middle of 1899. He was in urgent need of a thorough overhaul.

Brain fever meant he might be heard ranting and raving while his thigh healed and he put some weight back on his emaciated frame. Nurses would hear him addressing phantoms as "Your Majesty" or "Miss Amanda."

When released from the sanatorium six months later, Verner was re-energized and began work on various fronts at once. It was understood on both sides that Verner would never return to Africa under the auspices of the church. But the church and he continued to have uses for each other domestically. He worked occasionally for the Stillman Institute, as he had before. He canvassed for the mission and propagandized for its work while at the same time, as per his understanding with the Baron, parrying criticisms of the king.

His work had a secular side as well. J. B. Pond was a New York organizer who had sponsored speaking tours for H. M. Stanley and P. T. Barnum. In the first years of the new century

Verner traveled as far as Chicago for Pond's speakers' bureau to lecture on the ethnology, industry, and excellent prospects for commercial development of central Africa. Verner's interests and those of Leopold converged in this respect. The king wanted to attract American capital so it would weigh in with him against attacks from other quarters. Verner wanted to be part of a moneymaking enterprise, good for Africa and for himself, at King Ndombe's across the sea.

He wrote copiously. An article on the Batwa was accepted for the August 1902 edition of the *Atlantic Monthly*, and he was completing his voluminous *Pioneering in Central Africa*, the story of his missionary years, in which religion is decidedly an afterthought to all his other adventures and concerns, and is barely mentioned in the book's generally favorable reviews. ("You may not read Mr. Samuel Phillips Verner's *Pioneering in Central Africa* without sharing in no small measure the author's enthusiasm," wrote the *New York Times*.)

In 1902, he felt financially secure enough to marry. The bride was Hattie Bradshaw, an Alabama schoolteacher and daughter of a large, established southern family. Within the next two years he fathered Mary and Julia, the first two of five children.

In the same year, he began negotiations with W. J. McGee. The two may have already become acquainted at the Smithsonian, McGee's previous employer, when Verner tried to rent Kondola and Kassongo to the institution. Now the Chief was organizing the greatest display of traditional peoples ever mounted.

The anthropologist Frederick Starr was recruited to go to remote Japanese islands to bring back "hairy" Ainu. The U.S. government, in celebration of its recent triumph over insurrection in the Philippines, offered hundreds of Moro, Igorot, Negrito, and other Filipino tribesmen. It was understood that any number of native Americans, many already veterans of display, were to be made available once again.

But even a Buffalo Bill could display Indians, just as a P. T. Barnum could exhibit freaks. McGee's aims were more serious. He aspired to raise anthropology above the amateurish sideshows and ragtag miscellanies that had gone under the name at previous fairs. He wanted to be exhaustively scientific in his demonstration of the stages of human evolution. Therefore, in St. Louis, he required "darkest blacks" to set off against "dominant whites" and members of the "lowest known culture" to contrast with "its highest culmination." He thought he could find the giants of the human family among the Patagonian Indians. He was on the lookout for someone to bring him pygmies.

Verner started negotiations off with a proposal that could not fail to intrigue McGee. He would get pygmies to the fair and return them to Africa when it was over for the price of one thousand dollars. The low bid—plus Verner's written work, good relations with the king of Belgium, friendship with Ndombe, and well-publicized knowledge of the Batwa—succeeded in capturing McGee's attention.

Shortly after McGee accepted, Verner heard from one African he had already transported to America; he received his last letter from Kassongo. On September 16, Kassongo wrote from Birmingham, where he had gone to work in an iron foundry. He let Verner know he intended to return to Tuscaloosa shortly, where he would continue working to put himself through school. He ended:

> I am well just now. Brother Kondola has come to Birmingham and has a job at a stable. When will school open. Please let me no.
>
> Yours in the Lord
Kassongo

Three days later he was dead.

On September 19, Booker T. Washington spoke at the Shiloh Baptist Church in Birmingham. This pre-eminent leader of black America was turning his attention to stories of atrocities in the Congo Free State. Kassongo did not want to miss the opportunity to see and hear him. Kondola was interested but said something in his heart told him to stay home that night. He tried to persuade Kassongo to do likewise, but the prince laughed off his minister's advice as fuss and worry. Kondola spoke of those occasions when his heart had been right. Kassongo reminded him of those times when he'd been wrong.

The meeting was packed, with three thousand people inside the church, the same number waiting to get in, and only a narrow stairway separating the crowds. As Washington finished his address, two men in a front row pushed and pulled at each other for a seat. A woman cried, "Fight!" The crowd heard it as "Fire!" Panic ensued, and a mad rush toward the single point of exit, the stairs. Washington himself was only spared because a woman told him to be still and shielded him with her body.

Those on the stairs, blocked by the crowd outside, were trampled by the charge from within. A hundred people were pummeled into what one survivor described as "human pavement." When the dead were separated and identified Kassongo was among them.

Verner rushed to Birmingham as soon as he heard. By then Kondola had already shed his tears. When Kassongo opened the door that night to walk to the church, Kondola knew, without knowing how and without being able to do a thing about it, that he would never see his friend again, and he had begun to grieve. By the time Verner arrived, Kondola was calm and quiet; it was not Kondola but Fwela who needed comforting.

Full of self-recrimination, Verner asked whether it was his fault that Kassongo had gone to church, and whether he could be blamed for panic in the aisles? Wasn't the boy doing well at school? Didn't he want to be in America? Hadn't Kondola begged for both of them to come along? Mightn't the same have happened in Africa and maybe sooner, what with leopards, the Force Publique, the snakebite, and the boy's own pride? Could he have stayed by Kassongo's side day in, day out? Could he have sat up and watched him every minute? No matter how he freed himself, his last question always put him back on the dock: Wasn't he responsible?

Kondola put his arms around Fwela and held him as one might a vibrating object about to fly apart.

In a letter from the mayor of Birmingham to Secretary of State John Hay explaining the disaster, Verner was officially exonerated: "The probable cause of the said Kassongo's death was suffocation. From all the evidence of the case it appears that no one, either the said Kassongo or his guardian Dr. Samuel Phillips Verner, or anyone else was responsible for his death, it being purely accidental." To Verner's mind there was no reason why accident and responsibility could not coexist.

This tampering with fate, this effort at transplanting, might work with seeds, most parrots, and even fifty percent of monkeys but was not necessarily to be recommended in the case of men.

One African was dead, and Verner humbled. And then he resumed negotiations with Chief McGee to bring eighteen more Africans to St. Louis for the fair. Was the self-reproach sincere? As sincere and as potent as the forgetfulness and the ambition.

McGee raised Verner's opening bid from the impossible to the merely unlikely: $8,500 was allotted, $500 of it for salary and the rest for expenses, with $1,500 more kept in reserve. The Chief was still uneasy; he wanted reassurances from Verner that no diplomatic obstacles would be put in his way. Verner replied that he had recently received a letter from King Leopold himself, "couched in the kindest terms." What further guarantees could be required? "There will," wrote Verner on October 5, "be no difficulties there."

The deal was finalized October 22, 1903. On World's Fair stationery, McGee pronounced Verner a "Special Agent," authorized to conduct "an expedition into the interior of Africa," where he would offer "certain natives the opportunity of attending the Exposition in person." He was furnished with an extensive, detailed shopping list, as if the Congo were laid out like one of Chicago or New York's major department stores—and Verner merely had to point and pay.

The shopping list called for twelve pygmies—including "One Pygmy Patriarch or chief, One adult woman, preferably his wife ... Two infants, of women in the expedition," and "Four more Pygmies, preferably adult but young, but including a priestess and a priest, or medicine doctors, preferably old." Verner was authorized to bring back "one fine type" of what were referred to as "Red Africans." This fine specimen, preferably, would be Ndombe himself. There were to be three more "Red people" and two more natives left to Verner's choosing but "of a distinct ethnic type from any of the above."

He was also to bring back as much of the Congo as necessary in order to provide an authentic setting for the assorted Africans. The extensive list of supplementary items included "one most primitive house," and "one least primitive house," a "full set of religious emblems and ceremonial objects," and "a Blacksmith shop." Verner was responsible for taking photographs of fires, religious rites, funerals, and graves, and for "full and accurate anthropometric measurements." He was to become a fund of information on topics such as variations in color, albinos, rites, relations to apes and monkeys, folklore, chastity, and concubinage, and would be amply equipped with salt, cloth, brass wire, cowrie shells, matches, and hats for use in barter and the propagation of goodwill.

In November, press from around the country and beyond focused on the expedition. According to a St. Louis paper, Special Agent Verner was embarking on "one of the most difficult and dangerous of all World's Fair assignments." He was going to face the "unhealthy climate . . . hostile tribes and wild animals" of darkest Africa, where "at the bottom of the ladder," according to the New York Sun, he would find the pygmies: "There could be no group in the world more difficult to get."

His reward would be "eighteen of the most interesting specimens of the human race that will probably be seen at the World's Fair," according to the St. Louis Globe-Democrat. The benefits to science would be immeasurable. A New Orleans paper pointed out that pygmies and other guests of the Anthropology Department were to be subjected to tests of "power and acuteness of vision, delicateness of hearing, sensitiveness to touch and temperature, quickness of response to sense impressions, etc." The result would be a statistical method of distinguishing "the savage from the enlightened man," a numerical index of "what may be called the citizen value of an individual."

On November 28, a full-page article in the Duluth Herald struck an unusually cautionary note, reporting that forest dwellers had not survived previous attempts by anthropologists to bring them to Italy or Germany for study or display. They were, it seemed, "unable to live long away from their native forests." "Perhaps," the reporter wrote, "Mr. Verner's enterprise will meet with better success."

Other members of the press reported on Verner's departure in the spirit of improvisation that was to make the Anthropology Department such a delight to write—and read—about, and contributed so much to its success: "He will be accompanied by a couple of native Indians. It is expected these men will endure the climate better than white men," wrote a Cleveland paper, as Verner prepared to leave.

One of the "native Indians" turned out to be the singular and steadfast "John" Kondola. He was indeed one of two African natives who accompanied Verner when they shipped out of Africa to New York in 1899. Kondola was but one "native" now to depart from New York at the end of November 1903, bound first for Brussels and then for his African home with a heavy heart over the loss of Kassongo, his friend from childhood. The other man who accompanied Verner was the Reverend Alonzo Emiston, a graduate of the Stillman Institute. Emiston was as American as Verner himself, but a black man whom the Cleveland paper could not apparently distinguish from other "native Indians." He was a Presbyterian missionary following the footsteps of Sheppard and Phipps.

9

THE VILLAGE OF THE BASCHILELE

It came now very warmly upon
my thoughts ... that I was called
plainly by Providence to save this
poor creature's life.
—*Robinson Crusoe*

Evolution was very much the theme as Professor Special Agent Reverend Doctor Verner—the titles awarded him by the press—sailed out of New York harbor in 1903. The first time Verner had gone to Africa it was to a continent known only through fantasies and books, and by reflection, through the descendants of African-Americans like those his grandfather had owned as slaves. He had gone to Africa to escape the curse from which Robinson Crusoe fled, the blight of using life up in the safe but deadly middle station. He had wanted to brush against the root—the evolutionary, evangelical, psychological, and sexual root—of a racial question that disturbed him as a boy, and tantalized him as a young man.

Now, this second time, nearly eight years to the day after setting forth with Phipps—and after Reverend Sheppard and the Force Publique, King Ndombe and Chief McGee—there was no vagueness at all about Verner's purposes. Pygmies: they were the reason for his going to Africa. He was going to collect "the Pygmies of Herodotus, the fabled dwarfs of Ethiopia in reality and truth," as he called them that day when he followed the diminutive meat salesman into a conveniently located tribe of Batwa.

Pygmies were to be the core of the African Exhibit. They were evolution's enigma, anthropology's drawing card. Because of pygmies S. P. Verner had become a Special Agent.

Verner and Kondola arrived in Europe early in December. They spent the next month getting outfitted and dealing with Belgian officials. It is likely that Verner met with Leopold II in Brussels. Sixty-eight years old in 1903, the king was bloated, gloomy, and calculating, terrified in nearly equal measure of germs, his Congo critics, and the Kaiser.

Verner shipped out of Europe via Antwerp, bound for the Congo, the easy part of his journey over. He and Kondola arrived on the west coast of Africa in mid-January, where they began the trip by steamer up the Congo River, followed by the railroad ride along the passes of the Crystal Mountains. Verner had planned to be at Ndombe's by February 1. It was already February 17 when he began a twelve-day journey on the waters of the Kasai. At the beginning of March he was waiting on the banks of the river for yet another steamer to take him further on.

Nearly immediately upon his arrival in Africa he had fallen ill, a target once again of mosquitos. "Vicious little torments," he called them; they made him writhe "as if the coil of an electric battery were wrapped around my body, and the current playfully turned on by some fiend of the inquisition."

Malaria's parasites feast and hide but do not reproduce within the human bloodstream. That occurs within the stomach wall of the female anopheles mosquito. When she feeds on an infected human being, she becomes contaminated. When she feeds again, she injects fresh generations of parasites through her salivary glands into the bloodstream of her host. Man and insect both are integral to the parasite's life-cycle.

Soon Verner was cycling back and forth between the disease's various stages—the stage of cold chills, vomiting, and headache in which the parasites rupture their host red blood cells; the hot stage of fever and paroxysms during which they hunt new cells to enter and devour; and the wet stage of sweats and exhaustion between attacks. In addition to the huge distances he was covering on land and water, he was logging uncounted extra miles on the ups and downs of malaria. Strength stored up by months of rest in a Baltimore sanatorium and years of relative quiet in the United States was being rapidly depleted.

Verner's letters to McGee cry out about tribal warfare, fever-stricken steamship captains, and a Belgian administration that, curiously, was not living up to its promise to be of help. McGee, as if Verner might somehow have forgotten, as if it could have slipped his mind, redirected the Special Agent to the task at hand: "As on the last writing, I make but a single plea—*get the Pygmies.*" He told Verner that "Some who do not know you seem doubtful as to the success of your expedition; but those who have seen you are satisfied when I say—*he will bring the Pygmies.*"

In response to McGee's prompting Verner vowed, "We are not going to fail unless death comes."

While waiting for the steamer to take him the last leg of the journey to Ndombe, he did some exploring, dropping in on a village belonging to a tribe known as the Baschilele. The Baschilele were in fairly constant rebellion against the Belgians. A populous grouping, they had succeeded in preserving something of their independence, and with it, their tradition of selling slaves.

During Verner's stint as missionary, the Baschilele, mistaking him for a representative of Bula Mutadi, were the only group to try and kill him. They had fallen upon a convoy of canoes under his command.

The rear canoes never made it to a rendezvous. Ten men were slaughtered in the Baschilele ambush. When Verner came upon the severed arm of one of his companions that had washed up on the shore, it seemed to him that all his "youth dried up," and that his boyhood came to its conclusion. "I seemed to grow old," he wrote, "the warm enthusiastic blood chilled, another man rose from the wet sands of that bloody island and dragged himself listlessly into the canoe."

Verner is unforthcoming about why he entered the village of the Baschilele in March 1904. It may have been the rumors of the slave market that drew him, the urge to inspect one of the sources of his family's bygone wealth. It is undeniable, however, that in the slave market of the Baschilele he found and bought a pygmy for St. Louis. The cost was nominal: about a pound of salt and a bolt of cloth. "The first pygmy has been secured!" he wrote to Chief McGee on March 30. "He was obtained from a village in which he was held captive having been taken prisoner at a remote point in the great . . . forest twelve days march from any white settlement."

It is impossible to know precisely how long Ota Benga had languished in the village of the Baschilele before being bought.

While Verner had been swatting mosquitos and plying the Kasai in his race to find the Batwa, Ota had been hunting.

It is not unusual for a pygmy on the trail of an elephant to be gone for days, to stay away for as long as it takes. Nor is it uncommon for a pygmy to hunt an elephant alone. "Noise" signals discord and nonsense to a pygmy but means danger to an elephant. An individual pygmy has as good a chance of stealing close enough to an elephant for his wooden weapon to do some harm as a band of hunters working together.

There are elephant hunting songs in which a group of voices enter just before the previous singers finish. Before the new singers draw their breath, another group locks in. It is a structure not unlike that of the forest itself, with branches laced tightly together in the canopy. Finally the old men sing, casting their voices above the others, like the bull elephant with its snout upraised. Such a song was sung for Ota before he left.

A hunter stores the details of the hunt away in memory. If he succeeds, that is to say, if he survives, the details of the hunt will have their place in the story to be recounted later.

And there is a dance in which men wear leaves on their chests and sway alluringly in imitation of women. Women fix branches between their legs and thrust themselves mockingly at the hunters. This dance of boundaries melting, role reversal—forest burlesque—is reserved for the sweet completion of an elephant hunt.

Forest dweller and elephant—as ancient and intimate a lockstep between hunter and hunted as obtains anywhere on earth between man and beast. Every victory over the elephant is a sign that the pattern still prevails, proof that whatever is happening outside, the pygmies' way of life remains tenable,

intact; the forest still provides. "The forest," as the song of the
molimo goes, "is good."

When an elephant falls to a pygmy's lance, a hunting band
pulls out all stops. Drunkenness, storytelling, dance, songs,
feasting are the only possible response; nothing is held back.

Ota had celebration in mind when he set out on his hunt.
He had followed the elephant for miles as it stopped to dine
delicately on leaves, to shake a tree for fruit, or to strip bark off
with its tusks. He had made himself imperceptible.

Finally, from close by, as if in a trance, he listened to the
shuffling and snorting, the leathery flapping of ears, the low
trumpeting that seemed to go through his bones before he
dashed from cover and thrust his spear into the beast's under-
side, then disappeared again before the animal could find and
crush him.

From a distance he followed the wounded elephant as it
trampled and battered the forest in pain before loss of blood
forced it slowly to its knees. The camp could be summoned to
the feast.

But the camp Ota had left behind had ceased to exist.

What Ota saw when he returned was different enough
from what he remembered to make him doubt his eyes. Were
those his children resting face down on the ground without
moving? Was that his wife's bloody head lying in the ashes?
Could those corpses be the elders whose song still echoed in
his memory?

Ota knew of a spirit world that intruded into the world of
the hunt through dreams and was said to sweep up forest
animals that inexplicably eluded hunters. It was conceivable
he had, like those animals, blundered into the parallel world
of spirits. If so, and if those spirits were playing at looking
human, they were doing a poor job of it. There was blood
everywhere.

His own camp, his real camp, could be near at hand, the
path to it beginning anywhere.

The Force Publique had been deflected toward Ota's camp by
the villagers who lived on the outskirts of the woods. The
villagers pointed toward the trees, and told of a tribe of little
people, half-savage, with teeth filed to sharp points to tear the
elephant meat that was their daily fare, who laid up vast stores
of ivory.

Conscripting the villagers as guides, the Force Publique penetrated the forest, pushing terrified villagers ahead of them as shields against pygmy archers.

The villagers knew nothing about the current whereabouts of Ota's camp. It was purely by accident that the Force Publique stumbled upon an inhabited clearing. The marauders shoved the villagers ahead of them into the camp. The appearance in their midst of villagers, bound to each other by the neck like slaves, brought all activity to a halt. Children dropped miniature bows, arrows, and toy cooking utensils to heed the whistle, the sign of danger, that went up from the central campfire. All eyes scanned the forest as the men remaining in the camp made for weapons that had never been used against human beings.

The one constraint placed upon the tax collectors was that they not squander their allotment of ammunition. Hands were severed, smoked, and piled in baskets to be brought back to Bula Mutadi as proof that bullets had not gone to waste.

The Force Publique kept their shooting to the minimum necessary for killing or maiming most of the thirty or so individuals in Ota's camp. By the time they themselves marched into the clearing there was no resistance—only groans, half choked shrieks of fear, and the beginning of hysterical sobbing from villagers and pygmies alike.

It has been documented that bouts of madness leading to suicide were not infrequently the result when a man returned home in the Congo Free State to find his relatives killed or enslaved. Perhaps it was the sight of a Force Publique captain, a big man very much like the monster, half-man, half-elephant, of whom he had dreamed, that spurred Ota into action. He charged, only to be disarmed and bound by many hands.

He and the other survivors were treated at length to the chicotte, the hippopotamus-hide whip said to dig truth and compliance out of victims, but torture was of no avail. The pygmies had no store of ivory to disclose. Even if the forest dwellers, like the dwarfs of mythology, were of a mind to amass treasure, the task would have been beyond them. The nomadic lifestyle does not allow for hoarding.

Ota and the other survivors were marched for many days out of the forest, beyond the village, and along a river to a land they had never seen. There were many stops at villages beside that river. At each, one or two of the forest people were left behind. At last Ota himself was left as a slave in the village of the Baschilele.

No *molimo* ritual had been or ever would be performed to seal his period of mourning. No spirit called to him, telling him to give up hopelessness for the certainty of revenge, as happened to Geronimo on his third day of grief. Instead, one day in March a white man arrived at the slave market of the Baschilele. The opening of the Louisiana Purchase Exposition was only weeks away when Ota Benga found himself staring up into the keen, blue, and, some would have said, slightly mad eyes of a *muzungu*.

S. P. Verner bent down and pulled the pygmy's lips apart to examine his teeth. He was elated; the filed teeth proved the little man was one of those he was commissioned to bring back. He saw himself as saving Ota. With salt and cloth he was buying him for freedom, Darwinism, and the West.

Ota had lost his family, his world, and the world view that framed it. He had looked on a great deal of death. There was no reason for him to think of this white man as anything but death come back in different form, a personal summons from the land of the dead. On the other hand, there was no reason for him to refuse to make that journey in the company of the *muzungu* rather than to remain a slave in the village of the Baschilele.

"He came nearer and nearer; at length he came close to me, and then he kneeled down again, kissed the ground, and laid his head upon the ground, and, taking me by the foot, set my foot upon his heart . . . I took him up, and made much of him, and encouraged him all I could." So said Robinson Crusoe when he saved Friday from the cannibals.

"I thought it well to secure him at once, even if we get all we wish from Ndombe," Special Agent Verner reported to Chief McGee. Later, in a piece for *Harper's Weekly* published with the World's Fair in full swing, he amplified: "He was delighted to come with us, for he was many miles from his people, and the Baschilele were not easy masters."

The imputation of delight to Ota Benga was made months after the event. Verner mentions nothing about delight, or any other show of enthusiasm, in that first letter to McGee. By the time of the *Harper's* piece, he was already well on his way to fictionalizing the encounter, humanizing it, simplifying it, making it more comprehensible to himself and his readers—making it play more like Friday's first encounter with Robinson Crusoe.

Sweating profusely, stinking profoundly, burning up in fevers, and cooling down in shakes, Verner rattled on to Ota as they waited together for the steamer after leaving the village of the Baschilele. He told Ota about a great water, a land of white people, a place called St. Louis, a man named Stanley who had explored Ota's world. Would Ota like a chance to do the same to the white man's world? To visit the land of the *muzungu* and live to tell the tale?

Occasionally Ota ventured a question, such as why he, Verner, had left the land of the dead. Didn't he like it there? Had it become too crowded for him?

In the language of the forest, to the ears of a pygmy, Verner was a living, breathing god of noise. The most reassuring thing Ota heard in his first days of travel with the *muzungu* was the soft voice of Kondola offering water while Fwela raved; the most convincing thing he experienced was the long ride on a river steamer.

Atrocity brings with it the added anguish of disbelief, the shattering of faith. Ota's world could never be fitted back together in original form.

It was not long after S. P. Verner and Ota Benga made each other's acquaintance that the American press lost track of the African expedition. On April 8, the *St. Louis Post-Dispatch* threw in the towel. "EXPOSITION ENVOY PYGMIES' VICTIM," read the headline; "FAIR OFFICIALS HAVE NOT HEARD FOR TWO MONTHS FROM EXPLORER SENT TO AFRICAN WILDS." Pygmies, who "live in thatched huts in trees and are more at home in the trees than on the ground," had "ambuscaded" Verner's party before it had "an opportunity to make its mission known." Verner and friends circled wagons but were hopelessly outnumbered. The "savage tribe of pygmies" shot poison arrows first and asked questions later.

Of course, nothing like this ambuscade befell the travelers. In fact, Verner and Ota Benga were getting to know each other in privacy, away from the glare of world publicity. On March 31, they steamed into sight of Fwela's old campground at Wissman Falls, twenty miles from Ndombe's. The waters of the Kasai were at flood level. The only way they could get to shore was to by grabbing onto an overhanging branch and climbing down.

Midway on the hike to Ndombe's, the king's son came out to greet them. "Fwela, Moiyo," said the prince as his father had some years ago—"Life!" Yet the drums of welcome were not the only rhythms being played; they were interwoven with the drums of war. Verner had arrived at a delicate point in the history of the kingdom. "The confusion," he reported, "was terrific."

War between Ndombe and a neighboring kingdom threatened over the issue of a kidnapped (or runaway) bride. Moreover the state was once more bearing down upon Ndombe. Fwela would have play his hand well to preserve Ndombe's life and kingdom without alienating Bula Mutadi.

The state had devised a new scheme for procuring rubber. A state-sponsored mining venture had discovered not gold, as hoped for, but only copper, and Congolese copper was not doing very well on the world market. Natives were required to pay taxes with copper crosses they purchased with rubber. (Congolese rubber had continued to do very well in the world market.) If they were delinquent, or flat out refused to gather the rubber there were visits from the Force Publique.

Verner saw it unfolding before his eyes: the state pressing in, Ndombe once again being forced to prepare for combat. He didn't want to burden McGee's "scientific soul with all these crosses," as he put it, but, confidentially, just between himself and the Chief, there it all was, the same game going "merrily on, wheel within a wheel, while Sambo is caught between the upper and nether millstone."

Ndombe was summoned to bring the taxes directly to Free State officials. It would be the first time he ever left his kingdom. Was it a scheme to take him hostage? Would there even be a kingdom left if and when he was permitted to return? Ndombe turned to Fwela for advice. Verner told his friend to trust the Belgians. In early May, Ndombe and a good portion of his aristocracy departed.

He put Ndombe in their hands, but Verner was nervous about the Belgians. The Batwa, anticipating trouble with the Force Publique, had begun to melt away into the forest. Verner felt betrayed. "Underneath all their bland assurances," he wrote to McGee, the Belgian purpose all along was to "defeat me in a way in which their interference will not directly appear."

Verner had seen too much; he might go public someday. "Seeing too much" was code among the Belgians; Reverend Sheppard had seen too much. Based on their experience with Presbyterian missionaries, the Belgians might suspect all Americans of seeing too much, but Verner was interested only in keeping silent and bringing the pygmies home.

He had to do it soon. There was a riverboat due any day now. With the dry season coming, it could be the last boat until September. If Verner didn't make the right connections he would wind up in St. Louis sometime after the exposition closed.

The moment had come to approach the Batwa. But at the very sight of Fwela, mothers shrieked, grabbed their children, and disappeared into the bush. So Verner presented Kondola to put their minds at ease. He said Kondola had gone with him to America, and here he was again.

Where, the Batwa responded, was Kassongo?

Verner remembered the Batwa love of salt, and so he salted them. Salt did more for the cause than argument. First he salted the children. "Soon they swarmed, screaming, dancing, whooping with delight. Their mothers emerged from their tiny leaf-colored huts. They, too, were salted. Then came the old men." Fwela had turned into a great salt shaker in the bush.

Still they refused to trust him. They called him a wizard, and wondered why anyone would choose to travel with him.

Finally, an unexpected ally stepped into the breach. Ota Benga had arrived at his decision. He had immediately recognized the Batwa as his kin. Their songs, if not necessarily their language, were like his own. He knew he could build a life among them if he chose. On the other hand, he had lived in close proximity to the muzungu for weeks now, and found that the muzungu had redeeming qualities. He could be entertaining: his constant, fever-driven chatter kept Ota's mind from circling back in futile reconnoitering to a place of pain. The facts of his existence—white skin, clothes, hat, shoes, corn-tassel hair—teased Ota into curiosity. And he had saved Ota's life.

Ota surprised Verner now when he announced he had a yen for travel. He had decided to go with Fwela and Kondola.

Why didn't the Batwa come along? Why not see what opportunities for hunting presented themselves in the land of the *muzungu* across that water in which—or so said Fwela—animals swam that were bigger by far than elephants? With Ota's vote of confidence, nearly twenty Africans were moved to accept Verner's invitation to the fair.

The night before the riverboat was scheduled to depart was one of torrential rain, and, for Fwela, the worst attack of fever yet. The morning brought last-minute doubts and hesitations. The number of pygmies dwindled to four, not counting Ota. There were also three men from Ndombe's village, one of them a nephew of the king.

No women or children would be going. As for the Batwa elders, their attitude was summarized by one who said, "if the boys mean to go to the devil, they can go, but you shall not catch me." Verner's haul fell far short of McGee's initial specification, the shopping list that called for eighteen Africans, but it would do.

The whistle blew. The anchor was lifted. Verner paused for a moment from frenzied activity to write, "We were off. But as I gazed upon the mighty tomblike forests about us, and upon my little band of comrades, a lump rose in my throat at the thought of this affecting exhibition of implicit faith."

Steamer, train, and steamer once again took the travelers to the coast. There, Reverend Sheppard climbed aboard the same oceangoing vessel bound for America. Despite vast differences in their points of view, Sheppard remained cordial to Verner. (It was another missionary who expressed some doubts about Fwela's sanity, and still another who attributed his "somewhat peculiar" behavior to "having been affected by the sun"; and it was Roger Casement, the British consul whose report on the Free State led to Leopold's undoing, who categorized Verner as "cracked.")

In St. Louis, opening-day ceremonies for the Louisiana Purchase Exposition had already come and gone. Native Americans and other "picturesque peoples" had marched up and down the length of the Pike, not, as in ancient Rome, in a crass display of the vanquished before their conquerors, but in homage to anthropology.

The journey westward across the Atlantic from the Congo to New Orleans served as a kind of initiation into what was to come. "The utter amazement," wrote Verner, "at the swift-moving train, the great steamer, and, above all, the mighty ocean, in the minds of the Africans from the far interior, may be imagined."

There were spirits in the boiler room. There were wizards in the captain's cabin. Powerful medicine men had been hiding in the locomotive. Sorcery pulled the steamship by spiderweb-thin threads across the ocean. Pygmies are normally naturalists. Ironically, it was exposure to Western technology that made them turn to the supernatural for explanations.

A chair was a confrontation with novelty. The pygmies descended on a chair two or sometimes three at a time. Sitting close together, smoking the cigarettes they had been given and scattering ashes everywhere, they wondered about the sources of *muzungu* transportation. Good spirits, bad spirits, sometimes the whole thing made them laugh. Sometimes the whole thing seemed like noise.

They spent hours looking over the side of the boat.

No environment more different that the forest could be imagined, but there were connections. The whales of which Verner had spoken were being hunted down for oil, baleen, and ambergris just as African elephants were being killed for ivory. Some whaling captains, when the chase went badly, had been known to sail around to Zanzibar to fatten on the slave trade. Occasionally, to the pygmies' astonishment, a free-swimming humpback or finback hove into view.

The pygmies lost a chimpanzee to illness, a sign of deaths to come. Few of their pets would survive the Fair. Ota and the Batwa gave the monkey a solemn burial at sea.

As for Verner, his fevers had risen so high in Africa that "both his journals and the chain of his memory were broken repeatedly." Aboard ship, he suffered relapses "superinduced by a hot calm encountered in the Gulf of Mexico, whereby he was completely incapacitated." He was returning to America in the manner to which he had become accustomed, harrowed, worn to a bone by "fevers, labors, anxiety." It was mid-June when the *Glenarm Head* containing Verner's unusual cargo steamed into New Orleans. The functionary coming to greet him with McGee's congratulations called for a stretcher. Completely unconscious, surrounded by a retinue of Africans, Special Agent Verner had to be carried ashore.

With Kondola acting as interpreter between "the Pygmies

of Herodotus" and the Western world, the Africans were taken by rail along the Mississippi up to St. Louis. Verner was taken to the New Orleans Sanatorium on Carondelet Street, where, in a few days, he had recovered enough to read a note from Chief McGee: "Your little folk . . . are attracting much attention, though less than they would receive were they . . . under the direction of the only man in America competent to look after these things."

10

ANTHROPOLOGY DAYS

Here education found new forage.... The chaos of education approached a dream.

—Henry Adams

McGee had drawn most of the major figures and institutions of the new science of anthropology into involvement with the St. Louis Fair. Franz Boas of Columbia University and the American Museum of Natural History lent his name to the proceedings. Frederick Starr of the University of Chicago, who had brought the Ainu—always "hairy," just as the Patagonian Indians were always "giants"—from Japan, remained on the fairgrounds to teach. Instrument makers donated anthropometric measuring devices. Dr. R. S. Woodworth, Professor Starr, and other anthropologists focused on such questions as:

Were dark-skinned peoples capable of discerning the color blue?
How did the barbaric races compare with intellectually defective Caucasians on intelligence tests?

Was the ratio of head size to body size a reliable index of cleverness?

How would native peoples react to optical illusions?

How quickly would they respond to pain?

There was a passion for measurement. Scientists recorded and graphed the height, head size, and nose size of the people exhibited at the fair. The press had a different agenda. The following indicate the kind of stories that turned up on a daily basis in the news.

There was the ongoing story of the Zulus. A St. Louis promoter had come up with the idea of recreating the decisive battle of the Boer War twice daily on the Pike. General Piet Cronje, the Boer commander, many of his regulars, and many of the British troops who defeated him at the Modder River in South Africa in 1900 were brought to St. Louis. To provide authentic background—the showmen were as committed to authenticity as the scientists—a hundred Zulus were induced to come as well. The Boers and the British were local favorites, wined and dined throughout the city, but the Zulus were never paid the four dollars a week each they had been promised. They began to rebel.

The press carried accounts of the Boers and British stopping their mock battles with each other and uniting in earnest against the Zulus; of runaway "Kaffirs" tracked down by Boers, police, and immigration officials; and finally of twenty Zulus who escaped into the black community never to be found. (After the World's Fair closed General Cronje, the British, and the remaining Zulus continued to perform at Coney Island.)

There were newspaper accounts of a hairy Ainu man and his tattooed bride taking their honeymoon in the Anthropology Department, and of Geishas, members of the Japanese Exhibit, requesting permission to ply their trade in the United States. Little Willie, the black eight-year-old orphan, moved in among the Igorots, and the Kwakiutl Indians asked for a fence to be built around their campsite to protect their totem poles and handmade baskets from the "taking qualities" of World's Fair tourists.

On otherwise slow news days reporters tended to congregate around Geronimo. They hoped, at first, to get a glimpse of the notorious blanket he was said to own, knit from the scalps of one hundred whites. When the blanket did not appear, re-

porters settled for Geronimo saluting the American flag he had
once opposed, roping a steer, riding the Ferris wheel, or, tears
in his eyes, being reunited with a daughter he had not seen in
decades.

A favorite story concerned the Igorots from the Philippines. They had arrived in St. Louis dressed in loincloths but
President Roosevelt took a personal interest in their appearance and insisted they wear pants. The United States had just
won a protracted war against Philippine insurgents: questions
had been raised about American conduct in that war; Mark
Twain called certain American commanders no better than
"Christian butchers." Roosevelt hoped that dressing up the
Igorots would encourage visitors to think that Filipinos were
respectable and that the war had been worth the effort.

Arrayed against the president were the Igorots themselves,
the anthropologists, who regarded the idea of pants as an insult to authenticity, and the Board of Lady Managers which
ruled there was nothing wrong with loincloths. The press carried cartoons of an immensely overweight governor of the Philippines, William Howard Taft, pants in hand, chasing agile
Igorots, and published anti-trousers poetry:

> The Igorrotes must wear clothes!
> Impossible! Ten thousand No's!
> Four billion nits! Twelve billion
>   Can'ts!
> Great Ceasar, anything but pants!

In late June, just as President Roosevelt was resigning himself
to the Igorots remaining in their loincloths, Ota Benga, the
Batwa, and Kondola (whom the press called a "blue-gummed
educated African") arrived in St. Louis. The *St. Louis Post-
Dispatch* responded with a fact sheet about the pygmies who
were said to excite "the greatest interest of any race specimens
shown." Some of the facts were taken nearly verbatim from
Stanley, while others seem to have been freely improvised:

> They are very agile, leaping about like grasshoppers.
> Their women are described as "nut-brown little
>   maids," pretty and pleasing, with very lustrous
>   eyes.

If caught young they are said to make excellent servants.
They seem to be controlled by an impulse that makes
them find a delight in wickedness.
They are pigeontoed.

One among the pygmies appeared to reporters to stand
somewhat apart from the others. A feature article described
Ota Benga as "a dwarfy, black specimen of sad-eyed humanity." He was sad because the other pygmies were Batwa but he
was not. He was sad, furthermore, because he had been a slave
in the hands of the Baschilele from whom he had been redeemed only to be brought to St. Louis. It made him sad to be
a prisoner of his limitations, unable to assimilate into Anglo-
Saxon civilization. Most of all, he was sad because he would
rather be home putting his sharp teeth to the dubious purposes
for which they were filed.

The press cautioned visitors to consider those sharp teeth
carefully before giving in to pity, and to note well that every
time he opened his mouth to show them he expected to receive a nickel in return. Yes, this "Artiba," as he was called,
was "pitiable," but the reader was cautioned to remember he
was also "to be feared and shuddered at."

Scientific American focused on "Otta Bang" as well, describing him as perhaps twenty-seven years of age and the
father of two (the magazine made no mention of what had
happened to his children). On account of his stature (four foot
ten inches), and his beardless face, he looked "more like a boy
of sixteen or eighteen years." His sharp teeth recommended
him to the visitor on the "lookout for sensation."

It wasn't his teeth, though, that brought Mrs. Caroline
Jayne to Ota Benga. She was doing research for her book String
Figures at the fair, when, between the American Indians and
the Patagonian Giants, she came upon the African Exhibit. The
Batwa were present, but it was Ota Benga whom she singled
out. He existed, as was obvious, it seems, to all comers, at an
odd angle to the other Africans. He was available to outsiders,
and they, in turn were drawn to him.

Mrs. Jayne, who always carried string with her, showed
him a variation on Cat's Cradle. Ota beckoned for her to give
him the string. He moved his fingers quickly then held his
hands out so she could study a complicated pattern she named

"Pygmy Diamonds." Mrs. Jayne had been under the impression that string figures were not practiced in Africa, and certainly not by pygmies, so remote from other cultures.

She gestured for him to do it again, slowly, and he did. She did not know why Pygmy Diamonds so closely resembled a Carolina form she knew, but in her book thanked Ota Benga, that "bright little man," for demonstrating the pattern to her.

Not all encounters were so amiable. "ENRAGED PYGMIES ATTACK VISITOR," read a headline in the July 8 *St. Louis Post-Dispatch.* "H.S. GIBBONS . . . PHOTOGRAPHED THEM . . . HE WAS PURSUED AND BEATEN."

They fell upon him. . . . Several white men rushed to the assistance of Gibbons. He was pulled out of the way into a corner and the Africans were cuffed and kicked out of the building [the trading post]. Yelling with rage, they made a rush and tried to get back into the building, but were stopped by a wall of white men . . .

No warning signs have been placed so that visitors do not know the risk they run in attempting to take pictures. The fight was the third which has occurred within a few days. In each instance the photographer has taken refuge in the trading post.

The pygmies weren't the only guests of Anthropology who hated being surprised by photographers. Their opposition to the camera was less adamant than that of the Moros, Filipino Moslems who wore "rather repellent expressions" even when they agreed to snapshots. The pygmies, on the other hand, only wanted to get paid. The more the pay, the better the pose. McGee signed an order stipulating that anyone who wanted to photograph pygmies had to get a permit from his office. Kondola said the pygmies agreed to stick by this rule—no permit, no photo—except in those cases where photographers were willing to pay unusually well.

The pygmies were all for being bribed. One headline— "COULD NOT DECEIVE PYGMIES: AFRICANS KNEW THE DIFFERENCE BETWEEN STEEL DISCS AND REAL MONEY . . . 'No money; no good' "—illustrates the reason for many of the brawls: Fairgoers repeatedly tried to cheat the pygmies.

One official World's Fair photo shows Ota playing a large

hollowed-out tube while the Batwa dance. The tube is clearly a *molimo,* but the anthropologists, nominally interested in authenticity, did not appreciate the sacred instrument. They described it as "fashioned like a bludgeon and covered with skin." When played it resulted only in the production "of sounds not musical."

In another official photo, the pygmies, Kondola, and the two other Africans are lined up before their makeshift huts. (With no pygmy women to build them in the traditional way, the huts were thrown together out of bamboo, thatch, and whatever other materials were available.) There is a surly, mugshot quality to the Africans' faces, as if they were imitating the Moros' patented grimace toward the camera. (Residents of the Anthropology Department did visit each other; in particular everybody was taken on a tour of the enormous Philippine Exhibit.) The sourness may reflect the fact this was an official photo and nobody got paid. Most likely this is how the Africans felt that day about the great World's Fair and the entire land of the *muzungu.*

They had reason to feel that way, as Verner discovered when he finally left New Orleans and caught up with the fair. At the end of July Verner, usually in a straw hat, begins to show up in official photos, sometimes with all the Africans, sometimes alone with Ota.

He was quickly faced with two problems, the first being the pygmies themselves as they grew increasingly restive under conditions of *muzungu* hospitality, or the lack of it. When Fwela came to Africa, they said, he was met with songs and presents, food and palm wine. Drums. He was carried in a hammock. The Batwa reminded him that at Ndombe's he was given "everything that could be desired." How were the Batwa treated in St. Louis? With laughter. Stares. People came to take their pictures and run away. *Muzungus* came to fight with them.

The masses that came to see the pygmies were a second, more threatening concern. Ota and the Batwa saw most of the parrots they had brought with them and all their pet monkeys succumb to "lighted cigars and other vicious gifts forced on them by too-attentive visitors." The Kwakiutl, complaining of the Americans' "Taking Qualities," had it easy by comparison. They lost no more than totem poles to predatory hands. In the case of the pygmies, it seemed the crowds would not desist until they had snatched a live one for a souvenir.

On Sundays, after having put in a six day week as exhibits, the forest dwellers retreated with Verner to the wooded areas around the fair. Trees! It revitalized them just to be in the presence of branches, leaves, and shade, to see New World birds, plants, and mammals.

They rarely escaped for an entire day. Crowds got wind of their whereabouts. People filled the spaces between the trees, bringing with them the lit cigars, the noise, the jabbing fingers, the memories of dead pets. Verner had contracted to bring the pygmies safely back to Africa. It was often a struggle just to keep them from being torn to pieces at the fair.

Repeatedly the Anthropology Department attempted to mount educational events. Professor Verner scribbled a few notes on the black board—HOMER HERODOTUS STANLEY—made some opening remarks, then introduced the crowd to the Africans standing behind him.

Inevitably, people left their chairs and inched forward to feel the pygmies. All the attempts by Professor Verner and the Anthropology Department to educate the public ended in the same way. The crowds became agitated and ugly; the pushing and grabbing took on a frenzied quality. Each time, Ota and the Batwa were "extricated only with difficulty." Frequently, police were summoned.

On July 28, the pygmies tried to turn the tables in a dance performance on Plaza St. Louis. They had sensed the white man's hunger to see savages, wildmen, murderous flesh-eating terrors—to be titillated by demons, frightened by the apparition of their worst fears come to life. This time, for an afternoon, they were going to enjoy the role of aggressors. When they finished dancing, they yodeled war cries, brandished bows and arrows, put on their meanest faces, and made directly at the crowd, "as if to cut their way through the seventy five thousand people closely packed about the limits of the plaza."

The initiative was all theirs. "Seeing Unclad Africans Advancing Toward Her, Brandishing Their Spears, Woman Screams and Crowd Follows Her in Terror." What should they do next? How could they send out a signal that now the fun was over and they were turning back into themselves?

While they hesitated, the crowd regrouped, coalescing into the pygmies' own nightmare. The pygmies did not like to dwell too long on the thought that the land of the muzungu and the land of the dead were in reality one and the same place. But now it seemed the worst-case scenario of the muzungu had come to pass. The crowd heaved forward, scattering police lines effortlessly, like the living dead no longer to be denied.

The pygmies huddled together until the First Illinois Regiment arrived to separate the two sides.

After the confrontation on Plaza St. Louis, the Africans fell back to a more subtle line of self-assertion. They did what they were past masters at doing: imitation, mimicry with a twist, parody.

Marching bands were all the rage at the fair, from John Phillip Sousa on down. The Philippine Village had its own marching bands, the best known of which was led by Walter H. Loving. When Loving, a black man and a second lieutenant, was prevented from leading a regimental marching band for the U.S. army because of his color, he lent his talents to the residents of the Philippine Exhibit. The American Indians, too, had a marching band.

With all this marching going on around them, the pygmies decided to form an ensemble of their own. They hadn't been supplied with instruments, so they let the Indians, practicing within earshot, provide the musical accompaniment.

"PYGMIES ORGANIZE A MILITARY COMPANY . . . After watching the marching and evening drills at the Indian school, the Pygmies have appeared as a military organization, Capt. Latuna [Ndombe's nephew] commanding," the *Post-Dispatch* reported. The pygmies' aims were different from those of marching bands that made a fetish of order. In keeping with the best traditions of the forest, the pygmies emphasized an autonomy and spontaneity that verged on chaos.

At a whistle from Latuna, the pygmies came to a halt, "standing like statues," until he whistled again, at which point they resumed marching "to suit their own fancy, marching and countermarching in all directions."

"All through the drill," the paper reported, "the company keeps perfect time to the music of the Indian band . . . in spite of the fact that they are marching in any and every direction . . . Not once during the entire drill did they interfere with the Indians except to keep them convulsed with laughter."

The Indians were glad to be positioned next door to the

pygmies, whom they came to look upon as a tribe dedicated to the cultivation of comedy. When Geronimo came chanting toward Ota Benga that summer day in Forest Park and offered him the arrowhead, it was payment in kind.

With his marvelous feather headdress on, Geronimo faced the pygmy and chanted solemn sounds at him for some time after he dropped the arrowhead into his hands, raising dust with his buckskin boots and turning in a circle. When Geronimo completed the impromptu ceremony Ota looked into his eyes and had the impression for a moment that he was flying. Below him was a dry red landscape of rocks, gorges, and animals he had never seen before.

In August, Verner and Ota traveled to the Academy of Science in Davenport, Iowa, to do a show about pygmies. Verner was thinking ahead and plotting his next career move. It occurred to him he might have occasion to do some barnstorming with Ota. He was planning a letter to Hermon Bumpus, Director of the American Museum of Natural History. Verner hoped the museum would commission him to bring back African artifacts, but was waiting for the World's Fair awards to be announced before making his approach. It would preferable to introduce himself as a winner of the Grand Prize for pygmies at the St. Louis Fair.

They returned from Davenport to what one paper called "TRYING ORDEAL FOR SAVAGES"—a "Special Study of World's Fair Tribes" by the anthropometricists and psychometricists who had gathered at the fair. Their exposure to the intimate embraces of the crowds the whole summer long had prepared the guests of Anthropology for the touch of the dynamometer, the pulse controller, the cephalometer, aesthesiometer, pantograph, sphygmograph, and tape-measure. The anthropometricists resembled the crowds in their love of prying, poking, pricking, and jabbing. But they did not employ lit cigars in any of their experiments, and they recorded their results.

The scientists concluded that on intelligence tests "African Pygmies, behaved a good deal in the same way as the mentally deficient person, making many stupid errors and taking an enormous amount of time."

"Anthropology Days," an Olympic competition for savage races, came closely on the heels of the anthropometricists. After poor performances in such events as the shot put and javelin throw by the Igorots, Indians, Patagonian Giants, Hairy Ainu, Negritos, Eskimos, Kaffirs, Moro tribesmen, and pygmies, scientists reasoned that "lack of necessary brain" interfered with the workings of brawn.

One barbarian set a record "almost any winner of a schoolboy event would eclipse at will." Another put in a "such a ridiculously poor performance that it astonished all who witnessed it." A third performance led an anthropologist to mutter, "this is ludicrous."

The disgraceful records set by the ignoble savages almost caused their sponsors to lose their scientific detachment: "It can probably be said, without fear of contradiction, that never before in the history of sport in the world were such poor performances recorded."

The Ainu restored ruffled tempers by setting records in matters of decorum. They drew compliments and applause for being "without doubt the most polite savages . . . ever met." The Ainu "willingly, and with pleasant bows to the officials and everyone else, took part in every sport they were asked to."

The pygmies got their usual negative score for behavior, being "full of mischief" and taking absolutely "nothing whatever seriously." It was hard to get them to agree to Anthropology Days at all. They showed enthusiasm for one sport only, the mud fight, where their performance was called "clever," and their "dexterity in ducking, throwing and running" went some way toward redeeming their reputation.

They participated in some of the track events, but showed more interest in jumping all over the man with the starting gun than in getting to the finish line of the 440-yard run. The pygmies backpedaled and did woozy figure eights on the hundred yard dash.

Everybody, pygmies included, loved the baseball. This pure product of America exerted a "weird fascination," according to the scientists, a universal appeal. Small, stone hard, smooth, it seemed made, it *was* in fact made, for throwing. The aborigines lined up for their chance.

When Ota finished squeezing it and was getting ready to throw, he noticed Geronimo looking at him from the stands. After hurling the ball a mere 111 feet, he saw Geronimo smile. Kondola's toss was measured at 200 feet.

Anthropology Days were understood to buttress, "complement and on the whole fully conform with" the anthropometrical data "of function and structure" arrived at in the lab. The fair was built with the assumption that Caucasians were superior. Now the builders had compiled the numbers to prove it.

Anthropologists exercised a "half-cruel constraint," to keep the Africans out of garments that "would have interfered with the functions normal to their naked skins and brought serious if not fatal results." So, when chill winds blew through the fairgrounds in the autumn, the pygmies retreated to their huts. This irritated some fairgoers. Not only was it risky to photograph pygmies, it had become difficult just to see them. One fairgoer heaved a brick into their hut in the hopes of rousing them. They charged out and once again had to be restrained.

For some fairgoers, there was a profound sense of loss associated with the closing of the Louisiana Purchase Exposition. "When that last glimmer went," one woman recalled, "something really went out of our lives."

Ota, like many of the people displayed, was of divided mind. There was the Pike, but then there were the crowds. There were the marvels, the tetrahedral kite, the cars, the airships, and the Ferris Wheel. There was also the boredom, the insults, and the malice. There were the sights, but also the extraordinary fact that they themselves were chief among the sights. Ota could accept what he had seen or reject it, but he could not so easily extinguish all traces of the feelings it had evoked.

In the land of the muzungu, they took men and women and arranged them next to each other like buildings. Were the muzungu cannibals? In a sense, yes. They swallowed all other tribes.

On the first night of December 1904, President Francis made his farewell address. He spoke at length of the value of the fair, ending with the idea that only after the passage of time could it become clear if "the thought and the labor and the sacrifices that have entered into it were not ill-advisedly bestowed." On December 2, the New York Times reported, "WORLD'S FAIR CLOSED, OVER 18,000,000 SAW IT."

Promptly at 4 o'clock all the great exhibit palaces were closed and visitors were excluded. In the Palace of Agriculture onslaughts by souvenir hunters were made on some of the exhibits . . . but prompt action put a stop to the threatened turmoil.

As the night drew on, throngs concentrated in the main avenues to view for the last time the magnificent electric illumination. As the midnight hour was tolled by the great clock the glowing electric bulbs slowly began dimming, the pulsations of the great engines that drove the cascades gradually died away. The light faded steadily, diminishing until but a faint glow was perceptible. Then followed darkness, and the Louisiana Purchase Exposition had passed into history.

For the guests of Anthropology, there was a procession outward, with scheduled stops in President Francis's office. When it was the pygmies' turn for the ceremony of adieu, they were allowed at last into clothing more "close-fitting" than loincloths. On December 4, the St. Louis Republic reported that the Africans sported their "unaccustomed clothes as to the manner born, and any one of them might have been taken for a cake-walking swell from the classic precincts of Lower 'Mawgan' street." The pygmy taste in decoration was only the last of the innumerable ways they had of delighting the reporters: "One of them had pasted squarely in the middle of his shining forehead a sticker advertising a favorite brand of chewing tobacco."

"John" Kondola was there, as was Chief McGee and S. P. Verner, the pygmies' "resident interpreter, guide and philosopher," when "the little band of ebon manikins" bid farewell to Francis.

President Francis asked, through Verner, "How have you enjoyed yourselves? And what did you think of the Fair?"

The pygmies answered him among themselves with raised voices, frowns, and much head shaking.

"Great," said Verner, translating loosely. "They say they loved it."

Francis then asked, "Would you then prefer to remain in this country?"

The answer this time was "unanimous and emphatic, though given with some alarm by the pygmies."

"No!" was the response.

The St. Louis Post-Dispatch noted how cheaply the fair made good its farewell to the Africans:

GIFTS TO ROYAL PAIR COST $2.50
President Francis Makes Happy the Hearts of World's Fair
Pygmies for $8.35

PRESIDENT FRANCIS' GIFTS TO THE PYGMIES

Cask of salt for King Ndombe	$2.00
"Pearl" necklace for Ndombe's queen	.50
Watch fobs for nine pygmies	4.50
Spending money, St. Louis to Africa	
15 cents each, nine pygmies	1.35
Total	$8.35

On December 5, while Verner and Ota Benga took a train
to Washington, D.C., the Batwa rode the train to New Orleans
with Kondola, who agreed to a wage of five dollars a week for
"taking care of the 8 Africans, sleeping with them, and watching over them, until they are ready to leave."

An odd affinity had arisen between Verner, frantically
scrambling for a purchase in his own culture, and Ota, whose
society had been cut out from under him. Ota had never become completely absorbed into the Batwa. Verner, by virtue of
conflicting desires, ambitions, and a touch of madness, stood
in uneasy relation to other whites. That the two men could
never know each other completely, that the mental workings
of the one would always remain somewhat opaque to the other,
only increased the sport.

By the time Verner was carried comatose from the *Glenarm Head* in New Orleans, he and Ota had achieved the first
chancy stages of a friendship. The bond between them deepened in St. Louis. At the very least, they traveled well together.

Verner went to Washington for a visit with the Belgian
ambassador to collect his reward for staying mum about what
he had seen in the Free State. Ota mostly stared out the window while Baron Moncheur awarded Verner a concession in
land in the area around Ndombe's. Ota was glued to the window by the sight of the sky disintegrating. White rain. When
he got outside he fashioned perfect baseballs out of his first
snowfall, and plastered Fwela repeatedly.

After D.C., there was a brief stop in Tryon, North Carolina,
near the South Carolina border, for a family reunion. It appears
that rumors of pygmy cannibalism had traveled easily that far.
Verners and kin were so involved in preparations for their
barbecue they didn't notice at first that Ota and Ellen, a five-

year-old girl, had disappeared. When it dawned on them, they panicked. Verner got nowhere trying to convince them that if Ellen was with Ota, and they were in the woods, then Ellen was absolutely safe.

A posse was organized. The woods around town were searched until, totally unaware of the alarms that had been sounded and the conclusions that had been reached in their absence, Ota Benga and Ellen emerged from a clearing. He was carrying some small baskets he had woven for her out of local reeds; she was carrying pine cones she had collected for the fire.

They returned to New Orleans to wait with the Batwa for the steamer back to Africa. In the interim, World's Fair prizes had been announced, among them Grand Prizes to Verner for bringing the pygmies to St. Louis and to Professor Starr for bringing the Ainu. Kondola was awarded a Bronze, and Chief Geronimo a Silver Medal.

11

ANTHROPOLOGY NIGHT

> Now for the frantic leaps! Now
> for frenzy! . . . What wild—what ter-
> rible delight! The ecstasy rises to
> madness; one-two-three of the danc-
> ers fall—*bloucoutoum! boum!*—with
> foam on their lips and are dragged
> out by arms and legs from under the
> tumultuous feet of crowding new-
> comers. The musicians know no fa-
> tigue; still the dance rages on . . .
>
> —George Washington Cable,
> *The Dance in Place Congo*

When Verner and Ota arrived in New Orleans they found they couldn't be reunited with the rest of their party. The Batwa had caught chicken pox in their last days in St. Louis. Once in New Orleans, the disease broke out in the virulent form it assumes in those who contract it in adulthood. The Batwa were put into quarantine with Kondola assigned to care for them.

Ota, in a brief glimpse he was afforded of them, said it looked like they had been in the land of the *muzungu* so long they'd forgotten how to gather wild honey without getting stung by bees. The Batwa replied that the bees were inside their bodies, angry hives, and that their heads hurt.

From the other side of a closed door Ota told them about snow. By now they were ready to believe almost anything, even this. They looked at the sky. If snow came to New Orleans they wanted warning. They wanted to roll in it. Anything to ease the fearsome itch.

Their separation from the sequestered Batwa for nearly two months abandoned Ota and Verner to each other's companionship. Their days together turned into tours of the port city. Frequently, at night, Ota crouched at the other side of the closed door to report to the Batwa about what he and Fwela had seen together.

Often Ota and Verner took the streetcar together. It was still possible in 1904 for a white and a black man to sit next to each other on public conveyances in New Orleans. This was not because the white residents of the town were less zealous for segregation than others of their kind, but because the transportation company held up the implementation of Jim Crow on streetcars. There were, it claimed, insuperable practical difficulties in distinguishing white from black in a city that had recognized the shades in between to the point of honoring them with names—mulatto, quadroon, griffe, octoroon, white Creole, Creole of color.

The Louisiana Code of 1724 had allowed masters to free their nonwhite children and to endow them with property, a practice the French rulers of the city indulged in often. Thus was created that sophisticated, privileged, and propertied caste, Creoles of mixed blood, some of whom went on to become plantation owners and slave masters in their own right.

All of this comparatively nuanced attitude toward race was nullified by the Civil War. Louisiana Legislative Code 111 was passed in 1861. Its intent was that from then on you were either white or black in the eyes of the law; anyone in-between was black.

Sometimes on their outings, it seemed to Ota that he had never left the fair, that New Orleans was the fair spread out as a city. When they came to markets there was the familiar sight of American Indians, this time Choctaws, peddling berries and herbs. Just as at the fair, brass bands were everywhere making their blaring caterpillar progress down a sidestreet or curling around a corner.

The city was, in 1904, and had been for a long time, quite un-American in its open dedication to the pursuit of sensual pleasure, and especially, from Grand Opera to marching band, the art of music. It was a city that looked upon its houses of ill-repute as a resource sufficiently valuable to justify a guide, the *Blue Book*, which it published in the tens of thousands to help tourists and natives make an informed choice of brothel. In 1897, when alderman Sidney Story piously sought to restrict "any prostitute or woman notoriously abandoned to lewdness" to a given geographical location his motion carried, and that explosive, thirty-block area became known, after its legislative sponsor, as Storyville.

New Orleans was the port of entry for cocaine into the United States. The burly roustabouts who handled heavy Mississippi cargo liked to drop a nickel's worth into their beer for an extra boost. By 1900, cocaine was the drug of choice in the lower depths, both black and white, of Storyville.

In the early 1800s there were over eighty music stores in the city. In 1900, it was estimated that one thousand of the city's eighty thousand blacks looked to music for at least part of their livelihood. Perhaps that statistic, more than any other, is the clue to what was really happening in turn-of-the-century New Orleans—a black man who has been subjected to unremitting thought control toward the goal of making him forget that which is most crucial to him is on the verge of remembering: he is on the verge of an explosive reunion with his music.

That music had been considered so threatening by the slave masters that everywhere in the United States—except in New Orleans—it was forbidden for the black to play the drum. Now, in addition to the drum, he will play the cornet, the guitar, the piano. (There is a sense in which he will be playing the drum no matter what instrument he plays it on). The black man has taken his own instrument back and gained Western instruments; but the music he is about to play will be his own.

This was obvious on the streets. One of the things that came to Ota's attention first about New Orleans, as compared to St. Louis marching bands, was that some of the players didn't bother with sheet music.

Ota had noticed that, in general, whites read so they would know what to do. This was the secret to being white, this was how you became white, how blacks, when they read, were white too. The *muzungu* were hard to imitate because you couldn't really pretend to be one unless you could at least pretend to read. The whites read so they would know what to say. They called this making speeches. They read books so they would know how make things. They even read so they would know how to make music.

When they marched they attached pieces of paper to the ends of their instruments so they wouldn't forget how to play. But in New Orleans there were musicians who remembered how. They looked and sounded like it, and they had no pieces of paper.

Ota pointed this difference out to Verner, who responded at first that they had memorized their music. But when he really listened to what was coming out of their instruments he had some doubts that any of it could ever rest in peace upon the printed page. No, something was happening to the music that had a lot to do with a combination of remembering and inventing and very little to do with reading. It was a rebirth, a movement away from the triumphs of print and literacy toward something older, an event occurring among the descendants of slaves.

Ota considered it worthy of his nightly reports to the quarantined Batwa to mention that some people in the land of the *muzungu* seemed to have remembered how to play.

It was getting harder and harder to keep the Batwa bottled up. They couldn't go out to New Orleans, but some of New Orleans was coming to them. By night the long-distance note of King Buddy Bolden's trumpet could be heard. This was Bolden's well-known "calling my chillun home" note, and when the Batwa heard it they wanted to go home too.

As a boy, Bolden used to visit Congo Square, one of those places in New Orleans where it was lawful to play the drum. The hope was that by legalizing and localizing drumming the seditious influence of voodoo, coming in across the Caribbean from Haiti, would be more easily contained. The opposite occurred. The immense power of the Sunday dances in Congo Square exerted an influence over white spectators as well.

In Congo Square, where bullfights once took place, and which, earlier still, the Indians considered to be sacred ground, slaves and free blacks, descendants of Woloff and Yoruba, Ibo and Baluba, hurled themselves into an ecstasy that was old Africa in New Orleans. George Washington Cable, a chronicler of Creole life, put those Sundays into words:

> The strain was wild. Its contact with French taste gave it often great tenderness and sentiment. It grew in fervor, and rose and sank, and rose again, with the play of emotion in the singers and dancers . . .
> Hear that bare foot slap the ground! One sudden

stroke only, as it were the foot of a stag. The musicians warm up at the sound. A smiting of breasts with open hands begins very softly and becomes vigorous. The women's voices rise to a tremulous intensity . . .

Will they dance to that measure? Wait! A sudden frenzy seizes the musicians. The measure quickens, the swaying, attitudinizing crowd starts into extra activity, the female voices grow sharp and staccato, and suddenly the dance is the furious *Bamboula*.

Ten years after those performances were banned forever in 1885, some kid started playing trumpet with a sound that reminded anyone who'd been there of old Congo Square. That kid was Charles Bolden. On the one side his music was pure voodoo, with blues and gospel thrown in. On the other side, the music was of European descent, transmitted by the Creole.

The catastrophe for the Creole of color was tantamount to a blessing for the music. Classically trained musicians were thrown into the streets to struggle for their daily bread. At the same time many Western instruments, hocked during the Civil and then the Spanish American War, came into the hands of blacks unrestrained by sheet music or the old repertoire. The music that resulted was a fusion of Africa and the West, a synthesis of drum, cornet, trombone, guitar.

The Batwa heard it by day, in the jazz bands that swung around the hotel. They heard it at night in the gruff stomp of rhythm that came out of the clubs in nearby Storyville. They couldn't hear the words. They didn't know that if there were no police around, Buddy Bolden might edge into the Bolden blues:

> I thought I heer'd Abe Lincoln shout,
>> "Rebels, close down them
>> plantations and let all them niggers out,"
> I'm positively sure I heer'd Mr.
>> Lincoln shout.

> I thought I heer'd Mr. Lincoln say,
>> "Rebels, close down them
>> plantations and let all them niggers out,"
> "You gonna lose the war;
> git on your knees and pray,"
> That's the words I heer'd Mr. Lincoln say.

The Batwa had heard trumpets in St. Louis, but nothing that growled or chirped like this, nothing so funny or so sad, nothing that put them in mind of their own *molimo*, nothing so *molimoish*.

In the days after Christmas, bands and parades came by with greater frequency. Finally the Batwa could stand it no longer. One night they eluded Kondola and clambered down the stairs to join up with Ota and Verner waiting on the sidewalk for a parade to turn the corner.

When the parade swung into view it consisted of whooping black men dressed up as Indians and other black men dressed up to look like Zulus. The Batwa quailed for a moment. If this was what they had been missing for weeks, why didn't Ota tell them? If this was New Orleans, maybe they were better off upstairs.

One from among the New Orleans Zulu, a homegrown and seasonal tribe, no relation to the Zulus that had escaped the fair, stepped up to the wavering Batwa. Snare drums and trombones halted. He was wearing a leopardskin vest, a buffalo headdress with horns, and he was carrying a bone. Looking at the Batwa, who held their ground under the inspection, he seemed impressed. He uttered a few exploratory words. The Batwa answered all at once in Tshiluba.

King Bolden picked that very moment to point his trumpet at the moon in Johnson Park and call his chillun home with a blast that could be heard all the way to Lake Pontchartrain. Ota smiled, and the sight of those filed incisors convinced the Zulu witchman he had stumbled on to the real thing.

King Bolden blew again. It seemed this time he was going to hold that Jericho note until dawn broke, he broke, or until every last one among his children put down their things and danced. Bolden blew his summons to a party and since this was New Orleans and the days had lengthened into early February, the party was nothing less than Mardi Gras.

The wildman of the Zulus ushered Ota and the Batwa to the vanguard of the parade, looking Verner up and down with a shriveling, snorting look of disregard that emptied the Special Agent of the words he was about to speak as if he had been punched in the gut. Verner and Kondola were left behind.

Verner was crestfallen. He'd held onto the pygmies through ten thousand miles of travel, only to lose them on a moonlit night in New Orleans because some utterly ersatz overbearing Mardi Gras Zulu stared him down. Verner couldn't understand it. He had faced the wild Baschilele, braved and cowed the Force Publique. What was it about this gargantuan Louisiana Zulu that took all the fight out of Fwela?

As he pondered, the parade, which had disappeared down the street to his left, was approaching again. The pygmies had steered it around to come back for Fwela. Ota grabbed him by a sleeve and drew him into the procession. The Mardi Gras Zulu chief figured if this white man was good enough for the little guy with the teeth, well, he could put up with him.

> If ever I cease to love, if ever I cease
> to love,
> May oysters have legs—And cows
> lay eggs,
> If ever I cease to love.

> If ever I cease to love, If ever I cease
> to love,
> May the Grand Duke Alexis—Ride a
> buffalo through Texas,
> If ever I cease to love.

This song, lifted from a musical comedy, had been played in honor of Grand Duke Alexis Romanov, heir to the Russian throne, who, after a hunting trip with General Custer and Buffalo Bill, visited New Orleans in 1872. From then on it became the hymn to Rex, king of Mardi Gras, and Verner heard it that night from all quarters, as white men dressed in black face and black men dressed as Indians and Zulus converged on old Congo Square, terminus of the grand parade.

There were floats and plaster of paris statues in the night. There was something called a Missing Link, with an Abe Lincoln face and a monkey body. There was a sculpted alligator head with rows of teeth. There was a twenty-foot-high devil with a devilish smile.

At midnight, a rowdy Rex climbed to a podium, waved his scepter, and declared festivities at an end in the same words, or so it seemed to Verner, that President Francis had used to close the fair. Rex thanked all comers, reviewed the proceedings, recommended Carnival to the serious consideration of future generations, but when he was done talking not a single light was turned off, there was not a horn that did not resume its blaring, no one went sadly home. It was as if New Orleans was the same material of which St. Louis was made but inside out.

For Verner a barrier had lifted. He no longer had to stand above or to the side, as he had in St. Louis, to point out, explain, protect, inform, and misinform. He could take Ota by an arm and whirl him around without any loss in status. He was in New Orleans but was just as much in Africa, and he was also back home in South Carolina doing the country reels he loved as a child.

> If ever I cease to love,
> If ever I cease to love . . .

Earlier, he had stuffed a *Blue Book* in his pocket, a well-thumbed copy he had studied during his sojourn at the Sanatorium. Next stop was *Lulu White's—Lulu White's Mahogany Hall*. Verner had been saving that storied establishment for just such a contingency. "It would not be amiss," according to the *Blue Book*, "to say that besides possessing an elegant form [Lulu] has beautiful black hair and blue eyes, which have justly gained for her the title of the 'Queen of the Demi-monde' . . . As an entertainer Miss Lulu stands foremost, having made a life-long study of music and literature. She is well read and one that can interest anybody and make a visit to her place a continued round of pleasure."

Lulu advertised herself as maintaining the one and only house where you were assured of getting all of "three shots for your money," as in:

> The shot upstairs,
> The shot downstairs,
> And the shot in the room.

Verner thought it was the perfect night to ride Lulu's famous elevator built for two.

When Verner woke from revels a few days later there were some things he was glad to remember and some he wished he could forget. For the pygmies, the all-night dance of Mardi Gras was the closest thing to Africa they had known since

coming to America. It was America welcoming them at last at
their moment of farewell.

Kondola waved goodbye from a New Orleans wharf. He
was staying in America to continue his education. World's
Fair accounts pick the travelers up in Havana, where it took
two weeks for one of the Batwa to recover from a case of
grippe. Another two weeks were lost waiting for the proper
vessel. Finally, on May 3, almost a year after leaving Africa,
the travelers were tracked as being "presumably in the Lower
Kasai, working their way homeward about midway of a river
journey comparable to that from New Orleans to Bismarck or
Fort Benton, save that the transportation facilities are far in-
ferior."

12

WITCH BOY

"What you send Friday away for? Take [hatchet], kill Friday, no send Friday away."

—*Robinson Crusoe*

erner's journey to Africa to return the pygmies is, on one level, an adventure story, quintessential boys' reading, featuring any number of wild animals, a dance around the severed head of a crocodile, a wrestling match between man and beast, and hostile tribes subdued without a single shot by the wit and courage of the incomparable Fwela.

This is the mode in which Verner himself chose to cast his third trip to Africa, when, later in life, he serialized it for the Brevard, North Carolina, press. In these stories he appears exclusively in the third person. He is Fwela; a Tarzan type with a sense of humor and a fine eye for anthropological, zoological, and botanical detail. His traveling companion is that wizard of woodcraft, Ota Benga, faithful pygmy friend. In one of these stories Ota is introduced as "an extremely interesting little fellow, black as a coal, about 4 ft, 8 in. tall, somewhere near twenty-one years of age, weighing about a hundred pounds, active as a cat, lithe as a monkey, and extremely strong for his size."

From another point of view the third trip is the story of Verner's continuing quest for success, wealth, and the restoration of the family name. Batwa pygmies boast of being able to sing the life story of a man so well that his fame will spread all the way to the next village. Verner had already achieved a kind of localized acclaim in the village of St. Louis. He would have liked the story of his deeds to be sung so loudly and so well it would be heard in that grand village down the road, New York City, where he knew the next move in his career was waiting to be made.

He would have liked to be able to step up to some teller on Wall Street and to trade in a Batwa praise song, a Grand Prize for pygmies, the book he authored, and perhaps a battle-axe or two for a single salaried position in the field of African development. He would gladly have cashed in all other identities to emerge as one of the continent's commercial saviors.

From this perspective, his third trip is the story of the would-be developer, the exploits of a small-time rubber dealer and collector of plants, animals, artifacts, and, but for a single miscalculation, diamonds. It is the further installment in the annals of a divided man, one inspired by the example of David Livingstone, who nevertheless put his faith in a colonial regime that had become synonymous with greed and cruelty. In the words of Joseph Conrad, the Congo Free State was the site of the "vilest scramble for loot that ever disfigured the history of human conscience and geographical exploration." This is the regime Verner was rewarded for defending, though he never would have allowed himself to think that there was such a simple equation between his allegiance and material gain.

There is a dimension of Verner's eighteen-month journey to Africa that he chose to keep entirely under wraps. This is the tale of a renegade, once an ordained minister but now persona non grata at the mission station, a white man on a sexual adventure to the dark continent with one mistress for certain and others whose existence it may be safe to assume. The full story of Western sexual opportunism in Africa remains untold. When it is, S. P. Verner's liaison with the daughter of an African chief will surely deserve a mention.

Finally, there is an aspect of Verner's journey about which

he knew nothing, then or ever after, although it was taking shape from the moment of arrival in the Kasai. This is a story of hunter and hunted, and in it Verner, despite his rifle and his record of marksmanship, is entirely the hunted. He is being stalked by one so far superior to him in the art that when the trap is sprung he is unaware of being caught.

The man hunting him is Ota Benga, who from the beginning of this trip to Africa had his eye on its conclusion. Verner can be forgiven for being so easily taken, so easily wrapped up in the net of another's will; in this business of hunting and being hunted, he is, compared to Ota, completely outclassed.

Ota is no longer visiting the village of the muzungu across the sea, allowing himself to get hit by mud pies so as to provoke hilarity in disdainful St. Louis crowds. The return to the Congo is a return to reality, a return to the hunt. If his friend Verner is the principal quarry for the next year and a half, that is because to Ota's mind, rightly or wrongly, the white man holds the key to the rest of his life.

When Verner got back to Africa in the spring of 1905, it seemed that he remained in Mardi Gras mode. Much that he did had a magic touch. The first and most amazing thing he did was simply fulfill his contract with Chief McGee to put the Batwa right back where he found them. That became the stuff of song, dance, and recitations. News of it spread throughout the countryside. Fwela had taken the Batwa across the water to the very land of the muzungu. He had taken them to the land of the muzungu, which had swallowed so many others up, and he had brought every last one of them back home.

Naturally, everyone wanted to know what it was like across the water. Better for Verner himself to say nothing. More power to him when Ota Benga took up the refrain. "In the land of the muzungu there are houses so big that you could walk around in them without ever knowing if it was raining outside," said Ota. "In the land of the muzungu, white people put elephants, lions and leopards in cages and make them play tricks."

"You go so fast on land-steamers—trains—that if you stick your head out you lose your breath."

"In the land of the muzungu you get only one wife each."

"Men and women dance not in separate lines, but together."

Ota Benga plays the molimo—the sacred pygmy trumpet—at the St. Louis Fair, 1904. Anthropologists entitled this photo *A Savage's Idea of Music* and hoped the molimo would someday evolve into a flute. (*American Museum of Natural History, New York*)

David Livingstone (1813–1873). Samuel Phillips Verner was born the year Livingstone died and regarded himself as under the lifelong influence of the Scottish missionary, explorer, and opponent of the slave trade. (*The Bettmann Archive*)

Henry Morton Stanley (1841–1904), known in Africa as Bula Mutadi, The Smasher of Rocks. His writings established that pygmies were indisputably human and not some fantasy concocted by Greek poets. His forays into central Africa paved the way for Leopold II and the Congo Free State. (*UPI/Bettmann News photos*)

Ota Benga displays filed teeth at the St. Louis Fair, probably for the agreed upon fee of a nickel or dime, payable in advance. Fairgoers—and anthropologists—liked to think filed teeth were a sign of cannibalism. In fact, such cosmetic dentistry is still practiced in many parts of Africa and has no relation to man-eating. (*American Museum of Natural History, New York*)

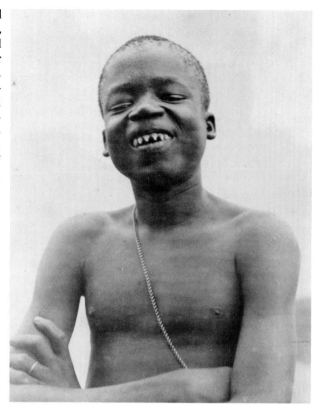

Samuel Phillips Verner (1873–1943), missionary, explorer, and would-be industrial developer of central Africa. Verner used this photograph on brochures for the lecture tours he gave, frequently with Ota at his side, during the St. Louis Fair. (*P. V. Bradford*)

Dr. William Henry Sheppard after his election to the Royal Geographic Society. Cofounder of the American Presbyterian Congo Mission, Sheppard was a leader of the American missionaries in their struggle against King Leopold. (*Collection of Arthur R. Ware, through the Hampton University Museum, Hampton, V.A.*)

This photograph, A Cannibal Graveyard, appeared in S. P. Verner's Pioneering in Central Africa. The anthropological value of this photo may be dubious, but Verner's grandson, P. V. Bradford, liked to scare his friends with it as a boy. (*The South Caroliniana Library, University of South Carolina, Columbia, S.C.*)

Slaves in transit, as photographed by S. P. Verner. The elephant tusks slaves were forced to carry from the interior were far more valuable than the slaves themselves. (*P. V. Bradford*)

Kassongo, a prince of the Batatela people, shown here at the Stillman Institute, Tuscaloosa, Alabama, where Verner enrolled him and his friend Kondola in 1899 after bringing them from Africa. On September 19, 1902, Kassongo attended a speech given by Booker T. Washington in Birmingham. Two men in the packed room began to jostle each other for seats, a woman yelled "Fight!" the crowd thought she said "Fire!" and Kassongo was crushed to death in a stampede for the exits. (*The South Caroliniana Library, University of South Carolina, Columbia, S.C.*)

Kondola, a.k.a. John Condola, (at right) Kassongo's childhood friend. Kondola helped Verner bring the pygmies to the St. Louis Fair, translated for them there but remained in the United States when Verner brought Ota and the other pygmies back to Africa after the fair's closing. Kondola continued his education at Stillman and Tuskegee and became a lecturer and itinerant preacher. He and Verner last saw each other in 1939. (*American Museum of Natural History, New York*)

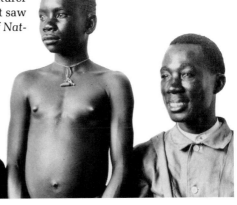

"A wonderful tribe of pygmies, some red and some black. Midgets as they are, they slay elephants with their tiny arrows and lances, and are as game and full of fight as a hornet. You'll enjoy reading about them and seeing their pictures." Quoted from the *St. Louis Post-Dispatch*, June 24, 1904. Ota is second from the left. (*The South Caroliniana Library, University of South Carolina, Columbia, S.C.*)

The pygmies perform before large crowds on Plaza St. Louis. Ota Benga, his back turned toward the camera, is on the right. (*American Museum of Natural History, New York*)

The Louisiana Purchase Exposition, or St. Louis Fair, of 1904 marked the centennial of the Louisiana Purchase. It was the largest, and most electrified world's fair to date, and the only one with its own Anthropology Department. (*Missouri Historical Society, St. Louis*)

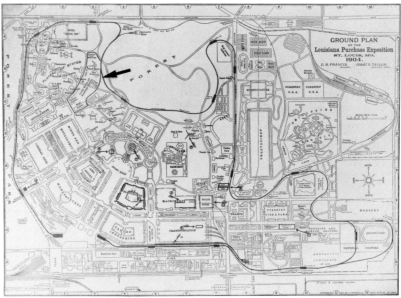

A ground plan of the 1,272 acre St. Louis Fair. The anthropology exhibits were at E–11, near the west (right) edge of the map. The large arrow at B–3 points to the area where the pygmies were housed. (*Missouri Historical Society, St. Louis*)

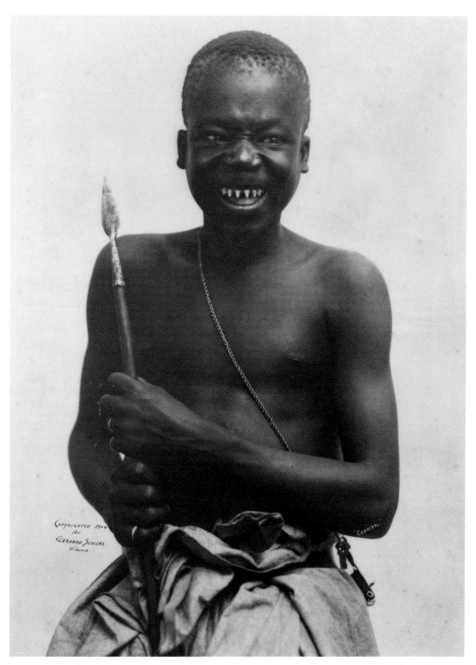

Ota, posing for the camera, was one reason the crowds thronged to the African Exhibit. (*Missouri Historical Society, St. Louis*)

Geronimo, a prisoner of war, sold bows and arrows, and autographed photographs of himself in St. Louis. Members of some fifty Native American tribes were displayed at the fair. (*Missouri Historical Society, St. Louis*)

Dr. William W. McGee, chairman of the Anthropology Department, St. Louis Fair. As an anthropological fieldworker, he described the Seri Indians as "zoocratic in government." He had greater success as an administrator. McGee's goal at St. Louis was to display "representatives of all the world's races, ranging from the smallest pygmies to the most gigantic peoples, from the darkest blacks to the dominant whites . . ." (*Missouri Historical Society, St. Louis*)

Madison Grant, trustee of the New York Zoological Society, endorsed and defended Director Hornaday's idea for displaying a man in the monkey cage. In later years Grant fought against further immigration to the United States from southern and eastern Europe, and authored or edited racist polemics such as *The Passing Of The Great Race* and *The Alien in Our Midst*. (*American Museum of Natural History, New York*)

Henry Fairfield Osborn, President of the Museum of Natural History, espoused many of Madison Grant's ideas and wrote introductions to his books. "The enclosed clippings are excellent," he wrote to Hornaday on September 28, 1906. "Benga is certainly making his way successfully as a sensation." (*American Museum of Natural History, New York*)

View of the American Museum of Natural History across the old Columbus Avenue elevated railway in 1908. The museum was the biggest building in New York City and there were plans, never realized, to make it the biggest on earth.

William Temple Hornaday, first director of the Bronx Zoo, and possessor of a scheme, as he wrote to Osborn, "for at once getting hold of the Public..." (*The Bettmann Archive*)

Starting on September 9, 1906, Hornaday's scheme came to fruition. See the Appendix for a partial text of these and other newspaper articles. (P. V. Bradford)

As visitors were not permitted to bring cameras on to Bronx Zoo grounds, no photos of Ota Benga in the Monkey House exist. Five official zoo photographs of Ota Benga and Polly, the chimpanzee Verner brought from the Congo, are part of the Bronx Zoo archives. (*The New York Zoological Society*)

Leopold II, King of Belgium and, as of the Berlin Conference of 1885, ruler of the million square mile Congo Free State. Leopold rooted out the slave trade but replaced it by a notorious system of forced labor. His rule over the Congo was opposed on both sides of the Atlantic by a movement that included Mark Twain and Arthur Conan Doyle. (*The Bettmann Archive*)

Daniel Guggenheim. Guggenheim and Ryan, invited into the Congo by Leopold to exploit its diamond, rubber, and mineral resources, formed the American Congo Company which employed Verner for a year. (*The Bettmann Archive*)

The young Bernard Baruch, Verner's confidant and protector among the millionaires. (The Bettmann Archive)

Anne Spencer, poet of note and friend of Ota Benga's, with her son Chauncey in their Lynchburg home. (*Chauncey E. Spencer and the Anne Spencer Home and Museum*)

A life mask of Ota Benga made in August 1906, when he was living at the Museum of Natural History. (*American Museum of Natural History, New York*)

"There are fire-wagons, cars, that go so fast you can't tell how fast they were going," he continued.

"The boat that crossed the great water to the land of the *muzungu* had more people than an entire village."

"In the land of the *muzungu* they fly about in bubbles, in balloons, in the sky like birds."

"They eat meat three times a day."

"More people came to look at us than live in the whole forest."

"There are truly more people in the land of *muzungu* than palm trees here!"

It was hard for the Batwa to convey an idea of the peculiar role they had played at the Fair. There was no correlate in Africa to the public display of people. Anthropology had not yet been invented there.

They turned to Fwela for help. With his assistance they put on a demonstration of just how it was done. They built the sort of wooden pen they might have used to enclose animals. They put Verner's makeshift rocking chair inside and piled some books on a little table. They added an Edison phonograph and a few recordings. As a finishing touch they added Fwela.

He contentedly rocked, smoked, read, wrote, and listened to recordings as he might have on a peaceful day on a porch back home. He was a *muzungu* exhibited in its natural state, its authentic habitat. The Batwa who had not gone to America gawked, stared, and could not help but laugh. What was Fwela doing in there?

He was being Batwa came the answer. You who are watching him are being *muzungu*. Now do you understand what happened there?

If Verner had gone to the Congo merely to deposit the Batwa he could have done so and been long gone. Nor would he have had much need for the litany of his accomplishments, the praise song of Fwela, that preceded him everywhere. But he had no intention of saying goodbye to the pygmies and turning on his heels. He had some buildings raised at Mt. Washington—his name for the land he had been granted near Ndombe's village—and even planned to build a hospital. Mt. Washington was to be his base of operation, the place to come home to after forays into the countryside.

He had been licensed by the Belgians to trade in ivory and rubber and hoped, by this means, to make Mt. Washington a going concern. The Davenport Academy of Sciences had asked him to bring back artifacts, the Missouri Botanical Gardens asked for plants, and he intended to collect enough African objects on his own to encourage the Museum of Natural History in New York to open its doors to him.

He had no lack of reasons to pick up and travel. But before setting out he made a cylinder recording of King Ndombe's voice. To check the results, he played the cylinder back on his Edison phonograph. Outside the cry went up, "The white man has stolen King Ndombe's soul! The King sits still, his lips are sealed, while Fwela forces his soul to sing!"

The technique of voice recording conferred a terrible power on Verner, and he quickly seized on its potential to scare "the wits out of would-be hostile groups." He did nothing to discourage rumors that "flew around the valley until they crystallized into a legend that Fwela could catch a man's soul and put it into a box and make it sing or talk while the man himself was standing by with his mouth shut tight, listening to his soul perform."

Ota caught on immediately to the import of voice recordings. Now when he sang the full litany of Fwela's deeds, this new talent of Fwela's had to be appended. Ota understood that Edison voice recordings worked by means other than magic. When Verner's porters showed signs of hesitation, when they refused to enter the domain of a hostile chief such as Chisakanka, it was Ota's job, and one he undertook with relish, to rally their support.

"Who's afraid of Chisakanka?" he would say, "Didn't I go with Fwela all the way to white man's land? Didn't it take us three moons to get there? Didn't we see more people than there are palm-trees in all this land?"

No one would own up to still being afraid of Chisakanka after Ota had put things in perspective. What were Chisakanka's powers when compared to those of a great white magician? Shamed by a pygmy, the porters would pick up their loads and prepare to enter the realm of Chisakanka or any other baleful chief.

It was a great advantage for Verner to have Ota along. It meant he never had to boast. He could hope for no better advance man. In the Congo, a pygmy may be mocked for his stature and his forest ways, but he is also secretly feared and admired; there is the suspicion that a pygmy is always in the know.

The Batwa stayed behind. They wanted nothing more than to be back among their kin, and to sing songs of the glamour of the land of the *muzungu* (while shying away from mention of the several indignities they had suffered there). Ota's disposition was not so simple; he had no kin. He had no home, only a choice of possible homes. He could have adopted the Batwa or Verner. For a while he kept his options open; he adopted both.

He married among the Batwa. Not much is known about his second wife, except that his marriage to her did not keep him bound to the circular huts in the clearing near the village of Ndombe. He traveled with Fwela all over the Congo Free State and up to the border with Angola, where the last holdouts against Leopold's rule gathered in rebellion.

He had assigned himself to Fwela. His marriage was genuine enough but perhaps it was the case that living in the old way could never again truly suffice. He was a hunter still, but one who required a broader range. Verner gave him that possibility. The roving *muzungu* and his retainers became the stuff out of which Ota's new hunting band was made. The quarry was no longer the forest elephant, but artifacts, specimens, rubber, and ivory purchased from the local population and then resold. The trips took longer—weeks, and sometimes months.

But after each trip there was the beginning of a new family to return to: his wife; the familiar ways of the Batwa; the hunt, carried out with bow and arrows dipped in a poison brewed from the heated sap of the Lulenga vine; the dances and the rhythms, common throughout the forest population of Central Africa; the all-night singing by the fire; the assurance of holding a certain place in a hunting band—no longer a youth, far from an elder—and the comfort of having peers.

Ota's attempt to strike a balance between these parts of his life—the ageless and the new, the poison-tipped arrow and the throb of the engine as he had felt it that first time through the floorboard of the steamer—was not fated to succeed. It is not known exactly when during this period the event took place, but Ota's second wife died, a victim of snake bite, and the die was cast.

Before then, Verner was the witch man. Ota, who seemed intimately connected to him, who had apprenticed himself to the white man, was known, but still often with admiration, frequently with affection, as the witch boy.

Now there were those who drew out the slow hiss of fear and hostility that enfold the word "witch" in any language. "Witch" was the sound unspoken, the sharp inhalation, as Ota passed certain houses in the town of Ndombe.

Witch—Some said Ota was responsible for the death of his wife.

Witch—He had been contaminated by the friendship of the white, Fwela, the man who stole souls out of bodies, the witch who left zombies.

Witch—Ota no longer belonged to any clan or family. He had chosen to stand outside in that void where no one chooses to stand, where no one can breath except witches like himself, and that was why his wife had to die.

For Verner every new allegation of sorcery was a feather in his cap, a new secret weapon, although a strain on his relationship with the Presbyterians over at Luebo. The final rift occurred over a dark-skinned daughter of a chief at the Mission School. Verner and the folks at Luebo had different ideas about her education.

The missionaries were trying, among other things, to instill in her the importance of learning how not to dance. Dancing was the wrong way to reach God. Or it was the way to reach the wrong god. The Presbyters were well-intentioned. They were going to teach her how to read instead.

What they succeeded in doing was concentrating all her dance into her eyes. Verner liked to dally with the notion that it was worth a trip to Africa just to see them. The first time he looked into them, quite by accident as she was walking by, he nearly lost his balance.

A tug of war broke out over her further education, and she became a frequent guest at Mt. Washington. Verner (until caught and banned) became a frequent late-night visitor to the Mission School.

The charges of witchcraft were an entirely different matter for Ota Benga. He had started life in the heart of Africa. Events were conspiring to drive him outward, to smash every new handhold he managed to achieve on the continent: outward toward a void in which it seemed only the *muzungu* had learned to flourish.

From the moment his wife passed away Ota began to study Verner with a new attentiveness.

Verner's reputation for attainments in sorcery above and beyond the norm posed problems even for friendly chiefs. There were questions of protocol, fine points of etiquette. How should they receive him? What did he eat, assuming that he ate at all? One chieftain threw a banquet for Verner's men but nervously refrained from offering Verner himself a single bite. He wanted at all costs to avoid the possibility of making a mistake, offending Fwela and winding up, like the once great Ndombe, with his soul in one place and his body in another.

Yet, for all that, Verner's armory remained incomplete. There was one more sorcerer's item to be had, and this one slithered across his path. It was the snake, Ntoka, central Africa's deadly horned viper.

"Ntoka, Ntoka! Kill him! Kill him!"

This was the universal sentiment of the caravan when the viper crawled out of the sleeve of a jacket Verner had left on the ground. He grabbed his gun and was about to carry out the execution when he had second thoughts. He plotted a use for Ntoka in Africa and a career for it in the United States.

So far as he knew, no American zoo could boast a specimen. He imagined Ntoka, with inch-long horns protruding from just above its eyes, as a source of fascination to adults and children alike. In the meantime, like a great serpent on a ship's prow, Ntoka would serve as the insignia of his caravan.

Catching the snake wasn't as hard as might be supposed, although Verner's companions were shocked that he would want to do anything other than shoot it. He held its head immobile with a two-pronged piece of wood, stuffing its body into a large canvas bag that had once carried tobacco. The snake lashed and struck out but finally exhausted itself and settled down. Verner ran a long, sturdy pole through a loop he tied at the top of the bag.

Ntoka was ready to go, if only porters could be convinced to haul him. Wembo, the brawny warrior who had carried a wounded Verner down the mountainside nine years before, was in the caravan. Wembo took some time making up his mind to hoist one end of the pole. Ota took the opposite end and the deadly snake dangled between them in the tobacco sack as they resumed the march.

Now Verner's standing was impregnable. Opposition melted away at his approach, and if surly Baschilele, for example, were slow to clear a path, Ota would offer to arrange a palaver between them and Ntoka, or a kiss. Ntoka was the last word in witch's weaponry. Verner, with his evil reputation, his soul-stealing Edison, and his snake, was well-equipped for business in the Kasai, a large part of which was collecting artifacts for Professor Frederick Starr.

Professor Starr had lately arrived at Mt. Washington, intrigued with Verner's pygmies and intending to collect Congolese art objects. Unfortunately, he fell ill with malaria nearly immediately upon arriving. Too portly to be easily portable, he remained behind at Mt. Washington.

While Starr secured the home front, Verner scoured the backwoods for him, bringing back nine thousand objects. Many of these pieces displeased the professor—they were insufficiently authentic, so Verner had to go out again. Since the best proof of a tribe's authenticity was its having shut itself off from whites, he had to go mostly to where he least was wanted. He had to find those places where the dim opinion of the white man had not yet capitulated to fear and force. It was on these journeys that Verner filled his journals with the adventures that later became *Travels with Ntoka,* and *The Taming of the Baschilele.* He also had an encounter with the diamonds of the Tschikapa River, the site, a few years hence, of one of the world's more lucrative diamond mines.

Verner was on his way to Chisakanka's territory. The grass bordering the river he had to cross was high, posing the threat of ambush, so Verner had it burned. Ota was about to start the crossing when he turned back, drawing Verner's attention to the water's surface.

It was alive with hundreds of thousands of army ants who had begun their own crossing to escape the fire. It was necessary to move downstream where Ota scouted a place that was narrow enough to afford a crossing, but was, he reported, guarded by a thirty foot python basking on a rock.

Such a snake could easily crush a man to death. With it hiding in the grass, no one in the caravan would be safe. Ota suggested setting a ring of fire that would either burn the python or drive it into the river and away. The plan was adopted, and after the grass burned down the snake was nowhere to be seen. The men, after looking left, right, and down into the depths for crocodiles, began to ford the stream when, as Verner put it, the porters found "beautiful pebbles and brought them to the white man."

He held a number in his hands, and could not rule out the possibility that some of the sparkling stones might be diamonds. The others, he supposed, were quartz. How was he to tell? He fell back on college chemistry. Diamonds were made of carbon, he recalled; quartz of silicon. Silicon was the heavier element. Therefore the heavier stones were quartz, the lighter might or might not be diamonds, or so he calculated, leaving the heavy stones for the Guggenheims, among others, to salvage from the Tschikapa River.

The selection of quartz over diamonds was obviously not one of Verner's more inspired hunches. Years later, explaining his mistake, he told his readers, "Fwela had received a University education with high honors, but his studies had been chiefly in literature . . ."

Ota's relationship to Verner ripened on these journeys into the bush. The two men had always been intrigued by each other, but now Verner became fascinated with watching Ota assimilate Western techniques to his own purposes.

Years before when Verner had "prosecuted" his psychological study of the Batwa, he had been vaguely aware that the interest was reciprocated. Now, when he focused on Ota Benga, he was blind to the fact that the interest was once again returned, that Ota could, for instance, when Verner wasn't looking, turn in flawless imitations of the white man lighting his pipe, folding and unfolding his maps, cursing at mosquitoes, and scribbling in his journal. Verner didn't have as intimate an idea of his friend. Part of what intrigued him after all their months and miles together was precisely the fact that some part of Ota continued to elude him.

Some nights during their African travels, Verner knew exactly what Ota was up to. He could tell by the aroma that wafted up from the hammock where Ota rocked himself. Verner knew that two herbs were of special importance to the forest dwellers who scattered their seeds at selected locations in the woods. The Lulenga vine was used for making poison. Bangi was the herb of choice for relaxation.

There were many evenings filled with the telltale odor of

Ota Benga engaged in relaxation. Other times Verner had to be more actively engaged to discover what his friend was doing.

At times he spied, thinking this gave him privileged access to Ota in his natural frame of mind. Such was the case in the affair he later called *The Canning of the Crocodile.*

The story turned on the affection Ota had for the animals—Ntoka excepted—that the caravan acquired on the march. He was the primary caretaker of several chimpanzees, for example, and had acquired a pet dog. "A Christian dog," he later sang, "since its father lived in the Mission. A speedy, copper-colored dog."

Ota's dog had wandered down to the Kasai one day to take a drink, where it had the misfortune to disturb a crocodile. Noisily and obliviously, the dog continued to slake its thirst, and the crocodile attacked.

Ota asked Verner for a keg of gun powder, and Verner assigned a spy to give a full accounting of what the witch boy did. The man reported that Ota dug a deep hole under the nest where the crocodile hid its eggs and buried the keg of gunpowder. Then he poured a trail of powder all the way from the nest to a hiding place some distance away among the rocks where he settled down, puffing on a pipe, to await the crocodile's return.

Sometime later an explosion was heard in camp, and not long after that Ota Benga appeared, bowed down under the weight of a large portion of crocodile. He had a "victorious gleam in his deep-set" eyes, wrote Verner, but he wouldn't say what happened. Verner got the full story—the powder set alight, the crocodile blown up, and Ota himself bashed by a rock or two when he crawled up close to see it happen—later, from his spy.

That night Ota sang the praise song of his little dog, and credited Verner with a share in his revenge: "Ota Benga had a friend," he sang, "the white man with the corn tassel hair. The white man had the bang medicine. Ota Benga gave the bang medicine to the crocodile. Ho! Ho! Ho! That crocodile will eat dog no more!" Then, the choral part of his solo over, Ota threw himself into dance.

Verner was invited to participate. He knew how to dance, but not like this. He called on on bang medicine do his dancing for him, putting on a display of fireworks that awed those in attendance who had never before seen the sky blow up.

Then he set fire to the river. He poured alcohol on the water
and tossed in a lit match. The surface of the water rose in
flames.

It was a bluff show, but it was a one night stand, and in his
heart Verner knew he had missed the point. The point of a solo
in African dance is to bring individuality and variation to the
step, build the energy, show the impossible is simple, and
tighten the noose between drummer and dancer. Verner had
overshot the mark; the point is not to frighten the dancers
away.

Even if he had sufficient fireworks and alcohol to stand in
for him on a steady basis, it would still be lonely work. Fwela
the magician couldn't help him here. Verner turned to the
solace of words. While the others continued to dance, he filled
his journal: "Then the dancing went on full tilt. There is no
use trying to describe it—how often have I wished that
O. Henry, or Mark Twain, or Dumas could have stood in my
shoes sometimes to leave behind a really immortal record of
what used to pass under my eyes."

He summoned up the power of the dance, and then, more
poignantly, its effect on him:

. . . the whirling figures of the tribesmen across the sward,
the loud roll of tom-toms, mingled at times with stento-
rian shouts, and alternating with the shrill piping of fife
and whistle—and then, yourself, Caucasian, Anglo-Saxon,
product of the West, of school, church, college, of cities,
capitals, railways, steamships, books and all the rest—set
down in the midst, looking upon it with lonely eyes.

"Why do you dance so much, Ota?" Verner asked one
morning, when the sheer beauty of the African scenery went
some way toward compensating for the fact that at times he
felt he didn't understand the first thing about the place.

"Because they like it," said Ota.

"Who likes it?"

"They do," and Ota made a casual gesture toward the
trees.

So pygmies thought of themselves as dancing on behalf of
the trees, as representing them, as doing for trees what trees
couldn't do for themselves. Pygmies were short, dancing trees;

trees were tall, stationary, leafy pygmies. "Trees," wrote Verner in his journal, under the topic "dance."

Verner devoted many words to that topic. The ever-present dance puzzled and disturbed him, as it did most whites who encountered it; it challenged the presumption of superiority they brought to Africa. In self-defense, Verner patronized it: "The dance has been made the subject of universal comment by some horror-struck missionaries, though I could not see anything worse in it than in the gay and easy whirl of the round dances on American ballrooms." He intellectualized it—"Possibly the wonderful capacity for physical endurance exhibited by some of these people . . . is to be traceable in large part to . . . their dances," and he anthropologized it: "I have sometimes also thought that the physical frenzy into which some of the American colored people used to fall on religious revival occasions may have had its roots in the hereditary influence of those African dances . . . "

He even consulted Frederick Starr about it, in the hopes of having the subject illuminated by professional opinion. Starr informed him that "the phallic idea which underlies so many primitive religions" was at the root of the African preoccupation with the dance. Verner thought Starr's idea was hogwash.

Sometime in the early months of 1906 Verner and his caravan returned from one of their forays to discover that Ndombe had pulled up stakes. The king and his subjects had relocated, taking the town with them. A little research showed Ndombe had fled not from the usual threat—Leopold and the Force Publique—but from anthropology, or at least from anthropology as personified by Professor Starr.

Starr had asked Ndombe to show him the ceremony that makes a man a king. Ndombe had complied. The problem was that this was no mere replica; in the eyes of Ndombe's subjects and his rivals for the throne it was the thing itself. Starr was gratified by the superb authenticity of it all, but when word got round that Ndombe had transferred power to the white man, others were not so pleased. Rivals felt that if Ndombe was of a mind to surrender the throne it should go to them rather than to Joka Mpende, the White Elephant. War was in the offing.

Ndombe quickly sought advice from certain elders, the region's experts in matters of royalty. He was told that kingship was rooted in a place, a physical location. If he moved and his subjects renewed their pledges of loyalty, then he could be king all over again.

This was the situation as Verner found it. Ndombe was about to be reinaugurated some miles down the road. Meanwhile Professor Starr hadn't the faintest idea why everyone ran away from him. As Verner put it, Starr had been left all alone to rule over a kingdom consisting of "bananas . . . the guineas, and the parrots."

At the end of March, Starr gathered up his thousands of artifacts, thanked Verner kindly for his help, and started on his way back toward the University of Chicago. Verner too began to think of leaving. There was no way to justify remaining any longer. The bulk of his collecting was done, he was chronically short of funds, and he was, though it is easy to forget it, a man with responsibilities, married and a father. His wife had cooperated with him so far by nudging McGee, now director of the St. Louis Public Museum, into sending five hundred dollars as prepayment for artifacts, but that had been in November. By the spring Hattie wanted to know when, if ever, she might expect her husband home.

It was time to begin the round of goodbyes. Goodbye to King Ndombe, and to Joka. Amorous, guilt-ridden, night-long goodbyes to a certain bright-eyed daughter of a chief. A warm, thoroughly sentimental goodbye to Ota Benga, or at least an attempt at one. As it happened, Ota had other plans.

He wanted to learn to read, he said, and not at the Mission School, as Verner suggested, but in the land of the muzungu. He wanted to come with Verner to America.

As always on the hunt, there comes a moment to dash from cover and sink the lance into the elephant's side—too soon and the animal might still be on the alert, too late and it might have shifted position. Verner had reached the point analogous to a great bull elephant munching contentedly on leaves. He was sipping coffee, scribbling in his journal.

Walking softly up to him, and making sure he had his eye, Ota, in a matter of fact sort of way, said, "And if you do not take me, Fwela, then I will throw myself into the river and I will drown."

Verner acceded. He would take Ota along and the next time he came to visit Ndombe—there was bound to be a next time, his career depended on it—he would bring him back.

He told Ota to pack, never a very complicated procedure

for a pygmy. In a few moments Ota came back with a bow, some arrows, and a chimpanzee. It was a more elaborate ritual for Verner. It meant filling dozens of crates, trunks, bags, and boxes so as to bring back minerals, plants, animals (Ntoka among them), and artifacts. Packing took Verner days.

By June the travelers had set out. On the twenty-third, they stopped in Sierra Leone, where Verner, operating as always on a shoestring, sold a chimpanzee for £35. Soon they were once again aboard ship, heading north. The ship hugged the coast for a while, and Ota, watching from the deck, thought of his wife, his children, his second wife. He heard the word *witch* hissing by. He saw the forest, where he might have spent his entire life, as but a part of the enormous land mass fading from his view.

He looked forward to a language and to customs he didn't know. He had almost no English, yet he intended, as he told Verner, to learn to read. Reading was the secret that led to the place where all the other secrets were stored.

He was going to the village to learn its secrets, borrow its customs, take what was necessary, then go back home. His going—his forcing Verner to take him—was predicated entirely on his coming back.

He was not an immigrant, but might have found nothing to object to in being called a tourist. In that sense, with his bow and arrows, his loincloth, his chimpanzee, and his filed teeth, he presents a picture, as he steams toward England, of history's first self-appointed pygmy tourist of the West.

By mid-July he was in Liverpool, where Verner made reservations for transportation west. By the beginning of August, 1906, he was sailing into sight of New York City.

13

SEEING THE ELEPHANT

> Despite the fact that "freak hunt-
> ing" was now a full-time occupation,
> sending managers and their agents
> searching the world for people with
> anomalies strange enough to make
> them a premier attraction, there was
> a freak shortage.
>
> —Robert Bogdan, *Freak Show:*
> *Presenting Human Oddities for*
> *Amusement and Profit*

Connecting the lines of the places Ota had already been in the United States makes for an intriguing pattern. It can seem as if he had been traveling incognito, that he knew everyone, was privy to everything and chose the best way to cut to the American grain. It suggests a pygmy's preferred mode of travel—a series of unpredictable appearances and disappearances. Be visible one moment, gone the next. Materialize, dematerialize, don't overstay your welcome. Scorn the routine, keep the accent on mobility.

World's Fair, Washington, D.C., New Orleans—hadn't he, in a busy eight or nine months, seen more than enough of the land of the *muzungu?* He felt he hadn't, that his travels thus far were introductory. There was a secret or a truth beyond the spectacles to which he had been exposed, a source to the energy, inventiveness, and even to the vastness of the crowds.

If there was a center to it all, he was sailing up to it now. If such a place existed, it was New York City.

The Ivory City of the St. Louis Fair had been six brilliant months of novelty. New York, with its skyscrapers hurtling upward and its bridges outward toward the boroughs, was a more permanent installation. New York was after the twentieth century's Grand Prize for new.

The turn of the century was a time of breakthrough technologies, rapid transitions not only between ideas and things but between things and power. Edison, for example, was not only the renowned inventor but also the fierce corporate competitor. Alexander Graham Bell's telephone, through which a barely audible "to be or not to be" was transmitted at the Philadelphia Exposition, became, in short order, the seed of a huge conglomerate. Ideas became things became corporate entities—quickly.

The new sources of energy, the surge in technology, the infusion of population, the rapid pace of change in every area led to an acute case of giantism. Were New Yorkers in need of a new institution, a museum of natural history, perhaps? Yes? Then they must plan to house it in nothing less than largest building on earth.

Did they require a zoo? They did? Then they would conceive of it on a scale that dwarfed the comparable institutions of London, Paris, and Berlin. Or else, why bother to talk about it? Why bother to build at all?

Things were governed by the unstated assumption that giants were coming. Soon. Maybe in the next generation. Evolution was still going on, after all. Darwin had never declared a moratorium. When the giants arrived there had better be room for them. They would expect to be made comfortable. They would want access to the best that civilization had to offer. The blueprints had better see to it now.

Verner knew something of New York City. He had been there once before in not altogether different circumstances. In 1899 he sailed into New York harbor with a cargo of plants and minerals, a monkey, a wild cat, parrots, high hopes, a higher fever, and two Africans.

It was inevitable that he think of Kassongo now, the strong face, the princely bearing. And the horrible end in Birmingham, crushed, compacted into "human pavement."

He remembered that harrowing evening in February when he raced through a blizzard on unfamiliar streets, calling out names strange even by New York standards: "Kondola! Kassongo!" until he found the teenagers hugging each other and waiting.

It was seven years later now, and summer. Somewhere, probably in Alabama or thereabouts, Kondola was preaching and blacksmithing and, when he saved enough money, would go to school.

Verner thought of that first hectic voyage to Africa and back as a boy's errand, full of a boy's mistakes. Now he was a man. Oh, there were no doubt mistakes left to make, but they'd be a man's mistakes, higher-grade errors, the fruits of experience.

The Africans recognized the difference. Ndombe had taken him aside before he left. "Fwela," he said, "when you first came to us, we knew you as Fwela Mwana, leader as a boy, leader with smooth cheeks. Now you are called Fwela Kuluntu. You are a man. Now, Fwela, you are Leader All Grown Up."

One mistake Leader All Grown Up had no intention of repeating in New York City was that of leaving an African anywhere he wasn't sure to be wanted. The African he had in mind was standing but a few feet away. Verner had a view of Ota's profile as the pygmy held on to the deck railing and peered out for land.

He savored the warm night air and began to chat lazily to Ota about how any minute now they would swing into sight of the Statue of Liberty. He rattled on about what a noisy place New York really was, and did some low-key trumpeting and honking just to give Ota an idea of what was in store. Verner respected his friend's feelings about noise, and anticipated that for this reason alone the city might be a sore trial to him.

Ota was about to add some of his own braying and honking to the noises coming out of Verner. Not only did he like to help Fwela along when he took to carrying on, but he had long since learned that making nonsense sounds amused many whites, who took the gibberish to mean the little pygmy was trying to speak his own silly language.

Ota and Verner were already attracting more than the quota of attention that normally flowed toward them—a white man and a short African conversing in an unknown tongue—when Ota froze. There was a glow of light resting on the water, like that of a huge luminous snake that could float. In the midst of this hazy glow a shape rose up that he never thought to see again. It was a Ferris wheel, turning leisurely and sparkling silently in the night sky.

On deck, the passengers followed Ota's gaze. Not a word was spoken as the boat slid by the apparition of the giant wheel spinning out gold and silver light on the illuminated shore. The spell was broken only when the ship turned northward into the harbor, coming into view of that more placid and perhaps already dated symbol of freedom, the green-gray Statue of Liberty.

George Tilyou's Ferris wheel stood at the border of sea and sand, ocean and the New World. Tilyou was the Coney Island entrepreneur who got his start selling sand and salt water to tourists in 1876, the year of the Philadelphia Exposition.

At the Chicago Exposition in 1893, he admired the fair's Ferris wheel, its rotating rebuff to the Eiffel Tower. Built in 1889, the Eiffel Tower was elegant but immobile. The Ferris wheel was permanently in motion and democratic; people could ride on it, and it glowed in the dark.

Tilyou asked if he could have it next. It was already promised to the St. Louis Fair, but Tilyou was not deterred. He applied one of the first principles of showmanship, namely that the original item is usually unnecessary; it could be faked, and fakes were often just as good or better for purposes of display. Back at Coney Island, he posted a sign proclaiming the second coming of the Ferris wheel, bigger and naturally newer than the one at Chicago, which had seated over two thousand people at a time. When the new wheel debuted in 1896, it proved to be nowhere as big, but it didn't have to be; no one was measuring. Tilyou's wheel was big enough to make itself visible, on a clear night with its lights turned on, thirty-eight miles out to sea.

Electricity was still new enough to be exciting. It implied an aesthetic of illumination, an art form of pure light. "Thousands of ruddy sparks glimmer in the darkness," wrote Maxim Gorky of Coney Island (as Henry Adams had written of the St. Louis Fair), "limning . . . shapely towers of miraculous castles, palaces and temples. Golden gossamer threads tremble in the air. They intertwine in transparent, flaming patterns . . . mirrored in the waters. Fabulous beyond conceiving, ineffably beautiful, is this fiery scintillation."

This was Gorky's initial rapturous response to the two miles of Steeplechase, Dreamland and Luna Park—"By day a Paradise—at night Arcadia!"—along Brooklyn's south shore. Later, in language just as forceful, he took it all back. He saw lewdness beneath the gaiety, jaded tedium at the source of the mechanical energy, and, at the core of it all, something close to pure evil. He condemned Coney Island as a "slimy marsh of boredom," haunted by "weary faces . . . colorless eyes . . . debased tastes."

Whether Coney Island was heaven, hell, or both, it certainly had evolved far beyond those simple days when it was accessible primarily to Brooklyn residents and upper-crust, genteel vacationers. Walt Whitman, born in Brooklyn, used to retreat to "the long, bare, unfrequented shore," when he felt a need for privacy. Alone and undisturbed he would swim, then "race up and down the hard sand, and declaim Homer or Shakespeare to the surf and seagulls by the hour."

That was before mass transit, the media, and the amusement parks summoned the world—to the tune of thirty thousand people daily—and made the need for privacy the last possible reason to go to Coney Island. Millions were drawn to see the likes of Fatima, for example, the Hoochee-Koochee dancer who had been even more popular than the Ferris wheel in Chicago. After being banned from appearing at the St. Louis Fair she moved to Coney Island and performed daily on the Boardwalk under the name of Little Egypt.

The career of Tom Thumb's diminutive widow, Lavinia Warren, had a second flowering at Coney Island. Out of the three hundred dwarfs assembled in a wildly successful exhibit called Lilliputia, she was the featured attraction, not because she was only thirty-two inches tall but because of the places she had been, the people she had known. The man she liked to reminisce about most was the tall president who invited her and her husband to dine with him at the White House in 1863.

General Cronje never seemed to tire of his battles with the British at Coney Island, even though he was condemned to lose every one, and Carl Hagenbeck's Wild Animals were always on display. Blowhole Theater blew petticoats upward, and couples hugged and tumbled on the Human Roulette wheel or in the Barrel of Love. The Man in the Moon and his Moon Maidens greeted you after your rocket ship left Earth behind, and told you that the moon really was made of green

cheese. You could try the Scrambler, the Tickler, Helter Skel-
ter, or the Dragon's Gorge; Shoot the Chutes or 20,000 Leagues
Under the Sea.

Before the Ferris wheel, and just as tall, there had stood
the "Colossus of Architecture," Elephant Hotel. Not only
named for but shaped like an elephant, it had circular stairs in
hind legs 60 feet in diameter each, glittering glass eyes four
feet wide, telescopes on top and rooms scattered throughout
its body, thighs, and trunk. By the time it burned in the 1890s,
it had contributed a new expression to the language. "Seeing
the elephant" meant going to Coney Island, spending a night
in the Elephant's thigh or trunk, and doing what you would
never conceive of doing at home. Perhaps because when the
French tore down the Bastille, the ultimate symbol of repres-
sion, they put a large statue of an elephant in its place, the
elephant—especially Coney Island's 122-foot tin-skinned
pachyderm—came to symbolize release, fun, sexual abandon.

After Elephant Hotel, every American amusement park
and nearly every major New York institution had something of
the elephant about it, whether real, symbolic, stuffed and
mounted, or reduced to ivory. The beast played a significant,
often overlooked role in the first years of the twentieth century.

In addition to Elephant Hotel, Coney Island had its own
small herd of real elephants. They helped out with heavy lift-
ing and were entertainers as well, doing Shoot the Chutes
elephant-style, sliding down into a pool of water.

An elephant named Topsy was among these stalwarts of
the amusement parks. She is remembered less today for how
she lived than for her death, an unforgettable solo turn. It is
not easy to get the true story. Coney Island historians tell it as
if Topsy's final bow took place before tens of thousands of
spectators on a busy day at the height of the season; The *New
York Times* of January 5, 1903, reports it as having occurred
the preceding Sunday, a wintry day, with few people around
who were not involved in carrying out her execution.

Topsy was sentenced to die in large part because of the
misbehavior of her keeper, Whitey Alt, a cantankerous drunk.
A few months earlier, when he was arrested, Topsy loyally
followed him to the police station where, according to the
Times, she spent some time "trying to get her fat head in
through the door with doubtful success." More recently, un-

der orders from Whitey—"Stick 'em" were reputedly his words—she had charged a group of Italian workmen who saved themselves only by climbing the rafters at Luna Park.

Topsy's own character was not entirely without blemish. She had a temper, having killed a man in Brooklyn the previous year after he fed her a lit cigarette. With only the increasingly erratic Whitey to prevent it from happening again, Luna Park's owners decided the safest recourse was to put her down. Electrocution was the method chosen; as Elephant Hotel had burned, so would Topsy.

Whitey Alt refused to have anything to do with her death, though they offered him twenty-five dollars to lure her to the assigned spot. Finally, after a doctor fed her carrots stuffed with cyanide to no avail—"She ate them greedily, and waited for more"—Edison's men clamped the electrodes on her where she stood, and threw the switch. Topsy raised her trunk aloft as if to make one last remark, then commenced to smoke and sizzle while Edison's Vitascope cameraman preserved it on film. (The resulting short—*Electrocuting an Elephant*—was popular in the early days of cinema.) Ten seconds later, she "shook, bent to her knees, fell, and rolled over on her right side motionless." Her organs were donated to Princeton University. Her feet were made into umbrella stands.

The Ferris wheel occupied Ota Benga's thoughts when he disembarked. Maybe every important place in the land of the *muzungu* had one. Verner, too, had Coney Island in mind. He was daydreaming about what it would be like to compete with the amusement parks. His cargo gave him a head start if he wanted to try.

He had no elephants with him, but he did have a pygmy. Verner imagined Ota dancing and singing, once again chanting Fwela's praises. When that brought a crowd, he could dig out his old pal Ntoka, announcing that unfortunately, the snake had been taught only one trick.

He could also produce Kuba masks, Baschilele battle-axes, and other artifacts. He could put two Soko monkeys in Ota's willing arms and announce that the pygmies of Africa are a wily brood, very partial about how they apply the theory of evolution. When it comes to white men descending from the apes, they say they knew it all along.

He could finish the show with a further touch of Vaudeville, placing a parrot on Ota's shoulders and a recording of an African rowing song on the Edison phonograph. Then, arm in arm, he and Ota swing each other around. The parrot squawks, Ntoka hisses, the chimps hold tight, and the two men, battle-axes held high in their free hands, sing the Tshiluba chorus to the song.

This show had all the ingredients: humor, action, blarney, surprise—you didn't actually need an elephant to make them see the elephant.

He would have launched the show immediately if he were still back in Africa. Entertainments of that sort were the speciality of Fwela, great white magician. He could have put the show on the road in America, too, but he didn't want notoriety. He wanted attention, but something more respectable than the Coney Island kind. After a night at the reputable Hotel Belleclaire on Broadway and Seventy-seventh Street, he and Ota were going to drop in on the American Museum of Natural History.

Another member of New York's well-distributed herd of elephants was waiting there—old Jumbo, P. T. Barnum's world famous pachyderm.

14

THE MUSEUM

The houses are as big as icebergs
on a glacial bank . . . a steep chain of
mountains with innumerable can-
yons that serve as roads.

—Uisâkavsak the Eskimo,
describing New York City

By the time Ota got to know him, Jumbo had been reduced to a skeleton, his bones alone weighing 2,400
hundred pounds. In better days he had been an international star.

Barnum had bought Jumbo from the London Zoo in 1882,
but to actually take possession of the elephant he had to flout
the will of the English people. They didn't want to surrender
Jumbo and rallied, wrote letters, and brought the matter up in
Parliament. Lawsuits were filed to contest the sale. An editorial bemoaned the fact that Jumbo, used to "quiet garden
strolls" and "friendly trots with British girls and boys," would
now be thrown in with a "Yankee mob" and consigned to a
vulgar diet of peanuts and waffles. In private, the queen expressed her disapproval.

Barnum loved it. Jumbo was front-page news on both sides
of the Atlantic and hadn't even left his stall. Getting him out of

his stall, on to the ship, and across the Atlantic made for headlines and comic opera all along the way. When he finally arrived in New York City, sixteen horses and more than four hundred men were needed just to budge the crate in which he stood. Circus elephants helped haul him uptown. The procession labored slowly up Broadway from lower Manhattan to Madison Square Garden, where Barnum's circus was performing and Jumbo immediately took his place as star of The Greatest Show on Earth. Giant Jumbo was Barnum's greatest hit since tiny Tom Thumb.

In 1885, after only three years under the big top, he suffered a head on collision with a freight train. The train was derailed, but Jumbo was instantly killed.

The country's leading museums clamored for the right to provide a final resting place for the elephant's remains. Barnum made them wait. According to him, Jumbo's performing days were far from over. He had the 1,500 pounds of Jumbo's hide mounted over his skeleton, making sure he grew a little taller in the process. He continued to exhibit the new, improved Jumbo under the big top. And he gave him a posthumous mate, Alice, a London elephant Jumbo used to dislike who now was billed as his grieving widow. Finally, after a season of display, the American Museum of Natural History in New York, to the annoyance of curators at the rival Smithsonian, became the recipient of Jumbo's bones.

When Verner arrived at the museum with his cargo in August 1906, he belonged to a type familiar to Director Hermon C. Bumpus. The museum had become the dropping off point for geologists, paleontologists, and anthropologists since it opened to the public in 1877, and Bumpus had listened to the tales of many men coming back from the wild with crates, specimens, and occasionally even natives.

Sometimes these men were harrowed by their work. The dinosaur hunter Edward Cope, for example, was haunted night after night by animals he dug up during the day. Great beasts stalked him in his dreams, kicking him, crushing him, tossing him around. It was to the museum that Robert E. Peary returned from his trips to northern Greenland. Peary often brought meteors back with him. In 1897, after three attempts, Peary brought Ahnighito, or The Tent, which, at thirty tons, was the largest meteor ever removed from its point of impact.

Along with Ahnighito, Peary brought six Eskimos to the museum. Four of them died quickly. Capable of surviving arctic winters, their bodies had no defense against New York City's tuberculosis and common cold. With ghoulish haste, the museum moved to possess, clean, and mount their bones. When the last of the four, a young girl, died, the New York press asked some embarrassing questions. Had the Eskimo child willed her bones to science? Had she agreed to become a museum showcase? Had curators troubled to get her permission as she suffered through the last stages of her illness?

One of the Eskimos Peary brought with him, Uisâkavsak, survived New York and returned to Greenland, where he faced the daunting task of telling his people what he had seen. A Danish explorer heard Uisâkavsak trying to put New York harbor into words: "The ships sailed in and out there, like eiders on the brooding cliffs when their young begin to swim. There weren't many free drops of water in the harbor itself; it was filled with ships. You'd risk your life if you tried to go out there in a kayak, you'd simply not be noticed . . ."

To convey an impression of the number of people in New York City, Uisâkavsak said, "There are so many of them that when smoke rises from the chimneys and the women are about to make breakfast, clouds fill the sky and the sun is eclipsed." Streetcars were "big as houses, with masses of glass windows, as transparent as freshwater ice," he said. "They raced on without dogs to haul them, without smoke, full of smiling people who had no fear of their fate. And all this because a man pulled on a cord."

Uisâkavsak had to be careful. Unlike Ota and the Batwa, who vouched for each other's stories, he was alone. There was no one to say he was not a fraud. His people gave him the benefit of the doubt until he tried to describe the "distance shrinker," or telephone. A tribal leader rose in disgust and cried, "Uisâkavsak, go tell your big lies to the women!" Uisâkavsak, who had survived New York City and managed to keep his bones out of the hands of curators, was henceforth known in northern Greenland as "The Big Liar."

It wasn't a question of whether Verner had come to the right place but whether he would be accepted. Dr. Bumpus preferred advance notice. He relied on proper references and liked to leave a paper trail. Verner wasn't completely unequipped with the sort of credentials Bumpus favored. He still possessed a letter of introduction from Secretary of State John

Hay to King Leopold II. He was a winner of a Grand Prize in anthropology from the St. Louis Fair, and could be very persuasive when he needed to be.

He needed to be. It wasn't only the usual ambition that drove him, but poverty. He was beginning to rely on writing bad checks to cover expenses; one, to the Guardian Trust Co., was to hound his steps over the next few months. He knew if he was going to make it in New York he had to stake a claim now, before debts consumed him. First of all, he needed a safe place to store Ota and the collectibles, preferably one without storage fees or rent.

For all Bumpus knew, Verner's collectibles might actually be worth something to a museum, and Verner himself might be the sort of busy man just passing through town who ought to be cultivated. Verner tried to foster this impression—he barely had time to fit lunch into his schedule, he said; he was off to Washington, D.C. that very day, and then to his family in Brevard, North Carolina. Bumpus agreed to care for Ota in the interim—there was a room, often used for guests, where he could sleep.

The following day, en route South, Verner wrote Bumpus that he had "meant to get the pygmy some more & better garments, but . . . was obliged to let that remain one of the privileges of some one of your museum staff." He encouraged Bumpus to take Ota Benga home with him: "If you seriously wish to have him near you . . . for some days observation, of course feel free to do so."

This letter, like many in the next few months, contained a postscript in transliterated Tshiluba that was designed to be read aloud to Ota. Verner told Ota he was well, and that Ota should remain with Chief Bumpus, whose heart was white.

The next letter, written from Brevard, N.C., broaches the delicate question of funds and employment. Verner offered to sell the museum the right of first refusal on his collection, including his chimpanzees, though he made it clear his interest in New York City was longterm, and a salaried position more vital to him than a single sale. He was prepared to put together ethnographic maps, grammars, and dictionaries for Bumpus, requesting $175 to underwrite his first month in the city until the details of his relationship to the museum could be finalized. He provided forms for Bumpus to sign in order to expedite the agreement.

Verner's language is flowery, but something of the real financial pressures can be seen. Verner writes of his "valuable concession" at Ndombe's, which, unfortunately, had temporarily tied up his cash. He alludes to securities, held elsewhere in the country, which he planned to convert in due course. He assures Bumpus there was no "loss at all from my African Expedition—quite the contrary."

In fact, there is every indication his "valuable concession" had drained Verner's few reserves, and the chances of his owning securities of any value anywhere were slim. When he speaks, however, of possessing "some gigantic beetles . . . so rare as to be almost unique," he is absolutely to be believed.

Bumpus was not slow to detect the discrepancies Verner tried to conceal. The request for a stipend of $175 a month sped up the director's search for second opinions. Who was this man who showed up without an appointment, deposited his things, then presumed to ask for money? What had he actually done for the cause of ethnology?

Bumpus wrote to Dr. Clark Wissler, the museum's curator of anthropology, explaining why he had agreed to take charge of "his pigmy and Chimpanzees" in the first place. "He may be a crank with whom we wish to have nothing to do," wrote Bumpus, "but I hated to take chances." He also consulted Dr. Walter Hough of the Smithsonian Institution—"Is he a person that would make an acceptable assistant here?"

The response was mixed. Dr. Hough wrote that the material Verner contributed in 1899 had indeed played a significant role in building up the Smithsonian's African collection. His endorsement of Verner's professional abilities—"He could do more than anyone I know to build up your African collection"—was balanced by the information that the explorer had once gone "insane and was confined for a time," although he seemed to have "toned down" since.

By August 10, Bumpus had come to a decision. At a salary of $175 a month Verner had priced himself out of the museum market. "This is so much more than certain officers are receiving," wrote Bumpus, "that I fear it would lead to some internal dissention." He advised Verner to sell his collection to whomever he pleased, referring him, with respect to the animals, to the Bronx Zoological Gardens, although one of the chimps seemed to the director to be in the last stages of tuberculosis.

This lack of enthusiasm for either employing or buying

from him struck Verner hard. A note of resentment, an edge of bitterness creeps into his letters, despite the cordial, nearly obsequious language. Verner felt that his lack of academic credentials prevented him from getting the treatment that Professor Starr, for example, would receive. But Verner kept trying to interest Bumpus in his wares; if not the unique beetles then perhaps some sculpted ivory he had secured at great difficulty and would allow the museum to bid on first.

As regards Ota Benga, however, the news from the museum was better—"I have bought a duck suit for the Pigmy," wrote Bumpus. "He is around the museum, apparently perfectly happy, and more or less a favorite of the men." The only problem concerned the city's "decidedly aggressive" breed of reporters, one of whom, a Miss Reynolds, had spotted Ota on the premises and wanted to know more about "that black boy." Bumpus told her no further information was forthcoming. With dead Eskimos and negative press notices in recent memory, he wanted to steer Ota Benga away from publicity.

He succeeded. Ota did not become a sensation at the Museum of Natural History. The crowds that came daily did not come for him. They came for dinosaurs, meteors, and what was left of Jumbo. Ota followed the crowds into every corner. He was learning to be invisible in a foreign land, nothing but a snazzy dresser in a white duck suit keeping his mouth shut tight on his telltale teeth.

He roamed the cool corridors in which the bones of the elephant, tyrannosaurus rex, the mastodon, mammoth, and brontosaurs were mounted, softly chanting the vowel songs of the hunt to himself as monsters rose up on every side. He moved around Jumbo's skeleton, measuring himself against it, thinking of past hunts and feasts, and recalling nights when he and fellow hunters had crawled inside the carcass of a freshly killed elephant for protection from the rain. Not a trace of an elephant's odor clung to Jumbo's bones.

Stuffed animals didn't interest him much, though he noticed how the *muzungu* liked to show them to their children. In this way the *muzungu* resembled his own people who told long stories about animals to their young. He hoped he would someday learn a story about a bear. He could not help but wonder if he would ever again have young.

There were meteors, the Willamette with its pockmarked surface, sharp, cratered, cool, and The Tent, only recently dragged over from Brooklyn Navy Yard by fourteen teams of horses. Ota liked to rub his cheeks against the surface of this rock, put his ears to it as if listening for a heart, climb it when he could. Director Bumpus once caught him in the act and gestured for him to get down. Eskimos had worked over the course of generations to chip tiny slivers of iron from Ahnighito. A bare-handed pygmy couldn't disturb it.

But for Director Bumpus rules were rules. He gestured with his hands, reaching up and bending down. He was using mime to instruct Ota to dismount. It looked a little like he was praying to a superior being as he repeatedly reached up and bent down, while unconsciously mouthing the words, "Get down, get down." He was pleased and a little surprised when Ota complied. Now, like an explorer, he could control the pygmy.

Museum guards were congenial. Making the rounds with one of them at night, Ota was treated to private viewings of some of the most valuable jewels on Earth, the mysterious Star of India Sapphire crossed in six lines by the light, the DeLong Star Ruby, the Patricia Emerald. These and the other gems in the museum's Hall of Minerals were a gift from J. P. Morgan. Although the Museum of Natural History didn't arouse quite the same passions in the banker as the Metropolitan Museum, he had been involved with it from the start.

The museum's president, Fairfield Osborn, called him Uncle. When Osborn needed money for mastodon bones all he had to do was ask, making sure to keep the application secret, and a check from Morgan would arrive. Whether it was art or dinosaurs, Morgan was the Grand Acquisitor; Ellis Island itself where the naturalization of objects was concerned. When Tiffany's gem collection won a Grand Prize at the Paris Exposition of 1889, Morgan bought the entire set and gave it to the museum. He continued to send gems and minerals by the boxcar to Osborn's constantly expanding institution.

What Ota saw at the Museum of Natural History deepened an impression he had formed at the fair; the *muzungu* swallowed other beings whole. What they couldn't digest they deposited in fairs and museums. Totem poles, masks, pipes, hunting gear—the entire material world of the Kwakiutl Indians—were hanging from walls or the ceiling or displayed behind glass. It gave him a queasy feeling. *He* was skilled in weaving with straw, *he* owned a bow and arrows. His woven hats and baskets, his bow and arrow could be up there too.

What had at first held his attention now made him want to flee. It was maddening to be inside—to be swallowed whole—so long. He had an image of himself stuffed, behind glass, but somehow still alive, crouching over a fake campfire, feeding meat to a lifeless child. Museum silence became a source of torment, a kind of noise; he needed birdsong, breezes, trees. One day he smuggled himself into an exiting crowd. A guard caught him and diverted him back inside.

Bumpus was alerted; the pygmy looked unhappy, he had tried to sneak away. The director tried to restore order with charades. He led Ota to the museum doors, pointed to them and waved his hand back and forth in what he hoped was a universal gesture of no. Ota sauntered back into the vicinity of Jumbo's bones.

Bumpus brought Ota along to a gathering of friends and donors, hoping to get some use out of his tenancy. Ota was introduced to select members of New York's donor class, including Daniel Guggenheim and his wife Florence. Bumpus was ready with appropriate remarks. "Mr. Guggenheim," he said, "I have the pleasure of introducing you to Ota Benga, whose people, sir, have not yet progressed even to the need for stone."

"Well, I couldn't interest him in shares of aluminum, could I?" joked the magnate.

"Ota," said Bumpus, "would you be so good as to bring Mrs. Guggenheim a chair?"

Bumpus pointed to a chair at the end of the room. With a serious expression on his face and a shoveling sort of movement of the arms, he depicted putting a chair behind and beneath Mrs. Florence Guggenheim. Mouthing the words, "Get a chair, get a chair," he repeated the gesture several times, trying to make sure the pygmy understood.

Ota smiled at Bumpus, walked across the room, lifted the chair, paused for a moment—he was aiming—and sent the chair flying past Bumpus just to the left of Florence Guggenheim's head. In the uproar that followed Ota left the room to climb to the top of his favorite meteor. When Bumpus followed after him and performed his dismounting gesture—reaching up and bending down while mouthing the words, "Get down, get down"—Ota just ignored him.

On August 16, Director Bumpus wrote to Verner. The sen-

tences are clipped, the message urgent. "Ota Benga restless,"
he said, "Chimpanzees need attention. When can you reach
New York?"

Verner arrived in New York City at the end of the month.
Although he took rooms in a hotel only a block away from the
Museum of Natural History, he kept his distance from Bumpus. No new placement for Ota had materialized and he was
nervous that Bumpus would put Ota and fifty boxes back into
his lap. Besides, sheriff's men had turned up at the museum
looking for him on behalf of the Guardian Trust Co., which he
owed $262.80 plus interest for the check he had bounced on
August 2, his first day back in the United States. He kept in
touch with Bumpus primarily by mail, just as he had from the
South, and occasionally by phone. (Was Bumpus sure, he
asked once more, that the museum had no use for a gigantic
beetle?)

He worked out an arrangement with a museum guard
whereby he could turn up periodically at a side door and have
Ota delivered to him. The first time they got together, Verner
asked his friend what the hunting had been like at the Museum of Natural History. Ota told him about coming within
inches of braining some female *muzungu*.

They wandered silently for a while until coming to a store-
front, its windows covered with posters. There was a kind of
bird with the head of a rabbit, a fish with human hair, and an
apelike man, a humanoid, about which it was written: "MAN OR
MONKEY—YOU DECIDE." There was an illustration of a man with
white and black stripes running diagonally across his whole
body, and beneath it a caption reading, "King Zebra, Chief Of
The Zulus, Comes From Outer Zululand To Show You A Zulu
Trance."

Looking both ways to make sure he wasn't recognized,
Verner paid up two dimes and he and Ota ducked inside. He
had never been in one of these places before; he had heard
they all moved to Coney Island. It was one of Barnum's leftovers, a freak show, the kind with albino Africans, burrowing
Bushmen, dwarfs and giants, real and fake Siamese twins. It
was dark, filled with cigar smoke, and on a raised platform that
served as a stage a large black man in painted white and black
stripes was dancing. His back was to the audience as he raised
first one foot, then the other, chanting, "NAJA JIMBU WOOJY
SNORK."

"Gibberish," said Verner.

"Noise," said Ota.

Slowly, the man came around. When he faced them they could see who it was. It was Ota's old friend and Verner's nemesis, the Mardi Gras Zulu.

Ota Benga slipped onstage. He raised his hands skyward and swayed elegantly in his white suit, while the Mardi Gras Zulu rolled his eyes back into his head and stomped. The crowd ooohed and ahhhed when Ota showed his teeth, and Verner heard, "If ever I cease to love, if ever I cease to love," the song of Rex, King of Carnival, as clearly as if he were back in New Orleans. Ota returned to claim his seat.

The Mardi Gras Zulu never figured out where the little man came from that night or how he disappeared. Maybe he had never been there at all. Stranger things had happened to the Mardi Gras Zulu on his visit to New York City.

"AA BA ZA BA WA JA ZOT."

"OO EE OO EE OH EE OH."

There was little work for a Zulu in New York City—not that there was much in New Orleans—but what there was the Mardi Gras Zulu found and learned to do. When he was done dancing in the dime museum he made his way to Coney Island, where he spent a season among the real Zulus who were the backdrop for the daily battles on the boardwalk between the British and the Boers.

Verner spent the remaining days of August evading the sheriff (who eventually confiscated half his crates) and trying to find a way to sell his animals. Following a suggestion made by Bumpus led him to the Bronx Zoological Gardens and its director, William Temple Hornaday. With Hornaday he was able to establish the sort of rapport he could only dream about having with the frostier Bumpus.

On August 27, the museum received a farewell letter from Verner. "I have arranged to place the African in satisfactory hands," he wrote, "and hope to get him away to-day." Warm relations with Hornaday produced an unexpected bonus. Not only was Hornaday interested in obtaining the snake and monkey, he was eager for the zoo to have Ota Benga as well.

15

THE PYGMY IN THE ZOO

The training of wild animals
may, or may not, involve cruelties,
according to the intelligence and
moral status of the trainer. This is
equally true of the training of children, and the treatment of wives and
husbands.

—William T. Hornaday, from
Article 20, "The Wild Animal's Bill
of Rights"

Seals and sea lions churned the water. They floated
lazily enough, sometimes resting—dark shapes, boul-
ders at the bottom—as they did all through the hot
afternoons of late August and early September following Ota Benga's arrival at the zoo. When the afternoon feeding
began, they crashed the water's surface again and again, racing
excitedly, circling at high speeds around their outdoor tank,
delighting the children in the crowd.

The feeding was over in a matter of a few frenzied minutes. Keepers tossed fish or handed them out to the hungry
animals, taking care each got its share. Gulls added their rau-
cous calls to the proceedings, the tips of their beaks reddened
by fish blood as they challenged each other for scraps the seals
left behind. A bull seal, barking at the gulls, forced them to lift
off and hover, but as he did not claim the torn fish for himself
they soon settled down again. Only the baby seals, splayed out

on rocks in the center of the pool, remained aloof from the commotion. Their diet still consisted entirely of milk.

Pictures of spectators at the seal pool during the period in which Ota Benga resided at the New York Zoological Park show women in blouses, long skirts, and occasionally bonnets, and men in jackets and hats. The seal pool brought members of New York's old families together with new arrivals from Italy, Eastern Europe, and Russia. English may have been the most common language, but it was often heavily accented, and at moments of excitement—a seal flipping over backward to catch a fish, for example—some families reverted to Italian, Yiddish, or a Slavic tongue.

For nearly two weeks Ota wandered freely in Western clothes, occasionally helping keepers with their chores. He watched the seals and stalked the crowd, casing it as casually and adroitly as a pickpocket. He had resumed his old hunting ways. Fortunately for visitors he wasn't after wallets or purses. He was content to observe—and be unobserved. He was interested in seals; he had never seen them eat before. As always, he was interested in the *muzungu*. He was aware by now that the *muzungu* came in a variety of sizes, languages, and smells. Ota took no chances. Applying the techniques of assimilation he had practiced at the museum, he gave visitors no reason to suspect there was anyone among them as outrageous as a pygmy.

The trick of invisibility depended on working with the shapes and colors already available. There weren't many black men visiting the zoo, but there were some, and they provided Ota with camouflage. He was content to be stared at as if he were a solitary, unusually short, silent black American.

The feeding of the seals over, crowds divided slowly in favor of the zoo's other attractions. The seal pool was the centerpiece of Baird Court, a collection of buildings that in turn formed the core of the New York Zoological Park, or Bronx Zoo, as it was more commonly called. Baird Court was to the 260 acres of zoo woodland what the city is to the countryside. It stood above the rest of the park like civilization itself emerging from and guarding the entry point to a surrounding wilderness.

From the seal pool it was but a short walk to Baird Court's Elephant House. Ota had seen traces of New York's herd of elephants before, but now, like a hunter who had followed tracks to their source, he was finally face-to-face with a New

York elephant in the flesh. Since arriving from Southeast Asia in 1904 (he cost the zoo $2,340), Gunda had been the leading resident of Elephant House.

Director Hornaday liked to draw a sharp distinction between his institution and Coney Island, his highbrow elephants and the carny animals that belonged to circuses or amusement parks. Nevertheless, since his arrival at the zoo Gunda had been trained to entertain.

Most afternoons, he could be found giving children a ride on his back, or teaching lessons in frugality. Visitors were encouraged to contribute pennies to his act by dropping them in a deposit box, or by holding their hands out so Gunda could swipe the pennies with his trunk. Next, he would drop the pennies into another box, his "bank," and pull a cord. The cord in turn rang a bell. That was the signal Gunda had been a thrifty elephant once again and was due for a reward. His keepers would bring him a tasty piece of bread.

After a while Gunda mastered this exercise so thoroughly it didn't depend on visitors or the donation of new coins. A single penny was sufficient to keep him going the livelong day as he removed a penny already in his bank, plunked it back in, and pulled the cord.

Director Hornaday was aware that Gunda had begun to cheat. He made it his business to keep close tabs on his elephants. They were simply too big and could become too dangerous to take for granted. When bull elephants became sexually mature and entered into the seasons of intense desire known as musth, they could become virtually uncontrollable.

When Gunda suffered through acute onsets of musth, his keepers began whipping him to get him to obey, which set off a public outcry. Director Hornaday was compelled to explain. On a large sign posted outside Gunda's stall he proclaimed, "Whipping an elephant *does not hurt him;* but he *thinks* that it does." It was, and remains, one of the more subtle explanations in the annals of the zoo and may, by confusing them, have temporarily silenced some of the director's critics.

The whipping did not inspire Gunda to mend his ways; he simply would not accede to lifelong captivity without the prospect of sexual release, and became a menace to anyone who came too close. When he nearly killed his keeper it became apparent that Gunda, like many a New York elephant before him, would not die of natural causes.

Carl Akeley, who had hunted big game and mounted hides

for the Museum of Natural History, was summoned. He was asked to bring his elephant gun.

Gunda was a Bronx Zoo animal, a member of the elite, and he, unlike Topsy and Jumbo at the end of their lives, was not to be denied a certain dignity in the manner of his death. Gunda faced the firing squad in private. When the shot had been fired and Gunda crumbled to the ground, the *Times*, which had followed his career closely, declared, "Gunda is a 'good' elephant at last."

That was in 1915, nine years after Ota Benga knew him. In 1906, Gunda's criminal leanings showed themselves only in petty deceptions aimed at getting extra bread. These were thwarted easily enough. Nails were hammered up through the bottom of Gunda's bank. It became impossible for him to re-cycle pennies.

Gunda was only one of many large animals within easy walking distance of the seal pool. Sultan and Hannibal occa-sionally announced their presence with a roar that could be felt and heard the length and breadth of Baird Court. They were the lords of Lion House, which they shared with Senor Lopez the jaguar and other big cats. There was also Monkey House, southeast of the pool, where the chimpanzee Ota had handed over personally when he arrived at the zoo was housed.

Ota spent a good deal of time with the chimp, helping her become comfortable with her new surroundings. While with her, he noticed Dohong, the presiding genius of Monkey House. Dohong was an orangutan, an Asiatic breed new to Ota.

In the tradition of earlier Bronx Zoo orangutans, Dohong had been taught to ride a tricycle, and was encouraged to do so in front of crowds. He had also been taught to swagger about clothed Western-style in pants and a shirt. When he sat down to eat he looked just like an imitation *muzungu*. It brought to mind Fwela's joke about how only white people were de-scended from the apes. Dohong, waiting patiently with a knife in one hand and a fork in the other for dinner to be served, was living proof.

But why, in the first place, Ota was curious to know, did the *muzungu* place such emphasis on getting animals to act like people, as with Gunda and his cord and coins and Dohong pouring from a pot of tea? What exactly was the point? Did *muzungus* hope that in the end all animals would act like them?

Dohong would sit there immobile, his eyes going contemplatively back and forth from his trapeze to the bars of the cage. Sometimes he would insert his trapeze between two bars, leaning in hard, yanking with all his might, and eventually widening the gaps between the bars. Ota noticed the escape route Dohong was opening with his trapeze. If there was no one around, he lent his strength to the orangutan's efforts.

The forest dweller thought of Dohong as one good reason, and perhaps his best so far, for having come to the land of the *muzungu*. Here, he felt, was an ape worth knowing. Dohong manifested similar esteem for Ota Benga. No matter how crowded the Monkey House got, if Ota was about the orangutan would single him out, curl up like a ball, and somersault over to the bars to get a little closer.

When Ota was not blending into the crowd around the seals, or becoming more knowledgeable about orangutans, he might walk into the administration building to look up Director Hornaday. Before Fwela left the Zoo to go South again, he had said that Chief Hornaday's heart was white. Ota had not yet made up his own mind about Hornaday's heart. He dropped in on the director to see if Fwela had written one of those letters with a message for him in Tshiluba, something with such a greeting as "Life, Ota," or even, "Life of Fire, Ota Benga," followed by a mingling of noise and information— "My family is well. Obey Chief Hornaday, he is our friend"— and ending with another "Life," or "Life of Fire, Fwela."

If Hornaday had nothing to read to him on a given day Ota would leave the director's office, its walls decorated with the antlered heads of many elk and moose, and wander out of Baird Court into the zoo's woodland area. Here lay the twenty-acre buffalo range on which it had been hoped a self-sufficient herd of American bison would graze and grow. This, like so many of Director Hornaday's plans, went slightly but significantly awry. Bronx grass proved inimical. Buffalo died rather than prospered and new beasts had to be shipped in constantly to sustain the floundering Bronx Zoo herd. In the end, native grass was eliminated, the range paved over, and buffalo, like caged animals, had to rely on keepers for their feed.

Here, in the shady wooded areas of the zoo, Ota could disengage from crowds. Squirrels lived there. Many kinds of songbirds nested in the trees. Wild mink and weasels hunted, competing with newly arrived Italian immigrants who settled along the outskirts of the park and hunted within it. Finally,

there were Hornaday's rangers, armed with pistols, who descended on the immigrants with orders to catch them and kick
them out. As Ota contemplated the game of dodge that took
place daily in the woods, he considered getting rid of his
clothes, reclaiming the bow and arrow he had left in Hornaday's office, and joining in the fun.

The Museum of Natural History had been exactly the sort
of place about which he had once said, "In the land of the
muzungu there are houses so big that you could walk around
in them without ever knowing if it was raining outside." The
zoo was different. You could tell if it was raining. No one
stopped you if you felt like getting wet.

There was air, freedom of movement, an elephant, an orangutan, and lions. There were the poisonous snakes of Asia,
the Americas, and Africa—including Ntoka, courtesy of Fwela
and himself—safely deposited behind glass. There were animals he was familiar with and many, like Dohong, he had
never met before. It was as if he were inhabiting a forest, or at
least the muzungu's idea of a forest, a forest minus wilderness.
Ota felt he was the human resident of this interesting, instructive but artificial world. He felt he could survive for some time
at the zoo; it was a congenial place to wait for his journey to
resume.

Ota's stay was not allowed to draw to a natural or a simple
conclusion. Hornaday and other zoo officials had long been
subject to a recurring dream in which a man like Ota Benga
played a leading role. His presence activated dormant plans.
While he wandered, spying on spectators or marveling at what
an elephant did when it had nothing else to do, conversations
were being held and calls were being made.

A trap was being prepared, made of Darwinism, Barnu-
mism, pure and simple racism. It drew on the showboating
personality of William Temple Hornaday; S. P. Verner's habit,
formed when a grade school teacher sent him out to cry at
Copeland's Grave, of deferring to authority; and Ota's affection
for an orangutan. So seamlessly did these elements come together that later those responsible could deny, with some plausibility, that there had ever been a trap or plan at all. There was
no one to blame, they argued, unless it was a capricious pygmy
or a self-serving press. There was nothing to point to but the
age itself, transparent to those who lived in it.

When, on September 8, the trap sprung shut, it wiped out
in a single stroke all of Ota's work. No more remaining unno-

ticed and anonymous, no more observing while remaining unobserved. On the contrary, he was propelled into maximum visibility. His story became the material of headlines, his name a household word not only in New York City but around the world.

It was like the St. Louis Fair all over again. But it was New York City, the World's Fair that never slowed or dimmed its lights. The display area wasn't an African Exhibit this time, it was a major zoo. There was less warning. And this time, as compared to his days with the Batwa and Kondola, Ota Benga was all alone.

The Bronx Zoo officially opened, seven years prior to Ota's occupancy, on a gray November day in 1899. It fell to Fairfield Osborn, Columbia University professor, President of the American Museum of Natural History, and trustee of the zoo, to make a few opening-day remarks. He looked down from his platform at a host of familiar faces. Much of the city's financial and political elite had come uptown for the ceremony.

J. P. Morgan was there, and zoo secretary Madison Grant, author, in coming years, of anti-immigrant broadsides such as *The Alien In Our Midsts*. Osborn, Grant, and Theodore Roosevelt had worked together for years to situate a world-class zoo in New York City. All three were members of the exclusive Boone and Crockett club, which brought together upper-class New Yorkers with an interest in big game hunting.

Members of Boone and Crockett were firm believers in hunting for sport as opposed to profit. They were concerned that newcomers to America, hunting in order to make a living, would destroy what remained of the American wild. Madison Grant believed, moreover, that the Nordic race needed access to the wild in order to recharge itself. The great race, as he sometimes called it, needed a place to turn to now and then where, rifle in hand, it could hone its instincts.

Since the zoo was to be in New York City, it followed that it would, like all the city's newer institutions, be the biggest of its kind. It would have more land than other zoos, more than the National Zoological Park in Washington, D.C., and many times more than New York's old Central Park Zoo. The collection of animals would verge on the encyclopedic, and would be housed, so far as possible, in simulations of their natural habitats. As in anthropology, so in zoology, authenticity would reign supreme.

Osborn addressed this issue in his opening-day remarks. He spoke of the animals that predated the coming of "our Dutch and English ancestors." Elk, moose, deer, and beaver were named the original inhabitants of New York City. Osborn promised the zoo's first guests they would soon find these creatures restored "to their old haunts," along with "all the other noble aborigines of Manhattan."

By "other noble aborigines," Osborn meant the human beings who had been displaced or destroyed when New York was settled. The Bronx Zoo would make restitution to these men in a manner that would also be a treat to spectators. "Later," promised Osborn, "we shall find a place upon the Buffalo Range for the Indian and his teepee." From the first the zoo's organizers made no secret of what they regarded as the ultimate exhibit.

William Temple Hornaday was the perfect choice to be the first director. He believed in zoos; it was Hornaday's opinion that "there is no higher use to which a wild bird or mammal can be devoted than to place it in perfectly comfortable captivity to be seen by millions of persons who desire make its acquaintance." He maintained the hierarchical view of races held by Madison Grant but transferred it to the world of beasts: large-brained animals were to him what Nordics were to Grant, the best evolution had to offer. As such they not only had to pull their own weight but to compensate for the lower orders.

Much of Hornaday's "The Wild Animal's Bill of Rights" was aimed at protecting captive animals from cruelty and neglect. Article 16 made it clear that animals had duties in return: "A wild animal has no more inherent right to live a life of lazy and luxurious ease, and freedom from all care, than a man or woman has to live without work or family cares."

About the lower orders of animals, however, Hornaday entertained no illusions. Crocodiles were a case in point, the kind of beast whose behavior could not be modified. It would be a waste of effort to try to reform them: "The ways of crocodiles are dark and deep;" wrote the director, "their thoughts are few and far between."

Hornaday had been at the Smithsonian Institution when Barnum donated the bones of Jumbo to the Museum of Natural History in New York. It was a disappointment to Hornaday who, as a taxidermist, would have been involved in mounting Jumbo's bones. When applying for the post of zoo director, ·

Hornaday boasted of his own showman's instincts, emphasizing not technical expertise but his "creative faculty—the power to originate."

Hornaday harbored a scheme for attracting public interest similar to the one Osborn announced on opening day. In 1896, he wrote of "*at once* getting hold of the Public" by "illustrat-[ing] the houses and the house life of the aborigines of North America." He thought such a collection could "be made a very picturesque, striking and popular feature, at very moderate cost; and it would be 'something new under the sun.' "

Ota Benga came to Hornaday's attention ten years after he hinted at this plan. The dream of the aborigine had not faded in the meantime. It was only waiting to be implemented.

It didn't matter that Ota could hardly be taken for a North American Indian. He did own a bow and arrow; he was an aboriginal inhabitant if not of a pristine Manhattan then of a pristine Africa. That was close enough.

As Verner later told it in *Travels With Ntoka*, when he and Ota walked through the doors of the Reptile House, "Ota Benga almost howled with astonishment at the sight of so many snakes in front of him," and when the zoo's veteran herpetologist grabbed Ntoka by the back of the neck without a care, "Ota Benga had started back towards the Congo with a yell, and Fwela had jumped over the rail."

In a conversation with Hornaday in his office, it was decided that $275 was a fair asking price for Verner's chimpanzee. It was agreed that Ota would remain at the zoo. No one would be able to claim him without Verner's consent. Verner, however, could have him back at any time, either permanently or on a temporary basis, for use on the lecture circuit.

Ota Benga took up his residency at the New York Zoological Park. Hornaday instructed his keepers not to trouble the pygmy but to give him as much access to the animals as seemed plausible, especially the monkeys, and most of all Dohong.

Based on his conversation with Verner, he wrote an article for the October edition of the Zoological Society Bulletin. It may have been slightly disconcerting for some readers to encounter a piece called "An African Pygmy," photo included, on the front page of a zoo publication. The piece on Ota came directly before one called "The Collection Of Lizards."

Hornaday's article contained its share of inaccuracies (Verner, for example, did not meet Ota when he was returning the Batwa, but when he was trying to recruit them for the fair), but was no worse than most renditions, and was sober—zoological—in tone. The handwritten version calls the forest dwellers of Africa the "smallest racial division of the human genus, and probably the lowest in cultural development." The printed version drops the reference to stunted cultural development.

Ota was given straw and rope with which to weave. As the Zoological Society Bulletin reported, "He has much manual skill, and is quite expert in the making of hammocks and nets."

He found the doors to Dohong's cage opened for him whenever he wished. Keepers often invited him inside. He was encouraged to set up his hammock and sleep in an empty Monkey House cage that opened on an outdoor enclosure shared by Dohong and the chimps. On Saturday, September 8, a target was put together out of straw in that enclosure. Ota was given his bow and some arrows and encouraged to shoot.

That was the day Hornaday let the crowds know something special was going on at the Monkey House, "something," as he had once put it, "new under the sun." Crowds tended to wane with the passing of summer. The director had found a way to keep them coming.

They came and gathered at the Monkey House. On September 9, the *New York Times* carried the first headline: "BUSH-MAN SHARES A CAGE WITH BRONX PARK APES."

16

IS IT A MAN?

In this land of foremost progress—
In this Wisdom's ripest age—
We have placed him, in high honor,
In a monkey's cage!

        —*New York Times,*
        September 19, 1906

He didn't have to do much. He just had to be short and black. He had to know little or no English. It was even all right that he wore clothes; that made it all the more tantalizing that he was in the Monkey House. He wore trousers, a jacket, but on the very first day no shoes.

Was he a man or a monkey? Was he something in between? "Ist dass ein Mencsch?" asked a German spectator, "Is it a man?"

It had the fascination of Dohong the orangutan dressed fully for dinner or pedaling his bike around the cage. But Dohong was just an ape putting on a show. Even the children could tell. No one really mistook apes or parrots for human beings. This—it—came so much closer. Was it man? Was it monkey? Was it a forgotten stage of evolution?

Some people were uncomfortable. One man said about the spectacle, "Something about it that I don't like." But he didn't turn his back. He stayed. He too was numbered in the crowd waiting to see what would happen next.

Ota did nothing particularly unusual that first day on exhibit at New York Zoological Park. Still, it was more interesting to watch him drink soda than to see Hannibal the lion tear raw steak. It was so engrossing to see him shoot his arrows—he rarely missed—the crowds forgot all about the hour when the seals were scheduled to be fed. Gunda the elephant went begging for pennies, Dohong, who had never cared much for the exercise anyway, didn't even bother to ride his bike for people.

How did the pygmy like sleeping in the Monkey House, people wondered? How did he feel about living at the zoo? Next day the *Times* editorialized: "It is probably a good thing that Benga does not think very deeply. If he did it isn't likely that he was very proud of himself when he woke in the morning and found himself under the same roof with the orangoutangs and the monkeys, for that is really where he is."

In St. Louis the crowd had been curious about how Ota and the Batwa would react to a little pressure, how they would stand up to some pain. At the zoo, that pressure, in a sense, was already included; the pressure of bars and a cage. Ota, that first day, was locked into his enclosure, except when his keepers let him out. When he was let out of the Monkey House the crowd stayed glued to him, and a keeper stayed close by.

After wandering, Ota settled back indoors into his hammock. The crowd loved it. He resumed weaving his mats and caps, then shot his arrows again. If he missed the children made faces at him. Ota made faces back, and the crowd loved that. Day one, and he was already a sensation.

Overnight Director Hornaday made a few last minute additions and refinements. Saturday had been dress rehearsal. The real show was about to begin.

On Sunday, September 9, thousands "took the Subway, the elevated, and the surface cars to the New York Zoological Park, in the Bronx . . . " according to the *Times*.

There was always a crowd before the cage, most of the time roaring with laughter, and from almost every corner of the garden could be heard the question:

"Where is the pygmy?"

And the answer was, "In the monkey house."

There was a more elaborate setting in the Monkey House than had been prepared the day before. Bones were now scattered around the cage to increase the impression of savagery and danger. In addition, Director Hornaday had posted a sign on the enclosure:

> The African Pygmy, "Ota Benga."
> Age, 28 years. Height, 4 feet 11 inches.
> Weight 103 pounds. Brought from the Kasai River,
> Congo Free State, South Central Africa,
> by Dr. Samuel P. Verner,
> Exhibited each afternoon during September.

Dohong was admitted into the enclosure. The orangutan imitated the man. The man imitated the monkey. They hugged, let go, flopped into each other's arms. Dohong snatched the woven straw cap off Ota's head and placed it on his own. Ota snatched it back. He picked the monkey up and let him drop, then turned his back to walk away. Dohong jumped up on his shoulders to hold him back. Ota shrugged him off, turned again to walk away. Dohong grabbed an ankle with one arm. Ota took big, limping steps around the cage, shackled to the ape. The crowd hooted and applauded. Dohong and Ota hugged. If Hornaday had thought to supply them with canes and Derby hats, they might have obliged with an old soft-shoe.

Children squealed with delight. To adults there was a more serious side to the display. Something about the boundary condition of being human was exemplified in that cage. Somewhere man shaded into non-man. Perhaps if they looked hard enough the moment of transition might be seen.

If Saturday's exhibit had somehow been too subtle, Sunday's entertainment compensated. To a generation raised on talk of that absentee star of evolution, the Missing Link, the point of Dohong and Ota disporting in the Monkey House was obvious. ". . . the pygmy was not much taller than the orangoutang," reported the *Times*, "and one had a good opportunity to study their points of resemblance. Their heads are much alike, and both grin in the same way when pleased."

Day two of the Pygmy at the Zoo already contained the first whisper of controversy. In response to a *Times* reporter, Director Hornaday admitted men were not, as a rule, exhibited in European zoos, but saw no reason to apologize: the pygmy was completely comfortable in the Monkey House. Hornaday claimed he had the full support of the Zoological Society in what he was doing.

The press in general seemed willing to indulge Hornaday, asking a few easily deflected questions now and then to maintain a semblance of balance and fair play. The entrance of the black community into the matter of the pygmy in the zoo lent it an entirely new dimension.

Rev. R. S. MacArthur of the Calvary Baptist Church was an unsmiling face in the light-hearted crowd at the zoo on September 9. "The person responsible for this exhibition," he said, "degrades himself as much as he does the African. Instead of making a beast of this little fellow we should be putting him in school for the development of such powers as God gave him . . . We send our missionaries to Africa to Christianize the people and then we bring one here to brutalize him." Dr. Gilbert of the Mount Olivet Baptist Church vowed that "he and other pastors would join with Dr. MacArthur in seeing to it that the Bushman was released from the monkey cage and put elsewhere."

Meanwhile Ota Benga was given what the crowd was led to think of as his first pair of shoes. According to the Times, "He seemed to like the shoes very much. Over and over again the crowd laughed at him as he sat in mute admiration of them." Did he object to the crowd laughing at him? "He has grown used to the crowd laughing, has discovered that they laugh at everything he does. If he wonders why he does not show it."

On September 10, clergymen representing the Colored Baptist Ministers' Conference, headed by James H. Gordon, superintendent of the Howard Colored Orphan Asylum in Brooklyn, looked for Ota and found he was not displayed as advertised. While proclaiming that the exhibit would proceed as posted, Hornaday had in fact backed down, canceling afternoon performances until further notice.

Still, the Monkey House continued to be Ota's address, and the ministers found him in a cage with Dohong in his lap. The ministers asked if he was locked inside the Monkey House. Ota smiled; Dohong pursed his lips and blew a kiss. Was he physically mistreated in any way? Ota smiled again, lifted his behind and produced a shoe. Dohong clambered off and returned with its mate.

It occurred to Reverend Gordon and the others that it would not be so simple to represent this fellow. They had counted on his being upset and angry. He was neither; they were the ones who were upset and angry. The ministers conferred among themselves. Why leap into a struggle that could make them look ridiculous? Perhaps the whole affair had been exaggerated. Then they noticed Hornaday's sign, still posted on the Monkey House.

The sign was shortly to disappear without a trace. It never made it into the Zoological Park's otherwise exhaustive archives, but on September 10 still greeted visitors to the Monkey House. The ministers read it and when they were done, according to the *Times*, "they became indignant."

Rev. Gordon announced on behalf of the other ministers that the committee was going to apply directly to Mayor McClellan. As the zoo was chartered by the city, the mayor could put an immediate stop to "the degrading exhibition." If the mayor refused to help, the clergymen resolved to call for a series of "indignation meetings."

Over time, the committee detailed a number of reasons for objecting to Ota's presence in the Monkey House and, further, his continued presence at the zoo. They had heard blacks compared with apes often enough before; now the comparison was being played out flagrantly at the largest zoo on Earth. "Our race, we think, is depressed enough," said Gordon, "without exhibiting one of us with the apes. We think we are worthy of being considered human beings, with souls."

The ministers also opposed the exhibition because it teased the crowds with the specter of the Missing Link. Any reference to the Missing Link implied acceptance of Darwinism. As religious fundamentalists the ministers' creed ran counter to the theory of evolution. Gordon commented:

This is a Christian country . . . and the exhibition evidently aims to be a demonstration of the Darwinian theory of evolution. The Darwinian theory is absolutely opposed to Christianity, and a public demonstration in its favor should not be permitted.

Though it did not show itself immediately, there was, among certain members of the black community, the embarrassment of being associated with Ota at all. They accepted the prevailing notion that pygmies, as stated by anthropology (and restated by the freak shows), were defective specimens of mankind. The *Journal*, a black newspaper, complained that "a member, unfortunate and not all representative of the people of Africa" had been put on exhibition.

Gordon wondered who "Dr. S. P. Verner" was and accused him of having looked in all the wrong places when trying to find lodgings for the African. "We have 225 children in the institution to which I belong," Gordon declared, "some of them pretty large children. We will take this little African and be pleased to have him . . . If this does not suit, I will take him personally into my home and be responsible for him to the fullest extent."

In fact, Verner was elsewhere in the park on September 10, conferring with Hornaday and trying to keep a distance from the Baptists. He, like everyone else, had been drawn to the zoo by the headlines.

His days, since leaving Ota in the Bronx, had been spent looking for work. As there were no immediate openings for him in the fields of African development or anthropology, he had lowered his expectations. Ads were in all the New York papers for ticket agents on the subway. Verner had arranged an interview, during which he was asked if he carried any letters of recommendation. He produced the letter of introduction to King Leopold II, written on his behalf by Secretary of State John Hay, and was offered a job as a night shift ticket-taker for the IRT.

He wasn't particularly proud of his new post. In a letter to Bumpus he referred vaguely to his job as a "position . . . obtained owing to my one-time training and record in Railway Engineering." Verner brought a typewriter with him to work. When he wasn't selling tickets he pounded out articles on Africa for submission to *Harper's* and other journals. It was like his days on the Southern Railway all over again, when, after his postgraduate crack-up, he mended and mulled over what to do with his life. Then, as now, Africa had been the obsession. Then he was reading about it; now he was writing about it, recounting his own experiences, and touting the excellent and as yet untapped prospects for African development.

Then he had been single, and now he was married. He planned to go south within a day or so of his visit to the zoo to bring Hattie and his two children to New York. First he had to make sure he could leave Ota with Hornaday. He had managed a private conversation earlier in the day with the forest dweller, and they had agreed that Ota would stay at the zoo.

When reporters found him, Verner told them that if there was a sign on the Monkey House, it was put there only to answer questions. If there were restrictions, they were entirely for Ota's good. When reporters asked about Ota being presented it as the missing link, Verner denied it. "The 'missing link,' " he told them, "will never be found alive."

The reporters next sought out Hornaday's response to the Baptists. "I am giving the exhibitions purely as an ethnological exhibit," he said. "It is my duty to interest the visitors to the park . . . "

He was succeeding brilliantly. On Sunday, September 16, forty thousand visitors roamed the New York Zoological Park. The zoo was becoming a draw on the order of magnitude of Coney Island. The sudden surge in interest, as the *Times* attested, was entirely attributable to Ota Benga:

> Nearly every man, woman, and child of this crowd made for the monkey house to see the star attraction in the park—the wild man from Africa. They chased him about the grounds all day, howling, jeering and yelling. Some of them poked him in the ribs, others tripped him up, all laughed at him.

When the crowds cornered Ota, the reporter added, "they asked him how he liked America," to which he was heard to answer, "Me no like America; me like St. Louis."

Even as it reached new heights, however, the exhibit began to come apart. Because of the efforts of the committee of black ministers, Ota was never again formally displayed with Dohong in the Monkey House after the first weekend, and Hornaday's poster was consigned to oblivion.

The ministers called the end to those afternoon displays a victory. It was not necessarily a victory for Ota Benga. Formal displays meant Ota belonged the to crowd for certain hours of the day. At other times there was at least the possibility of being left alone. Now the crowds assumed he belonged to them always.

Other aspects of the clergymen's protest had mixed results as well. Attempts to enlist Mayor McClellan's support resulted in failure; he refused even to meet with them.

Through a secretary, he referred them to Madison Grant, who gave them "no very satisfactory reply." They continued to press their case, receiving letters of support from black congregations throughout the city and the South and resolving to seek redress through the courts. John E. Milholland, a white attorney, agreed to take the case and help defray the cost of litigation. Milholland was associated with activists critical of Booker T. Washington's leadership, which they regarded as conciliationist. His support indicates the affair was serving to unite blacks and their supporters across a wide range of political views.

Superintendent Gordon continued to press an appeal on simple grounds of humanitarianism. "You people," he was quoted as saying to some white men, "are on top. We've got to rise. Why not let us, and not impede us? Why . . . show that Negroes are akin to apes? Give us opportunities."

Hornaday's press allies began to desert him. The *Times*, while ridiculing Gordon and the other Baptists, concluded that no vital interests were served by continuing the display of an "African homunculus":

> It is most amusing to note that one reverend colored brother objects to this curious exhibition on the ground that it is an impious effort to lend credibility to Darwin's dreadful theories. . . . The reverend colored brother should be told that evolution, in one form or other, is now taught in the text books of all the schools, and that it is no more debatable than the multiplication table.

Criticism of Hornaday, distaste for members of the protest movement, and condescension toward Ota Benga himself were typical of positions taken by the *Times* during the affair, as in some stanzas published in the September 19 edition:

> From his native land of darkness,
> To the country of the free,
> In the interest of science,
> And of broad humanity,
> Brought we a little Ota Benga,
> Dwarfed, benighted, without guile,
> Scarcely more than apes or monkey,
> Yet a man the while!

It is possible the three-cornered dance between Hornaday, the press, and the protest might have continued for some time. What brought it to a swifter conclusion was the attitude of Ota Benga himself. Ota spent one afternoon bouncing a rubber ball with one hand while exploring the musical possibilities of the harmonica he was holding in the other. The harmonica, according to a reporter, produced "unearthly sounds," and the ambidextrous bouncing and blowing gave the crowd such a treat "as Benga hasn't furnished heretofore."

Ota went out of his way to steer mischief in Hornaday's direction. This was his counterattack, his revenge for constant ridicule he pretended not to feel, his payback for the fact that even with a police officer now assigned full-time to protect him, he was always in danger of being grabbed, yanked, poked, and pulled to pieces by the mob.

Ota brought the war home to Hornaday's office. There were mornings when the phone kept ringing—it was Supt. Gordon demanding the pygmy's release—while Ota blew "unearthly sounds" directly into Hornaday's free ear with his harmonica, and reporters took notes. Ota would string up a hammock up just when the director was talking to the press, and rock himself gently in a corner. Hornaday could never tell just when another loud, disruptive harmonica raspberry would assault his nerves.

On Tuesday, September 25, the Times carried the headline "BENGA TRIES TO KILL; PYGMY SLASHES AT KEEPER WHO OBJECTED TO HIS GARB." It had been a hot day. Ota had been playing with children when keepers found him and commenced to spray him with a hose. According to the report, "He enjoyed this, and grew so boisterous that he finally took off nearly all of his clothing." The keepers gestured for him to put his clothes back on. He responded by starting to remove the little he still wore. When they tried to put his clothes back on him forcibly, Ota ran away and came back brandishing a knife. He was set upon from all sides, disarmed, and hustled inside a cage.

Perhaps Ota's anger and deeply ingrained dislike for authority got the better of him in this case, and he instigated what he usually avoided, a direct confrontation; but it is difficult to be sure. Keepers often urged him to charge the bars of a cage, his mouth open wide, his teeth bared, to give spectators the impression of the wildman and to give children a fright. It was of a piece with the bones scattered around his cage. It is not impossible that something similar happened here, re-hearsed well in advance by Ota and his keepers.

Bronx Zoo photographs taken at this time show a very different side of Ota Benga than the mask of mischief he wore in his concerted attack on Hornaday's sanity, or the fury—real or not—manifest in "BENGA TRIES TO KILL." The photographs, taken by the zoo's official photographer, are, as visitors were not permitted to carry cameras with them, the only photos that exist of Ota Benga at the zoo.

The zoo routinely filed photographs of all its animals, but there was no filing category for human beings. Filing the pictures of Ota Benga posed a problem; as in the matter of racial identity Ota defied prevailing labels. The solution was to photograph him holding a baby chimpanzee. Archivists then filed the picture under the label reserved for monkeys; the pretense was that the chimp was the subject, the pygmy nothing more than background.

The chimp averts its gaze, content to be cradled in Ota's right arm. Ota's expression remains constant through all the pictures taken in what was probably a single sitting. He is calm—almost too calm. There is the suggestion of sadness, a hint of resignation, and something more: Ota, who had been the object of so much scrutiny, is not merely being seen in these photos, he is seeing. He is seeing back, seeing the camera, the cameraman, and the whole civilization that seems, in his gaze, to be arrayed directly behind them.

Who are you? he seems to be asking. It is, after all, the question he crossed an ocean to answer. He asked the question, in 1906, of his own age. Looking now from behind the vanished camera and the deceased cameraman at the man in a spotted loincloth, bare from the waist up, with a chimpanzee nestled in his arm, the question written on those features is every bit as earnest and unavoidable.

Under continuous pressure, Hornaday showed a talent for the multiple response. To Mayor McClellan he played down the entire incident. After congratulating the mayor for refusing to become involved in the "absurd matter" he added, "The whole episode is good comic-opera material, and nothing more. When the history of the Zoological Park is written, this incident will form its most amusing passage." Hornaday charged that the business of a pygmy behind bars had been grossly exaggerated by a sensationalist press; that none of the Baptists had actually *seen* the pygmy locked in a cage.

He was keen to accept congratulations from Fairfield Osborn. "The enclosed [press] clippings are excellent," wrote Osborn. "Benga is certainly making his way successfully as a sensation." Yet, on September 16, he wrote to Verner in Brevard: "Ota Benga has become quite unmanageable. Whenever the keepers go after him in his meanderings, and attempt to bring him back to the Monkey House, he threatens to bite them, and would undoubtedly do so if they should persist." On the seventeenth, panic mounting, he wired, "Boy had become unmanageable; also dangerous. Impossible to send him to you. Please come for him at once. Answer."

It was with lively regret he noted that as Ota had been "so much in the public eye, it is quite inadvisable for us to punish him." He agreed in principle that Ota should go to the Howard Colored Orphan Asylum. "Enough! Enough!" he cried, according to the *Times*. "I have had enough of Ota Benga . . . they can get busy tinkering with his intellect. "

Only Verner could authorize Ota's transfer to Rev. Gordon and the Howard Colored Orphan Asylum, but he, it seems, was stranded on a mountain top just outside Brevard, marooned by "a tremendous equinoctial gale & rain-storm, raising an immense flood in the . . . river, stopping the mail-carriers, breaking the railway, and doing all sorts of damage." It didn't seem from the tone of Verner's response that he had been infected by Hornaday's sense of alarm. In fact, there is the implication that until Hornaday paid up for the chimpanzee, he would be in no rush to come down from his mountaintop. In the meantime, if Hornaday could control Ota no other way, Verner suggests the director try a sedative.

Verner arrived in New York City the last week in September, and met with Ota in what he had come to think of as the forest dweller's office in the Monkey House. There was unusual awkwardness between the men.

"I heard you had a little trouble, Ota."

Ota looked as if nothing could be further from the truth. "Noise, Fwela, noise," he said.

"I thought Hornaday was exaggerating. As for Hornaday, Ota . . . "

"Fwela, his heart is white."

"I told you!"

"White as that snow I once saw."

"Excellent."

"White as a *muzungu*."

"Oh? You don't mind going with Rev. Gordon, do you?"

"Fwela, is his heart white?"

On September 27, Ota left the zoo for the Howard Colored Orphan Asylum. The *Times* noted that "The pygmy was glad to leave the zoological garden, and the authorities . . . equally happy to be rid of him." A few days later the paper published a letter from a sixty-seven-year-old Parisian woman who wanted to know if Ota was "in good condition," and if the zoo would "sell him to me not too dear as I am not rich."

When Ota Benga left the zoo on the twenty-seventh and crossed the Brooklyn Bridge with Verner, his name soon disappeared from the international press. There were no more letters sent from France, no more protests kindled in Yonkers and North Carolina. There was an end to crowds. Ota's tour of Manhattan's grand institutions had come to an end.

17

ORPHANS

> Moreover, all the customs and
> skills of the hunter-gatherer life are
> learned early in life and may leave
> an indelible imprint, making it ex-
> tremely difficult to acquire later in
> life the taste and even the necessary
> skills for a different condition. . .
>
> —Luigi Cavalli-Sforza,
> *African Pygmies*

Reverend James H. Gordon had distinguished himself from the outset in the contest over Ota Benga. It wasn't only that as head of the Howard Colored Orphan Asylum he had been in the unique position of being able to propose alternative accommodations for Ota. Gordon was also singled out by a gift for oratory. When, in the controversy, he put that gift in the service of a fundamentalist belief that humans were not descended from the apes and that Darwinism was an anti-Christian fraud, he and the other Baptist ministers were subject to ridicule on the editorial pages of the *New York Times*. Gordon's persistent, eloquent appeals for Ota's release on grounds of justice and fair play were not so easily dismissed.

The approach he chose was adversarial without being antagonistic. The following statement to the press was typical: "As far as I can see, this little black man is capable of development. Indeed he seems bright to me. We think we can do better for him than make an exhibition of him." Gordon's aim was not to humiliate whites or make it more difficult for them to concede, it was to avoid what he perceived as the humiliation of blacks.

Gordon's activism was very much in the spirit of his predecessors at the Howard Asylum. The previous superintendent had been William F. Johnson, a charismatic blind preacher who headed the institution from 1870 to 1902. Johnson had been one of the city's leading voices first against slavery and then, after the Civil War, for equal rights. In 1874, when his son was turned away from an all-white Brooklyn school, Johnson helped initiate a campaign to integrate the schools. The struggle reached fruition twenty-six years later, in 1900, when Governor Theodore Roosevelt signed a state law barring discrimination on grounds of race in public schools.

Integration, however, did not apply to orphanages. The Howard Colored Orphan Asylum was one of only two New York City orphanages that accepted black children (and therefore, by the rules of segregation, only black children). The other, the New York Colored Orphan Asylum, had been looted and burned during the Civil War.

In what may well have been the low point of the anti-draft riots that shook the city in 1863, whites surrounded the building housing the New York Colored Orphan Asylum on Forty-third Street and Fifth Avenue, chanting slogans such as "Burn the niggers' nest," and "Down with the niggers." The rioters blamed the war and the draft on blacks and did not bother to distinguish adults from children when it came to vengeance.

In the event, close to 250 children were secreted out a back way shortly before the mob burst in. The rioters made off with what they could carry, smashed what they couldn't (or tossed it out a window—one ten-year-old bystander was killed by a falling bureau), and finally set fire to the building. Firemen arriving at the scene were threatened and prevented from taking action. Their water hoses cut in two, there was nothing they could do to keep the orphanage from burning to the ground.

What the sack of the orphanage said about race relations was echoed by the trial that followed. Of the fourteen men caught and charged in connection with the attack, all, for one reason or another, were released.

By 1867, the asylum had relocated, under white Quaker leadership, to suburban 143rd Street and Amsterdam Avenue, but conditions brought on by the Civil War had made a single orphanage insufficient to the needs of New York's black community. The city's black population increased when ex-slaves migrated north. The number of homeless black children increased disproportionately when some mothers, learning they would not otherwise be hired as domestics, saw no way to survive except by abandoning their sons and daughters.

Answering the need for intervention, Sarah Tillman, a black woman, began welcoming this population of homeless children into her Manhattan home in 1866. Members of the city's black clergy came to her assistance, and they, in turn, enlisted the support of General Oliver Howard (the same man who lent his name to Howard University), head of the Freedman's Bureau. Soon wagonloads of children were on their way to the larger, more permanent address in Brooklyn where the Howard Asylum put down roots.

Like the New York Colored Orphan Asylum, the Howard Asylum was a charitable institution devoted to the care of black children. But Howard, unlike the New York Asylum, was a black institution in the full sense. The New York Asylum was run and largely staffed and financed by whites. Howard, on the other hand, strove to remain black-operated and staffed. It was located in the black community. It was a part of that community and totally aligned with its concerns.

This may have had advantages for the children. There were those—W. E. B. Du Bois among them—who argued that Howard offered its wards the kind of compassion and education a white-run institution could never hope to provide. It was also true that Howard's independence incurred certain disadvantages, chief among them added difficulty in securing funds.

Besides its being black, this was another major difference between Howard and the American institutions Ota had previously known. Unlike the St. Louis Fair, the museum, and the zoo, Howard made no loud boasts about America's place in the world. It was not born of imperial largesse, nor was it built to be the biggest of its kind. The Howard Asylum engaged in a constant struggle to stay afloat.

This did not prevent Gordon from sharing in the high hopes and optimism of the age. Gordon believed that Howard would one day be the northern equivalent of Tuskegee Institute, turning out, like Booker T. Washington's school, skilled, highly employable workers for agriculture and industry. Some industrial training was already available at the Brooklyn facility by 1906, and Gordon looked forward to making increased use of land purchased that year in the agricultural community of Smithtown, Long Island. He also hoped to boost Howard's educational offering beyond the primary-school level.

It was with obvious pride in what Howard had achieved in forty years and in what it might yet accomplish that Gordon promoted the institution during the controversy with Hornaday. It was with the same pride that the preacher met reporters at his door and invited them in to see Ota Benga.

Ota had arrived Thursday, September 27, wearing the white suit that had been bought for him at the American Museum of Natural History and the canvas shoes he had been given, in front of hundreds of spectators, at the New York Zoological Park. He entered the orphanage without his bow and arrow, however. Verner had convinced him there would be no hunting at all in Brooklyn. Reporters were not far behind.

Rev. Gordon felt he had something to prove by Ota. If he could teach Ota to read, write, and speak some English, if he could show him the rudiments of what was considered civilized behavior, that would speak volumes for blacks. To take a veteran of the Monkey House and turn him into a citizen worthy of respect would be an incomparable argument for the respect due the entire race.

Failure would only reinforce prejudice. But Gordon saw no reason to presume failure; there was nothing about the little man to indicate it. That he was bright there was no question; Gordon said you could see it in his eyes, and he responded immediately to instruction. He was immensely curious and loved going for walks around the neighborhood attended by a member of the staff.

On those walks he looked into everything. Sometimes there was a startling ferocity to it. It seemed as if he wanted to take this entire world apart with his hands, eyes, and mind to see what was inside, to find out how it held together. The other day it was nails, how nails held boards together, how they kept many-storied buildings standing.

Gordon had seen him laughing and pointing at a bent nail he held in his hand, nodding his head from side to side and singing out repeatedly, as if he had just surprised some deep-delved secret, something to the tune of "*Muzungu.*" Then he had done a little dance and held the nail aloft, as if in that single nail he had got to the bottom of New York City and found the means to set up his own version any time he chose.

Gordon explained to reporters that he bore no grudge against Professor Verner. The professor had done the best he could, according to his lights, for Ota Benga. Gordon sketched out the line of development he proposed to use in educating Ota, saying it was first of all necessary to respect the pygmy's manhood. Instead of sleeping in the dormitory with the children, he had his own room and could smoke there whenever he pleased. Nor would he eat in the mess with children; he would eat with the cooks, who had taken a liking to him.

Gordon produced a piece of paper on which there was scrawled in pencil the name "Ota Benga." It was Ota's first written work and had been composed by Gordon placing his hand over Ota's and guiding it through the characters as they pronounced the syllables. Ota entered the reception room. He required no introduction to the journalists. "How de do, how de do," he said to each of them in what, according to the *Times* were "accents so startlingly positive that one is tempted to make a further remark." When the reporter filled his pipe he found the pygmy to be responsive: "Ota Benga grinned and also drew out a pipe. 'Baccy?' he chuckled, and gratefully pocketed an extra pipeful."

Gordon told the reporters the story of Ota's first Howard Asylum pipeful. Professor Verner had still been on the premises, and when a woman came into view was able to communicate a fine point of etiquette in the pygmy's native tongue, namely that it was frowned upon in this country to smoke in the presence of a lady. It was astonishing how quickly he put out his pipe and hid it from view.

Gordon walked the reporters to the door and Ota saw them off with his all-purpose, "How de do." Gordon kept his real feelings about that first pipe to himself. He had been disturbed at the keenness of the look Ota Benga gave the woman as she passed. And he had remarked how Ota chatted with some of the fourteen-, thirteen-, and twelve-year-old girls at the orphanage. It didn't seem to matter that his English was still virtually nonexistent and that all his charm was exerted in a foreign tongue. The girls responded, giggled, and were tickled by his approach.

*   *   *

With the articles covering his first few days at the Howard
Colored Orphan Asylum, Ota Benga began to fade from the
press. There were occasional summary pieces in which tales of
cannibalism were jovially resurrected (as in an earlier piece
comparing Ota's first wife, slaughtered by the Force Publique,
to spareribs). Verner, who was settling in with Hattie on West
Fifty-seventh Street, spoke to reporters of his relationship with
Ota before the forest dweller rose to Bronx Zoo fame.

"We were simply two friends," he said, "traveling together, until, for some inexplicable reason, New York's scientists and preachers began wrangling over him, and the peaceful
tenor of our ways was so ruthlessly disturbed." He hoped Ota
would survive "scientific investigation, reportorial examination and eleemosynary education," so as to "rejoin me on our
further travels and be happy in the sunshine of the Kasailand."

"I saved him from the pot," Verner concluded, "he saved
me from the poisoned darts, and we have been good friends for
a long time. I beg New York not to spoil him."

After this last spate of articles, Ota Benga retired from
public view. Not for another ten years would readers need to
trouble themselves over the final installments of his story.

He was hunting, that's how he saw it. He was hunting the
alphabet, those extraordinary small shapes that retain sound,
and he was hunting the sounds themselves, the words and the
pathways between them. When he slammed the erasers together to clean them, when he washed the white chalk off the
blackboard, when he stood up in class to pronounce "robin,"
"squirrel," "cook," "umbrella," he was hunting.

Now he was truly living among them, no longer visiting.
When would he leave? He didn't know. He knew only that he
would know, and that for now he was far from finished.

How would he leave? Fwela would contact him.

The children and staff of the orphanage spoke often about
slavery. Ota spoke of elephant hunts, and sometimes could be
provoked to sing a song of the forest, but he said nothing about
his parents, his wives and children. He hardly even spoke of
St. Louis. They asked him about the zoo. He told them, with
relish, about Dohong. The children of the orphanage helped
Ota learn to speak English.

Nearly alone among them he received no visitors. Where
was Fwela?

*   *   *

Verner was hunting as well, or rather hoping to be hunted and trying hard to get caught.

In the summer of 1906, King Leopold of Belgium summoned the New York millionaire Thomas Fortune Ryan to a meeting in Switzerland. It was part of his campaign to secure American support for his continued sole possession of the Congo Free State. The American Congo Lobby had done as well for Leopold as could be expected, but the king wanted the sort of protection that only became possible when millionaires banded together to protect their investments and mold public opinion.

Leopold wanted the shield of American capital. Ryan, a Catholic, wanted the chance to make a further fortune and to negotiate, sign contracts, and be associated with royalty. Builder of New York's IRT, Ryan also happened to be Verner's employer. When he returned to New York City he contacted associates of past business deals, men like the Guggenheims, Bernard Baruch, and Rhode Island's Senator Aldrich.

These men had a sudden need for African expertise. Verner's closest approach to New York's men of their station consisted of the fact that the IRT post to which he was assigned lay directly under Wall Street. From there, as he put it, from "the ticket window at the mouth of Wall Street the Morgan house [across the way] looked bigger than Olympus."

Now the whereabouts of Verner the Africanist, author of so many articles, were investigated. Still in Ryan's employ, he was shown one day into a Wall Street office high above the ticket window. The collection of African objects Bumpus had scorned (the gigantic beetles, the magnificent tusks) were bought by Ryan at a far higher price than Verner had ever dared ask from the museum. Now there was a proper use for the orchids he had saved from his last trip to Africa; some were delivered personally to J. P. Morgan, the others given to Solomon Guggenheim, both these men being deserving and "well known patrons," as he put it, "of the orchid world."

Ota was willing to learn English; he was not willing to unlearn the ways of the forest. He was willing to study the beliefs of the *muzungu*; he was not engaged in forgetting his own. What it came down to was a test of wills, or rather forest stealth versus a four-square Baptist approach.

Ota looked at the girls at the orphanage turning into

women. Rev. Gordon saw him looking, and Ota knew that Gordon saw. It was a contest carried out in silence.

Gordon gathered his staff together and told them to be careful, though he didn't say of what exactly. The staff gathered the girls, passed on the superintendent's cryptic message, and everyone became extremely careful. It led to an overall atmosphere of tension, a general alert.

Nevertheless an incident took place between Ota and a young woman named Creola. The incident was hushed up, but it was thought better if Ota Benga spent as much time as possible at the Howard Asylum's rural facilities, under Long Island skies, away from Brooklyn, miles from Creola.

Of all the wealthy men with whom he now came in frequent contact, Verner gravitated most to Bernard Baruch. He needed an adviser, protector, and confidant. Baruch—Jewish, City College–educated but South Carolina–born—was his man.

Baruch's father had been a surgeon in the Confederate army and, afterward, as ardent an advocate for the return of white rule as any in the Verner clan. (One of Bernard Baruch's earliest memories, like Verner's, was of being part of the crowds cheering the end of Reconstruction in 1876.) The family had gone north in 1881 when Bernard, three years Verner's senior, was eleven. The move had to do not only with a desire to escape the devastated region, but also with a duel in which Baruch's father served as a second.

In the aftermath of the duel it didn't help that the Baruchs were Jewish; it certainly didn't help that the man Baruch's father seconded was far less popular than the one who lay on the ground with a bullet in his heart. Next day men on horseback showed up at Dr. Baruch's office. They left, but it was clear to Dr. Baruch they would come again, and when they came it would be at night, and there would be white sheets and burning crosses. Lynch law was rife; Dr. Baruch needed no further prompting to take the family north.

It wasn't too long after graduating from City College that Dr. Baruch's son discovered his calling—stockmarket speculation—and his metier—that of being a millionaire.

He and Verner had another thing in common besides being South Carolinians in New York, and that was rubber. Verner touted himself as expert in the growing and gathering of Congo rubber. He knew the men, the plants, and the conditions of their interaction. He knew firsthand about the Force Publique and understood, despite himself, why the Congolese product was referred to by E. D. Morel, Mark Twain, and by the Congolese themselves as "red rubber."

The New York investors, on the other hand, didn't want red rubber. If they were going to work with Leopold he was going to have to cut back on the bleeding and the mutilation of his laborers. They wanted to share in the king's wealth, not his infamy. Verner was prepared to recommend to Leopold in private that other forms of labor should be considered, if not on grounds of morality, than on those of efficiency—starving men were resentful and not the best workers.

Baruch had become involved with rubber in 1904 on behalf of the Guggenheims, with whom he often allied himself. He traveled to Mexico in that year to investigate the possibility of Mexican rubber meeting burgeoning world demand. In early 1907, he sent Verner to Mexico to study the several-million-acre farm he had established to grow guayule, the Mexican rubber plant.

The demands of the new work were unremitting. The trip to Mexico preempted Verner's giving a lecture at Harvard to which, as he wrote a friend, he "had been looking forward practically all my life," but work for the American Congo Company, or A.C.C., one of the two corporations the New York investors formed with Leopold, was well compensated. Verner started at ten thousand dollars a year plus stock considerations.

After Mexico, Verner was in Europe in March for meetings with Leopold who, at seventy-one, had capitulated to his phobias and peculiar affections. He was massive and found it hard to get around, his beard was swathed a good part of the day, and he doted on a mistress young enough to be a granddaughter who scolded him as she pleased.

When it came to the Congo, he was the same wily Leopold who had emerged from the Berlin Conference with his African prize twenty-two years ago, and who had seemed so sincere and benevolent to Reverends Lapsley and Sheppard on their way to the Free State in 1890. Verner's contention on behalf of the New York millionaires was "that trade and not force was the way to the Africans's heart." Leopold agreed to put no obstacles in the way of the American Congo Company instituting labor reforms on its estates.

Agreement in hand, Verner was off to the Kasai. A lifetime's ambition had come to pass. He was no longer Fwela, or leader, only to the Africans—Ndombe, Joka, and the Batwa—he was soon to see again; he was a leader as well among the whites. But before leaving Europe behind it occurred to him he had forgotten something. He was supposed to be traveling to Africa with Ota Benga. For so long, for all of his adult life, he had sat anxiously outside the doors to the great world. When he entered it was on tiptoe. By the time he began to put down his feet with some confidence he realized he had left his friend in Brooklyn.

As it turned out, Ota had developed his own ideas about when he wanted to return. By the time Verner contacted him he had decided now was not the time; Fwela would have to wait.

Verner got in touch with Ota through his wife, who had returned to the South after her husband's departure. Hattie contacted a business associate of his, an A. T. Wilkinson, who, on April 10, 1907, wrote to Rev. Gordon at the Howard Asylum. Hattie was suddenly thrust into the position of taking responsibility for her husband, and of bearing embarrassment for him. She attempted to excuse him on the grounds that he had been "so pressed with business immediately before his departure, it is quite possible that he neglected to see you about the matter."

A week later Wilkinson reported to Hattie on Gordon's response, as transmitted in a phone conversation:

> He says that Ota Benga has expressed a desire to stay in this country, and that as he considers him capable of judging for himself what is best, he thinks that his wishes in regard to the matter should be complied with. I told him that Dr. Verner felt responsible for him, as he was the means of his coming here, and that I would like to hear from Ota Benga himself to this effect. He said that he would have Ota Benga write me a letter, which I will foreword either to you or to Dr. Verner, as you desire.

The letter to which Gordon refers has not survived. Nor has any other example of Ota's written work.

In October, 1908, the efforts of men like Morel, Arthur Conan Doyle, and Roger Casement bore fruit. Leopold was compelled to cede his crown colony to the Belgian Parliament. The Congo Free State ceased to be; the Belgian Congo was born in its stead. The changeover did not guarantee an immediate end to massacres and forced labor. Leopold's critics continued to monitor the new regime, but the defeat for Leopold was a defeat for Verner as well. The New York investors paying his salary would not extend themselves on behalf of a man tainted by association with the discredited regime. There was also some hint of scandal—alleged by the Belgians, denied by Verner—in connection with his work for the A. C. C., but in the end it boiled down to a decision by the millionaires: if the Belgians didn't want him around they could see no reason to keep him.

Less than a year after accepting the job in the Kasai with the excellent pay and the unlimited prospects, he was back in South Carolina, unemployed. "Mr. Baruch told me . . . the BELGIANS THOUGHT I KNEW TOO MUCH," Verner wrote in February 1909, as he tried to come to terms with the shattering of all his hopes. Bernard Baruch offered him that precious thing—justification in the face of defeat. It wasn't his fault, he did his job only too well, the Belgians could not abide him for that very reason. He had been too intimately involved, privy too long. When he asked them to make changes, they knew he knew whereof he spoke.

Verner's letters from this period strike a plaintive note. He had bowed from the waist like a cavalier when presenting orchids to J. P. Morgan. He had met with a king in a king's chamber. He had been exposed for a while to the doings of some of the world's most powerful men. Now he was reduced to listing his abilities as follows to a prospective employer: he could do "Clerical work, accounts, type-writing, book-keeping . . . railway work."

Verner did not take one course of action that might have offered satisfaction. He had been fired for knowing too much, yet he refused to divulge what it was that he knew. He turned his reticence into a point of honor, boasting of his loyalty to the very men who had dismissed him. A publisher approached him with an opportunity "to enter the lists against King Leopold." Verner "steadfastly refused" the chance, although the "ammunition" he had was certain to "create a sensation all over Europe and America."

He stayed in South Carolina, advertising himself from

New York City to Chicago as skilled and employable. Some of his letters allude to a new scheme—never completely divulged—calculated to strike once again at the vital interests of the New York millionaires. He dreamed of a return to grace, an invitation back into the great world he had lost.

The Smithtown/Kings Park area of Long Island was first singled out to become a haven for havens—for asylums, orphanages, old-age homes, a Christian community, a Jewish farming collective—by William A. Muhlenberg. An evangelical Episcopal priest, Muhlenberg had earlier founded St. Lukes Hospital in Manhattan. He opened the St. Johnland Christian Colony on Long Island in 1864. With its utopian aspirations, St. Johnland included cottages, an orphanage, a church, a foundry, and a farm.

A railroad station was built to accommodate St. Johnland in 1872, and in 1905, drawn by one of Long Island's oldest synagogues, the Jewish Agricultural and Industrial Society (JAIS) bought land in the area. The JAIS was funded by the Austrian railroad magnate Baron de Hirsch. (The Rothschilds funded agricultural settlements in Palestine; de Hirsch funded them elsewhere in a range of territories extending from New Jersey to Argentina.)

The Howard Colored Orphan Asylum joined the other institutions around Smithtown in 1906. There was initial concern that residents would resent the intrusion of a black population. This did not turn out to be the case. One of Howard's preferred methods of training was to indenture its wards to local farms. This arrangement made cheap agricultural labor available. Accordingly, Howard's Annual Report for 1906–07 states, "We are assured by many of the residents of St. James that they do not consider our Asylum a menace to the community, but rather a helpful institution . . . "

By 1910 the Jewish experiment in Long Island agriculture was drawing to a close. Most Jewish immigrants preferred taking their chances in the city to raising poultry and growing potatoes, carrots, and beets in Smithtown. The JAIS put its lands up for sale. The Howard Asylum bought them all, except for a small plot that remained a Jewish cemetery, and black orphans replaced Jewish immigrants on land known locally as Indian Head.

The Long Island branch of Kings County Hospital opened

in the Smithtown area in 1885 and quickly became one of the area's leading employers. In 1907 the Brooklyn Home for Children, a white orphanage formed to rescue children before "habits of vice become in them hopelessly inveterate," set up nearby Long Island facilities.

Baseball brought members of these varied institutions together in Long Island. The umpire spoke Yiddish and was trying to master English, one team consisted of white orphans, the other of black orphans, there was a pygmy prancing off first base threatening to steal second. The makeshift stands held mental patients, inmates of the Long Island branch of Brooklyn's Kings County Hospital. Every now and then one of them broke away from staff, hurtled toward the field, and stormed around the basepaths.

There was no doubt that Ota brought speed and excitement to the Howard nine, but his antics on the basepaths tended to bring pandemonium down from the stands. After he slid into second, three of the inmates of Kings County's open air ward got away from attendants and slid into second too.

When Verner at last got a job it wasn't because of rubber or diamonds. It had nothing to do with King Leopold, Thomas Fortune Ryan, or Bernard Baruch. Nor did it pertain to typing, clerking, or bookkeeping. In a sense it was mosquitoes that got him his new position, anopheles mosquitoes and the parasites they had deposited in his blood.

The Panama Canal was being built in an environment rife with malaria. Verner's long years of experience with the disease won him a position as a medical officer in the Isthmus of Panama. It was there, while working for Colonel W. C. Gorgas, that he received a letter from Reverend Gordon.

Gordon admitted sadly to Verner that the educational experiment had failed. There had been high hopes of Ota finding refuge at Howard, but Ota remained a nomad. "His age," concluded Gordon, "was against his development. It was simply impossible to put him in a class to receive instructions, from a literary point, that would be of any advantage to him."

After Ota's removal to Long Island there had been no more intimacies, at least none that came to light, of the sort that had arisen between Ota and Creola. (Gordon once heard Ota describe relations of this sort as "rejoicings.") On the other hand, there had been a gradual loosening of all bonds between Ota and the orphanage. For a while he had worked part-time and attended classes part-time. He had spent one semester at the Baptist Seminary in Lynchburg, Virginia. When he returned, his English vocabulary was enriched, though he drawled, and he had become a Christian, having requested baptism.

Gordon had difficulty understanding the point of the conversion. It was different from conversions he had seen before in that it hardly seemed to affect the convert's behavior. If anything, Ota's relations with the Howard Asylum became still more tenuous. He resumed working as a laborer on the Obery farm for ten dollars a month, plus room and board, and soon ceased to attend classes.

He drifted back to the orphanage for special events. If there was a baseball game or barbecue, Ota could be counted on to appear. It was at these reunions that Gordon could gauge just how popular Ota had become among the boys. Ota's appeal ran counter to Gordon's own prestige. Gordon stood for certain clearly specified values, Ota for a vaguer, saucier alternative. The example Ota set undermined the orphanage. Older boys, especially, were tempted to follow his footsteps and drop out of school.

Gordon felt compelled to sever formal ties between Howard and Ota Benga. The institution would no longer take responsibility; so he told Verner in the letter sent to Panama in the last days of 1909. Soon there was more news. Ota had approached Gordon on his own. He wanted to return down south to the seminary in Lynchburg. He said it wasn't so cold down there and he had made some friends.

Gordon had no reason to insist on keeping Ota on Long Island. There was a well-established black community in Lynchburg, which Smithtown lacked. All in all, it seemed to Gordon that Ota's chances were better there. He helped make the arrangements and in January 1910, Ota left the New York City area for good.

"Goodbye pilgrim," said Gordon as he saw him off by train.

18

OTTO BINGO

"There is darkness all around us;
but if darkness *is*
and the darkness is of the forest,
then the darkness must be good."
—Colin Turnbull,
The Forest People

The countryside around Lynchburg was full of wildlife, and Ota came to know the woodlands as intimately as if they were his home, which in a sense they became. There were deer, turkey, rabbits, squirrels, and plenty of fish living in the streams. There were New World leaves, roots, and berries, which Ota tasted and brewed until he became conversant with their properties.

He gathered wild sassafras, and brought it to friends he had in town who would appreciate such a gift. He learned to brew dandelion wine. And every now and then he could be seen strolling back into town smoking bangi.

Ota arrived at a cultural compromise in his Lynchburg years. He would honor the ways of the black *muzungu* (who in turn, he discovered, had to stick by certain rules laid down by the white *muzungu*), up to a certain point. Beyond that point he resurrected the traditional lifestyle of a pygmy hunter and gatherer, down to the smoking of bangi while relaxing around a campfire. He would read—that's what he had come to America to do—and attend classes at the Lynchburg Seminary now and again. Otherwise he would hunt. He might live and sleep in the town, but he spent as much time as possible in the woods.

He constructed a new bow and carved new arrows, not like the one Geronimo had given him, with a stone arrowhead, but pygmy fashion, with just a sharpened wooden tip. He was not a traditionalist in all things. An excellent marksman when it came to Western weapons, he often brought a rifle or shotgun with him to the woods. When he chose to use the bow and arrow instead it was for a reason—miss with a gun and the animal would be long gone, miss with an arrow and you could have another try. This is the sort of advice Ota was likely to convey to his fellow hunters. Often he had companions with him in the woods.

In Africa the hunt enforces sociability on the forest dwellers. It compels them to work together, to overlook or laugh at tensions, to frown on noise. In Lynchburg, ten thousand miles away from home, Ota went some way toward recreating the traditional sociability and communalism of the hunt. The difference is that this, Ota's last hunting band, was not made up of peers. He was the only member of his age group, the only adult to be represented—all the rest were children. There was Chauncey Spencer, Anne and Edward Spencer's youngest boy, just four years old when Ota arrived in Lynchburg, and Hunter Hayes, son of Dr. Gregory W. Hayes, the seminary's president. Mrs. Josephine Anderson, the local grocer, often sent her son along as well. The band of hunters Ota led through Lynchburg's woods were boys from about five to eleven years old.

At the zoo, Ota had been teased by such children. His presence behind bars had been calculated to inflame them. They were inevitably driven wild when he charged the bars, wrestled with Dohong, bared his teeth. They jeered at him and he learned to jeer back. At the Howard Asylum, no longer separated from Ota by iron bars, the children admired him to such a degree that Rev. Gordon feared he would exert a subversive influence.

In Lynchburg black families entrusted their young to Ota's care. They felt their boys were secure with him. He taught them to hunt, fish, gather wild honey. Nearly eighty years later one elderly man recalled that when Ota strung a bow that was as long as Ota was tall, it sounded like Beethoven. Another spoke of Ota as having been a kind of hero, a "close relative," a pal.

Ota demonstrated the calls that would bring quail and wild turkey; he said it was better to draw game to you than to have to go out after it. He stood still on rocks above a stream, the spear in his hand poised for passing fish. Once a bear cub stumbled into one of his traps. Ota released it; it would surely find its mother, he explained.

The children felt safe when they were in the woods with him. If anything they found him overprotective, except in regard to gathering wild honey—there was no such thing as too much protection when it came to raiding hives. Ota was not the most sympathetic guide in this respect. A bee sting can feel catastrophic to a child, but Ota couldn't help himself, he thought bee stings were hilarious. Perhaps getting stung by a bee was a stock figure of pygmy humor, the forest equivalent of slipping on a banana peel.

Even on his hunting trips, Ota stayed within the terms of his compromise with Western ways. He wore trousers, pants, shoes. Early on in Lynchburg he had dental work done. Now even his teeth looked normal enough; it was no longer possible for him to flash his unnerving, sharp-toothed smile.

It was only on certain moonlit nights that he would drop the pretense and insist on doing things the right way, the forest way. Then he would smoke his bangi, build a fire, remove Western dress, put on a bark loincloth, and commence to sing the ageless songs of the forest.

The children were drawn to the ceremony and joined him in the dance. After watching Ota stoop and sway from a supple waist, they were eager to try it too, and were always more than welcome.

Ota's moonlight dances were not excuses for silliness, loudness, or any old gyrations. There was a right way to move, there was stillness and silence beneath the chant. There was energy and discipline all at once, even the suggestion of religion. When they asked, Ota told them this was how he had danced in Africa.

His African origins were not emphasized in Lynchburg. On the contrary, every effort was made to normalize and assimilate him. A dentist had capped his teeth. Even his name was smoothed into something less alien—Ota was transformed into Otto. He was now Otto Bingo in full, an unusual name to be sure, but not without a certain Southern plausibility. The name change visited upon so many immigrants at Ellis Island caught up with Ota in Virginia where he metamorphosed into Otto, Otto Bingo, the gentleman from New York.

It endowed him with an extra layer of experience. In addition to telling stories about Africa, he could be called upon to talk about New York City, a locale scarcely less exotic. The children heard about the Bronx Zoo, the keeper who prodded him to charge the bars, the bones scattered around the cage.

But he did not take them further into his story. He stopped short at the St. Louis Fair. The children heard nothing about the slaughter of his wife and children that preceded his first visit to America. They never became aware of Fwela, the white man who had bought him from the Baschilele for salt and some few yards of cloth.

Much remained to be contemplated in private, when Ota hunted alone half a world away from the forest where he had begun.

In trying to arrive at an overview of Ota's years in Lynchburg, it can be argued that the town proper was essential, the days and nights in the woods nothing more than recreational activity. Or it can be maintained the hunting was of the essence and the time spent in town secondary, like the days African pygmies spend repairing the thatch roofs of their farmer neighbors or playing drums in exchange for yams, bananas, palm wine.

How important was rabbit to his diet when compared to the fried chicken he got from Mrs. Anderson? Which played a greater role in his recreation, the bangi gathered in the woods, or the bourbon he sipped with Edward Spencer in the garden?

Such questions miss the point. What stands out about both sides of Ota's Lynchburg life—countryside and town—is its unity. Both sides display the persistence of traditional pygmy ways and point to an individual determined to translate an African lifestyle into an American context. Ota was still the nomad, avoiding routine, regularity, and any suggestion of a settled, indoor life.

When contrasted with the usual immigrant experience it seems that Ota, although alone, gave less ground. It can only be because he never intended to remain abroad. The goal remained what it had been since the day he threatened suicide unless Verner took him back to America. He intended to stay as long as he considered necessary, and then to go home. Of course, none but Ota could say when that point of saturation would be attained. And no one could say if, at that point, return would still be possible.

Home itself had become problematic. What was home for Ota Benga? All the members of his hunting band had been killed or sold into slavery; as proven by his lack of attempt to restore contact with them. Was home, then, the confederacy of peoples centered on King Ndombe? Was it a circular hut among the Batwa, not far from the village where he had first been hailed as witch boy?

Home had become indistinct. Perhaps that is why he refused Verner's invitation to leave in favor of prolonging his stay abroad. But even if, as a specific point on the map, home was indefinite, the concept remained crucial to him. Home was never anything other than the African forest, the world of the hunt, the fully elaborated society—men, women, children, elders—of his own kind. In America Ota carried fragments of that society with him, as pygmy women carry embers of a campfire from one campsite to the next.

Like them he was between campsites. In the meantime the image of home allowed him to stay abroad. He could adapt so well, negotiate so delicate a truce with alien ways, because he was sure the exercise was only temporary and because it remained his choice.

Tobacco growing and processing was Lynchburg's leading source of employment, to the degree that when the tobacco industry slumped or contracted, black population decreased. Given the weight of the industry in the local economy, it is not surprising that Ota put in a stint at a Lynchburg tobacco factory. Factory work was temporary, however. For the most part he preferred odd jobs, helping out with Mrs. Anderson's chickens in return for room and board, or doing chores on the grounds of the seminary.

The seminary was a center of Ota's life in Lynchburg, as it was for many blacks in the town. It provided him with shelter when he needed it, put him in contact with men and women who became his friends, and offered him food when he was not dining out on rabbit. It was to the seminary—its president, Dr. Gregory W. Hayes, and some of its staff—that Ota returned when he abandoned life in the North.

His face was familiar on campus. He attended elementary

school classes and liked to work the ropes that rang the bells in the campus tower. If the hunt was bad or he felt like eating indoors Ota was assured cafeteria fare. The seminary made Ota welcome, as it had John Chilembwe, an African who had attended classes there some ten years before Ota arrived.

The Lynchburg (or Virginia) Seminary, opened in 1890, was an unusual institution and only partly what it seemed: an industrial training school modeled after Booker T. Washington's Tuskegee, and obedient to his blueprint for black education as announced in his speech—later known as the Atlanta Compromise—made at the Atlanta Exposition of 1895. Under these guidelines, the seminary would offer no Latin, Greek, or humanities but rather the industrial arts and religious education.

This was a mask the Lynchburg Seminary wore, for instance, when representatives of the white Baptist Convention toured the premises. The white Baptists expected to see a lot of sewing machines, ironing boards, hammers and nails, saws, screwdrivers, and other implements of manual labor on campus, and so they did. After each such inspection they recommended the Baptist Convention pay the salary of the seminary's president for another year.

When the inspectors left, the seminary revealed a very different face. Some of the ironing boards and hammers remained, but out from hiding places in cellars and closets came history books, grammars and dictionaries, and works of literature.

The institution was once caught in this act of intellectual refurbishing, and President Hayes was threatened with the loss of white-sponsored salary. But Hayes refused to stop teaching the taboo subjects. Even at the cost of his subsidy he remained committed to the liberal arts.

With the Tuskegee camouflage peeled away, it seems clear Hayes and his supporters were much closer to Washington's rival, W.E.B. Du Bois. Educated at Harvard and in Europe, Du Bois rejected the notion that black schooling should be purely vocational. In 1909, the year of its formation, he lent his talents as scholar and writer to the NAACP. The NAACP once and for all disavowed the concessions Washington had made in 1895. It stood for the opposite approach—black advancement was possible only with full restoration of civil rights. Though it was not feasible in Virginia to agitate too openly or aggressively for such a position, still it can be seen where the real sympathies of the Lynchburg Seminary's staff and students lay.

There was yet another level to the seminary's political identity. When John Chilembwe, a native of Nyasaland, came to the United States in 1898, he chose to study in Lynchburg. A member of the Negro National Baptist Convention—the same organization that battled to free Ota from the zoo—brought Chilembwe to Lynchburg and introduced him personally to Pres. Hayes. The school, then, was already known for its sympathy for Africa and Africans, and believed, at the very least, in a missionary connection.

While studying at Lynchburg, Chilembwe, the future leader of a revolt against British colonial rule, organized an African Development Society that enlisted the support of Dr. Hayes and other staff members, as well as the participation of blacks throughout Virginia and in Washington, D.C. The prospectus of the African Development Society called for Americans blacks to aid in the "development of the rich resources" of Africa and to assist in the "founding of settlements" there. The seminary, then, subscribed to the philosophy of pan-Africanism, the belief that black life in Africa and America were intimately related, that blacks could take responsibility for each other across national boundaries and act as one on the world stage.

The idea of a return to Africa took another curious turn at Lynchburg. It had served, earlier, as a foundation for American missionary activity. For public figures like Alabama's Senator Morgan, it raised hopes of a decisive solution to the problem of the ex-slaves and their descendants: put an end to racial conflict (or the possibility of racial harmony) by sending blacks to Africa. The African Development Society showed the idea could be appropriated by blacks for their own purposes. Members felt that though they lived in America they were rooted in Africa. They were citizens, spiritually at least, of both continents.

With this sort of thinking prevalent on campus, it is not surprising that the Lynchburg Seminary was prepared, so far as it could be, for Ota Benga, and ready to embrace him.

Ota was a regular guest at the home of Dr. Hayes and often slept in the hayloft of his carriage house when the weather was warm. But no one in town was more hospitable to Ota than Anne Spencer. Born in 1882 and just about the same age as Ota, she graduated from the seminary and later taught there. Anne had attended classes at the same time as John Chilembwe and noted the African's "general unlikeness to the other students." She recalled his bearing, his claims for royal ancestry, his pride.

Ota was the second native-born African she came to know, and he presented himself rather differently. He brought wild sassafras to her garden and spoke not about royal origins but herbs and flowers. This alone would have been sufficient to engage her attention. The garden had been a center of her life since she and her husband Edward moved into the house on Pierce Street in 1903.

In addition to the love of flowers, Anne, ever since her mother had cured her of measles with a poultice of herbs that baffled the doctor, was a believer in the healing properties of plants. These were Ota's specialties. If she pricked a finger on a rose thorn or sprained an ankle he would be sure to know the right combination of herbs to staunch the bleeding or ease the pain.

Anne had some Indian blood on her father's side and sometimes dressed to accentuate it. She also had some white ancestry. On her mother's side she was descended from slaves who had worked for the Reynolds family, plantation owners at the time and tobacco magnates later. The master had taken the accustomed liberties with his female slaves, as evidenced by Anne's light skin.

The violations that had taken place on her mother's side of the family were a sensitive point. Anne much preferred to don a headband and a buckskin jacket, clothing that put Ota in mind of an Apache warrior he had known.

"Geronimo, look me like Geronimo," he would say to her. She set to work prying out the story of Ota's meeting with Geronimo, grammatical errors and all, grammatical errors especially—one of the things she liked best about Ota's conversation were the alterations and variations he imposed on normal English usage. A poet whose work brought her to the attention of the country's leading black writers and intellectuals, Anne Spencer had an ear for language.

Lynchburg was a frequent stopover point for travelers heading north or returning south, and the Spencer home frequently welcomed W. E. B. Du Bois, for instance, on his way to or from Atlanta. Booker T. Washington was known to pay a visit now and again, though never at the same time as his rival. Washington avoided Du Bois in Lynchburg as assiduously as he avoided him at conferences held in London.

In their opinions about Africa, the men diverged as widely as they did about most things. The question of the Congo was one of the few where their opinions converged. Each criticized Leopold's rule and was wary of his Belgian successors. Ota met both men at the Spencer home.

The house had a piano in the front room, and Ota listened while Anne played ragtime, some classical pieces, blues. Above the bookshelves in the study there were original wanted posters for runaway slaves—descriptions, pictures, and rewards.

Then there was the garden, already celebrated in the town, and the little garden house where Anne wrote poetry, as, in later years, "White Things," touched off by tales of a Georgia lynching:

> Most things are colorful things—the
> sky, earth, and sea.
> Black men are most men; but the
> white are free!

There would be readings aloud in the garden, Anne usually, but possibly Edward, reading to the children. To Ota, this was interesting. It was their way of storytelling, stories passed through books.

Never, though, for too long, even in the haven of the garden, could they stay away from talk of race: a lynching a county over; the tobacco factory suddenly refusing black labor; the new law about where blacks could sit on buses—blacks in back or not at all.

Anne preferred not to go out of her way to court her own anger. Feelings of inferiority on grounds of race never had a chance of poisoning her image of herself. She would live her life as best she could as if the aberrant notion had never been conceived. "I write about some of the things I love," she replied when asked why Jim Crow played so little a role in her published work, "but have no civilized articulation for the things I hate."

Back of the bus? She'd see about that. Would the bus driver dare throw her off? If he did she answered back enough to turn his white face red. She'd hitch or walk instead. There were other means of transport than by back of bus. It was considered scandalous to see a woman in her Sunday best stick her thumb out and load her children, and perhaps Ota as well, onto the first haycart that came along. She was raising rebels.

Her husband supported her raids on Jim Crow. He was the town's parcel postman, a job won by underbidding the competition. Dark-skinned as he was, a white man on his route objected to his delivering parcels by the front door: he was black first, a postman second, said the customer, and since when should a black man approach a white man's house by any other route than through the back door? Edward Spencer just stopped delivering there. The man had to go to the post office for his parcels.

There were some battles you could win, at least some rules you could bend a little. Anne and Edward Spencer showed Ota that. There were some rules, however, you could do nothing more than mock, leaving moot the question of who had won and who had been humiliated.

Once, Ota climbed aboard the bus without any money. "Owe me a nickel," said the driver. Ota offered him an egg instead. The driver refused. By its ears Ota pulled a rabbit out of a sack he'd carried with him. The driver hesitated. The passengers howled.

One grumbled, "Take the goddamned rabbit, Earl, and let's get going."

Another: "Hold out for a piglet."

Another: "Drive."

Soap Suds Bottom, Dog Alley, Pool's College, Pigeon Box— these were the town's black nightspots, as listed by the police. Not all the dealings that took place there were legitimate. Razor blades often made midnight appearances, guns were not unknown. Some of the regulars of Pool's College were wanted by the law. These were not establishments where Ota—Otto— might meet white people. Not at the seminary, not at the Spencers', not, in all likelihood, while stalking deer or turkey in the woods. But it could and did happen, at the market and downtown.

Some whites took an interest in him. One tall, stooped fellow with spectacles wanted to know where he was from to start with, and how he had wound up at Lynchburg. He had heard Otto was shy, especially with white folks, and was surprised when he so willingly told his story, unfortunately the only extant version of many such tales Ota doled out in exchange for root beer and sandwiches.

He recounted how, as a seventeen-year-old, he and his companions had been playing in his native land when a band of ferocious Englishmen descended on them. His friends were speedy and got away but he was a slowpoke and had to pay the price. The English loved to travel, and needed a servant. They kidnapped him and took him around the world a number of times, then tired of him. As they were in New York City at the time, they brought him directly to the zoo.

Ota went on to reminisce about Gunda, the banker elephant, and Dohong, the monkey—his neighbors in the Bronx. The rest had seemed plausible enough, but this part was hard for the tall, bespectacled man to take. A pygmy in a zoo? Living side by side with monkeys? Impossible. Ota insisted.

He was sent away to Virginia only because his hunger got the best of him, he said, taking another bite of his sandwich. They caught him sneaking up on Gunda with a spear. That's when they threw him out of the Bronx Zoo on his ear, and someone brought him down to Lynchburg.

Verner had many versions of how he first met Ota and was always ready to compose another. Ota showed he was just as good at dining out on tales of how he first came to America.

Ota thought of Fwela often, but once he moved to Lynchburg there is no evidence he ever heard from S. P. Verner again. Verner was trying to forget his abortive African career in Panama. Ota was trying to create a scale model of Africa in Virginia.

He dreamed. He was at the Museum of Natural History again. The man at his side was Fwela. It was as if they had never been apart. They walked by mastodon and brontosaur. Ota climbed a meteor. They continued by the fishing nets of the Kwakiutl Indians.

Verner was explaining how objects came to the museum, how rich men or explorers donated them. This gave Ota a surprising idea. He too would make a donation: He would donate himself. Would he not then be a rich man? No one else had yet donated a pygmy to the museum. Besides, he had nothing else to donate. He would give himself to Bumpus. Bumpus would put him to sleep behind the panels of his own glass case like a stuffed animal.

Ota continued to explain his idea but Fwela had already disappeared from the dream. When he woke, he realized there had been chanting throughout the dream, the interlocking chanting of his people, the grieving rounds of death.

He built a fire.

He had waking dreams as well. Bangi was like dreaming. There were places in the woods where the plant grew, places where he had buried its seeds. He'd smoke and imagine, in the woods of Lynchburg, he heard drumming ten thousand miles away. Forest to forest, tree to tree. He thought about his friends in Lynchburg, Anne and Edward Spencer, the children, Professor Hayes. Their great-grandparents had been brought against their will but now they themselves belonged here; he did not.

1916.

War was raging and he knew it. It was what they talked about. There were pictures in the paper. Belgian arms were insignificant in Europe. In Africa, though, they fought the Germans off. The war King Leopold dreaded was being fought throughout the Congo. There were photographs of thatch huts burning, huge trees lying on their sides.

March 20, 1916, he built a fire. Five o'clock in the afternoon.

Somehow he had stopped. There was no more going forward. The only way was back. It was as if all at once there were no more animals in the forest, just wind blowing in the leaves. It was sudden and absolute. Ota knew he was finished here. Whatever it was he had come for, he already had. There was nothing else to take.

He began to check the price of steamship tickets. It filled him with despair that he could not come close to buying one.

He no longer knew how to find Fwela, and Fwela had not come.

Hunters do not, as a rule, worry about the future. It would be folly. Worry is a dubious invention that belongs to other lifestyles, farming for example. No amount of worry can summon or secure next month's game.

Pygmies do not store meat. They do not save. Ota had no way of getting back to Africa.

At the vernal equinox, outside the carriage house where he slept when it was warm, he built a fire and broke off the caps placed on his teeth.

The boys, Chauncey Spencer, Hunter Hayes, and the others, asked him to take them hunting. They tugged at him, tried to lift him to his feet. It was frightening, their friend and teacher, grown suddenly heavy and immobile, so unresponsive. When he spoke, and it was seldom, they could see tears in his eyes, and he told them he wanted to go home.

They'd always thought this was his home.

He stripped to a loincloth. A crowd gathered to see Otto dancing, singing around the fire. The boys tried to join him as always. This one time he chased them all away.

There was one thing left to do. He had no motion left for anything else. He had no English any more. He had the vowel songs, the leaden, bloody onset of memories, things he had survived by putting out of mind, the past appearing like a hole in the ground he had to prepare himself to leap into, to sing within. The forest dweller's song of reconciliation:

> There is darkness all around us;
> but if darkness *is*
> and the darkness is of the forest,
> then the darkness must be good.

He had stolen undetected upon an elephant and speared it in its vulnerable stomach. With the song, the dance, the fire in front of him, he was stealing in upon himself. He was coming close with a wooden spear, hunting, coming into sight of himself, a man dead tired of the hunter who had been trailing him for days.

He had hidden a revolver he had stolen earlier that day. In March's afternoon shadows he retrieved it from under the hay in the carriage house and, still singing, turned the gun upon his heart and fired.

Next day, Chauncey asked his mother why. Anne had been thinking of a story she knew, *The Story of Bras-Coupé* by George Cable. It told of a dying slave who is asked by a priest where he thought he was going after death. The slave answers not to heaven, as expected, but whispers instead:

> with an ecstatic, upward smile . . .
> "To—Africa"—and was gone.

Anne Spencer told her ten-year-old boy Ota Benga had sent his spirit back to Africa.

19

PRAYER MEETING

All that I can make out of it is
the fact that somehow I have kept up
the fight for forty-five years now,
since I stood trembling and almost
terrified before the little congregation
in the church at Walhalla.

—S. P. Verner

Ota's death set off a last round of headlines, starting, on March 22, with the local press. "PINED FOR NATIVE HOME," said the *Lynchburg News*, "Sad Story of Young African Who Committed Suicide Here." The article was sympathetic, alluding often to Ota—referred to for the most part as "Bingo"—and his desperate desire to go home. To clear up the mystery of how he came to America in the first place, the paper had recourse to the story given by the tall, bespectacled man. Readers were treated in earnest to an account Ota had planted like bangi seeds, just for fun. They read about the speedy, globetrotting Englishmen, the slow pygmy, the trips around the world, and the zoo, the least likely element and the only one that was true.

In describing Bingo the reporter said that his "legs were very short, but his body was long," and that he "responded quickly to kind treatment." A few weeks later the *Lynchburg News* carried another, less sympathetic piece, consisting largely of the expert opinion of William Temple Hornaday, whom someone had written of Ota's suicide. Hornaday claimed it came as no surprise to him that Ota put a bullet in his heart. "Evidently," wrote Hornaday, "he felt that he would rather die than work for a living."

On July 16, 1916, the Sunday edition of the *New York Times* weighed in. The bulk of the article is a response to Ota's death by Verner, who had heard the news in Panama. Verner rose to salute his friend: "he was one of the most determined little fellows that ever breathed . . . A brave, shrewd little man who preferred to match himself against civilization rather than be a slave to the Baschilele. All honor to him, even though he died in the attempt!"

A somewhat fuller version of Verner's communiqué was printed in the Zoological Society Bulletin, the same publication that had featured Ota once before. Verner flew to Ota's defense; no shame was attached to his having died a suicide. On the contrary, such a death elevated him to the company of great men, Hannibal and Marc Antony, "big souls that succumbed in the same way after they saw they had undertaken the impossible."

Verner wished he could have been with Ota to help cheer him up, though he trusted that Ota's Lynchburg friends did all that could be done. He wrote that even if Ota had managed to get back to Africa he might have been no happier: "His country is now torn by war made by the white men among themselves, and a war far more terrible than any the pygmies ever waged. In fact, I have lately heard that Ndombe's peaceful kingdom was utterly broken up by the Belgians . . . and that Ndombe's son was put in prison on some trivial charge."

In the past Verner always climbed from doubt back to optimism, from game-pits, even with their poison stakes embedded in his thigh, back into the sun. This is the first public utterance in which the darkness gets the better of him; doubt and bitter sorrow demand and get their due. "Between the impossible conditions of Ota Benga's own land," he wrote, "and those which he could not surmount in ours, the homeless pygmy found no abiding place." The problem of "no abiding place" was one with which Verner did not find it difficult to sympathize.

In 1920, he and his family returned from Central America to Brevard, where he became a teacher and superintendent of the

county school system. Most of his pupils were children of
local mountain folk. Verner told them stories about his adventures in Africa until their eyes grew round and their mouths
fell open. Then he would send them out for recess and lay
down for a snooze.

His efforts to forget Africa had come to nothing, despite
nine years in Panama trying. On the contrary, it was Panama
that faded like a dream. When Verner addressed his students
and told about the horned viper called Ntoka, the pygmy
known as Ota Benga, and the great King Ndombe, he was
Fwela once again, Fwela back in action, outsmarting baleful
Chisakanka, or putting another one over on the Force Publique. He was also noted as a dynamic teacher of American
history. He had it in his bones, from Colonel John, who fought
in the Revolutionary War, to Uncle Charles, who with nothing
but a Bible in his hand headed off General Sherman at the pass
in the war between the states.

Of all the men in New York he had met, he stayed in fairly
regular touch with only one, William Temple Hornaday. Verner wrote Hornaday about an improved strain of hybrid
chicken and a new, humane animal trap. Verner's diagrams for
the trap look like proofs of some advanced Euclidean proposition, and he had letters from New Yorkers eager to try the
trap on noisy alley cats they wanted removed to other neighborhoods. Wouldn't the millionaires be irresistibly drawn into
a project that promised such unlimited demand for tin and
copper?

Hornaday politely tried to redirect Verner's attention elsewhere. How did Carolina orchids grow, for example, or did
they? Would there be a book resulting from the Panama years?
Would Verner please not forget to let the director know of any
further developments in that marvelous idea for a hippopotamus farm? They steered clear of the subject of Ota Benga. That
didn't mean either man had forgotten him.

In the 1920s, as Verner entered his fifties, he became involved once more in the Presbyterian Church. In 1926, ten years
after the suicide, Verner led a prayer meeting in Ota's honor. He
took as his text not a verse from the Bible but the African phrase
he had heard used so often: "His heart is white, Fwela" or
"Fwela, his heart is black." A white heart was a good heart, a
black heart was evil, spreading harm like mayhem.

To his audience, this sounded like the familiar hellfire
sermon with an African twist, predictable since this was Ver-

ner—look deep within, pluck out the evil thought before it matures into a deed. Except Verner was saying the evil thought was a deed already. Well-aimed it was witchcraft; widespread and loosed in all directions it materialized as war. What was better, he demanded of his all-white listeners, a white man who saw no further than skin pigment, or an African who judged by the shading of the heart?

He told the story of how he had first met Ota Benga—one of the many versions at his command—and how Ota had lived in New York, Long Island, and the South. He challenged the audience to answer the question, had he been sufficiently his brother's keeper by bringing him to America? He spoke of Ota's marksmanship, his prowess as a hunter, and asked if they could measure how much loneliness there must have been for such a man to turn a gun against his own heart. The whitest heart, he added, he had ever known.

His eyes reddened, his voice broke, and S. P. Verner cried.

He established a reputation in Brevard as liaison between the races, speaking before black congregations and becoming a spokesman for their needs. He had always wandered across railroad tracks and oceans separating cultures. In a small way in a small town he made himself a link.

In the late 1920s Kondola let Verner know he was planning a visit. Loyal, cautious "John" Kondola, given to premonitions; a living connection to Verner's earliest African adventures. It had been years since Verner had seen him. At last there would someone to whom he would be Fwela once again.

Kondola, unlike Ota, had made the transition to living in America. He had fewer problems identifying with American blacks. Like Ota, he too spoke of returning to Africa. The urge, however, never became absolute. Unlike Ota, Kondola was able to come to terms with its indefinite postponement.

Starting with his family, Verner had told many people in town of Kondola's imminent arrival. His youngest daughter looked forward to that day as to the coming of a prince. No doubt Verner had something to do with raising her expectations, mixing a little of Prince Kassongo into his description of Kondola.

But Kondola hadn't survived so long without learning the mores of the South. When the great day came he entered unobtrusively through the back door, bitterly disappointing Laura, who grabbed him by a hand and tried to lead him outside to start all over.

Verner and Kondola appeared together before both white and black congregations. And those who had begun to doubt there ever had been such a man as Fwela beyond the reaches of Verner's imagination had to hold their tongues.

> The bright shy smile of a pygmy.
> The eyes of far-famed King Ndombe,
> "large as a quarter of a dollar."

Verner continued to write and talk about Africa. Some thought it couldn't possibly all be true—the endless tales of snakes crawling out of jackets, game-pits, hippos, the trumpeting of elephants down the mountain, the flocks of parrots wheeling way on high. Other listeners were impressed by Verner's tales: here, clearly, was a man who far exceeded the small-town conventions of Brevard and whose broad experience no doubt included, in addition to confrontations with wild beasts, a fair share of enviable indiscretions.

He published the African stories that comprise the manuscripts for *Travels with Ntoka* and *How We Tamed the Baschilele* in the Brevard press. In them he is Fwela, the white magician, marksman, and adventurer traveling with the wily and "ever-faithful pygmy" who "became famous afterwards under his name of Ota Benga."

In the late 1930s, weakened by complications due to chronic malaria, he began to dictate fragments of an unfinished autobiography. The autobiography discusses parentage and lineage, slavery and the Civil War, Joe Copeland and Miss Amanda, and the first decisive reading of *Robinson Crusoe*; but perhaps its most memorable passages are reserved for expressions of heartsickness and regret.

Verner truly unburdens himself here, delivering at last the unfettered cry of doubt and torment he had spent a lifetime trying to keep down. Looking back on his childhood, he writes: "There are children who shed undesirable suggestion as the duck does water; and they are the darlings of the Gods. But the rest, to whom some tar will stick, make up the vast bulk of humanity . . . " If God did not show some mercy toward that morally frail majority, "the human race would dwindle down to dependence upon those few immunes, and they would not be numerous enough to make a dent in the vast wall of nature around, with its ravening and ever-open maw."

Verner did not number himself among the immunes. The consequence was to "suffer the torments of remorse to an extent that makes me wonder whether the emotion at some stage . . . may not border on insanity."

If ever I cease to love,
If ever I cease to love . . .

He that fights Fwela must fight Ndombe also; and when Fwela dies than will Ndombe die also.

Near the end of his life old personalities disintegrated, like red blood cells left behind by malaria plasmodia, to be replaced by new ones. Verner took to wearing his overalls backward. Now and again he would stuff himself into one of his wife's dresses, but he could still pull himself together. He was the effortless center of every gathering. Grandchildren and others remember a booming voice calling down calamity on anyone foolish enough to use racist epithets in his hearing. As he admired North Carolina sunsets he told tales of other sunsets, far away. All his children learned a favorite Tshiluba rowing song.

when Fwela dies
Je—sus, Thou art stand—ing

He died in 1943, seventy years of age. He had specified a plain gravestone with only his name and dates. His had not been a life characterized by dreams come forever true, or summits reached and permanently held. He had fallen far short with respect to restoring family fortune. He had held diamonds in his hands only to walk away with quartz. In respect to the tombstone Samuel Phillips Verner got his wish.

EPILOGUE

All songs are implicitly sacred.
"The forest gives us this song," the
people say, meaning, "The forest is
this song."
—Peter Matthiessen,
African Silences

everend William Henry Sheppard led a life that has,
perhaps, been inadequately explored by historians.
First visitor to the Forbidden Land of the Kuba people
and first American witness of Free State atrocities,
Sheppard's effect on the development of the Presbyterian Mission to the Congo is hard to overstate. That mission, in turn,
played a vital role in the struggle of reformers against King
Leopold II.

After long years in Africa, Sheppard returned to Louisville, Kentucky, where he continued to write and preach. His
collection of Kuba ceremonial objects, donated to the Hampton Institute in Virginia, remains one of the finest of its kind.

Rev. Sheppard died in 1927.

Roger Casement, the British Consul to the Congo in 1904,
brushed against our story first by issuing the report, based on

his travels in the Free State, that was crucial in turning world opinion against King Leopold. Secondly, he pronounced S. P. Verner "cracked."

As has been noted, Casement's frustration with official British response to Congo atrocities was one of the factors that led him, an Irish Protestant, toward the cause of Irish nationalism. In 1916 he was in Berlin, slowly losing hope that the Germans in World War I were prepared to significantly extend themselves for Irish independence. He was smuggled back to England by U-boat, only to be picked up immediately by a British patrol.

The British wanted to execute him for treason and, to erode any residual sympathy for him, circulated a copy of his diaries, the notorious Black Books of Roger Casement, which were purported to document years of homosexual activity. The diaries, particularly a section known as the Cash Notebooks, contain the details—including amounts of money that changed hands—of sexual encounters in Africa, Latin America, and Europe. There is even a language of ecstatic nonsense sounds designed to express the delight Casement ostensibly took from these encounters.

Many, including W. B. Yeats, who devoted two poems to Casement, denounced the diaries as a fraud and a forgery. The behavior of the British, who did not permit public inspection of the documents and withdrew them almost immediately from view, lent credence to this charge. More recently, however, it has been shown the diaries were in fact authentic. It has long been known that Casement's goal in returning to England was not to promote the Easter Rebellion (crushed, but immortalized by Yeats), as the English charged, but, on the contrary, to call it off.

Roger Casement was hanged on August 3, 1916. "It is a cruel thing to die," he wrote to his sister not long before the execution, "with all men misunderstanding."

A year after the St. Louis Fair, Geronimo rode in Theodore Roosevelt's inaugural parade. (When asked why he had invited this "greatest" of "single-handed murderers" to appear in the procession, Roosevelt answered, "I wanted to give the people a good show.")

Afterward, Geronimo was granted an audience with the president. He knew this was his last, best opportunity and appealed eloquently for the right to lead the remnants of his people home. "Great Father," he said to Roosevelt, "my hands are tied as with a rope. My heart is no longer bad. I will tell my people to obey no chief but the Great White Chief. I pray you to cut the ropes and make me free. Let me die in my own country, an old man who has been punished enough and is free."

Roosevelt heard him out, then answered, "I do not think I can hold out any hope for you. That is all I can say, Geronimo, except that I am sorry, and have no feeling against you."

In 1909, his exact age unknown, though he was probably over ninety, a drunken Geronimo fell off his horse and spent a midwinter night on the cold, wet ground. As a youth his spirit ally promised he would never die of a bullet wound. His body was pockmarked by the countless bullets that failed to kill him, but he had never been promised protection against old age and pneumonia.

As he lay dying, two young Apaches appeared to him in a vision, asking him to once and for all break with the past and accept Christianity. Geronimo had struggled for years with the ways of the missionaries. He answered it was too late for him, and that he could not abandon the old ways.

He died on February 17, 1909.

In 1924 Director Hornaday received a letter from a man named John Cromartie, who had obviously never heard of the pygmy in the zoo. Cromartie proposed that "If placed in a cage between the Orang-outang and the Chimpanzee, an ordinary member of the human race would arrest the attention of everyone who entered the large Ape-house." He volunteered for the role, and furnished the "particulars of [his] person" for Hornaday's consideration.

Had Hornaday accepted the proposal, a new sign placed on the Monkey House might have read as follows:

Race: Scottish	Height: 5 feet 11 inches
Weight: 11 stone	Hair: Dark
Eyes: Blue	Nose: Aquiline
Age: 27 years	

Instead, in reply, Hornaday wrote that Cromartie had roused the restless "ghost of vanished Ota Benga, pygmy negro of the Congo," who had once upon a time "flourished in our Primate House, against a background of picturesque chimps and orangs." If it were not for "the idiosyncrasies of Mankind," continued the director, and the intervention of a "militant" and meddlesome reporter, Ota might well have happily "continued here to this day."

With the benefit of eighteen years' worth of hindsight, Hornaday continued to refine the story of the pygmy in the zoo: not only had Ota "flourished" while being fed to the mob, but he had also been paid for his labors. He had been, or so it now seemed to the director, an employee in good standing of the New York Zoological Society. Consequently the reporter and the preachers not only did the public out of an interesting exhibit, they did the poor pygmy out of a job.

In 1922, Hornaday published the results of a lifetime's rumination on animal behavior, *The Mind and Manners of Wild Animals*. In its preface the author, growing morose over the implications of World War I, suggested that zookeeping had its philosophical rewards, and that a visit to the zoo might fend off feelings of despair. He cited his own experience as an example. "During these days of ceaseless conflict, anxiety, and unrest among men," he wrote, "when at times it begins to look as if 'the Caucasian' really is 'played out,' perhaps the English-reading world will turn with a sigh of relief to the contemplation of wild animals. At all events, the author has found this diversion in his favorite field mentally agreeable and refreshing."

The book contains much lively, if anthropomorphic, writing. The Indian crocodile, for example, is "a shameless cannibal." The most "philosophic" birds are "parrots, parakeets, macaws and cockatoos." Out of all mammals, the gray wolf is the most "degenerate and unmoral." The book features a photo of Rajah the orangutan pedaling his tricycle against a background of drums and a toy piano, and there is a complete version of "The Wild Animal's Bill of Rights."

On the subject of animal intelligence, Hornaday reserves his greatest praise for the "inventive genius" of an animal whose "faculty for mechanics . . . not only challenged our admiration, but also created much work for our carpenters." This animal, of course, is Dohong. How Dohong, by himself or with the chimps he recruited for their weight, cracked or bent the bars of the cage; how, after a session of demolition, he liked to stick his head out and take a good look around—all this is recounted in affectionate detail. The book contains not a word about the pygmy in the zoo.

William Temple Hornaday retired from the post of director in 1926.

The life-cycle of the Howard Colored Orphan Asylum was delimited by war. The Civil War, and freed slaves coming north, created the need for the orphanage. World War I brought blacks north once more in search of work but was the death knell to the boundless optimism that underlay the St. Louis Fair, and brought about the end of the orphanage in a more immediate way.

The purchase of war bonds replaced many other forms of discretionary spending. Just when there was reason to expand (and those like W. E. B. Du Bois, normally opposed to industrial training, willing to help), Howard was forced to the financial brink. Wartime rationing, directed, at the highest level, by Bernard Baruch, dealt the final blow.

In the winter of 1918 desperately needed fuel was late in arriving. There was little heat and no hot water. Pipes froze and burst. Ice formed on the floor and some children's feet became frostbitten. First aid incorrectly applied aggravated the situation, and two children had to undergo amputations. As a result, the orphanage was condemned, its doors closed, its wards sent their separate ways to various hospitals and to the New York Asylum.

The Howard Colored Orphan Asylum survives today only in the form of a scholarship fund.

In the 1920s, Anne Spencer's poems were included in that flowering of black literature known as the Harlem Renaissance. Writers such as Langston Hughes counted themselves among her friends. She lived to see the dismantling of the Jim Crow system she so despised, and against which she strove to armor herself and those close to her. She died in 1975 at the age of ninety-three.

Today the Spencer home, once a focus for dissent, is an historical landmark, and a featured tourist attraction in the town of Lynchburg. The garden, if no longer as spectacular as when she tended it and Ota Benga brought her flowers, is still intact. The wanted posters for runaway slaves still hang on the walls of the study. Her books remain on their shelves.

Her son, Chauncey, has settled across the way from the Spencer home. One of the first blacks to make a career in aviation, Chauncey helped desegregate the United States Air Force (only to be slandered by Roy Cohn and Joe McCarthy for his pains). Today, well into his eighties, he leads tours of the Spencer Home. A tour with Chauncey can mean a journey back to those days in his childhood when he hunted with a man he knew as Otto Bingo.

Leopold II of Belgium died December 17, 1909, suffering acute stomach and intestinal pain, and too obese to move. His last official act, the result of months of campaigning on the theme of the threat of war, was to sign an Army Bill into law. Earlier, by surrendering the Congo to the Belgian Parliament, he had removed an obstacle to establishing an alliance with Britain.

"Let God watch over Belgium," wrote Leopold in his testament, "and be merciful to my soul."

There had indeed been diamonds in the Tshikapa River; Verner had waded through a fortune's worth. In their Congo investments, Thomas Fortune Ryan and the Guggenheims did not compound his failure to exploit the situation. While Verner was running afoul of King Leopold—KNOWING TOO MUCH about the Free State's labor system—and thereby losing his position with the American Congo Company, its sister corporation, the Forminiére, was building diamond mines along the banks of the Tshikapa. Those mines continue to yield up gemstones today.

A troupe of Batwa currently heads up a revue of traditional African music known as Africa Oyé, which fills houses in Boston, New York, London, and Tokyo. The Batwa's role is to open the show and, by an invocation to the ancestors, legitimize the performance to follow. It is the same on stage as it is in central Africa, where their Bantu neighbors still rely on pygmies to address forest spirits, and where the Mbuti pygmies start a hunt by naming those who hunted in time gone by.

The forest dwellers of Africa still arouse the interest of science. Biologists seek them out to test their blood and to bring back samples of their DNA. They are drawn by new forms of the same questions that once vexed S. P. Verner and Chief McGee: What role do pygmies play in human evolution? What relation do they have to the original human type, and, needless to say, why are they so small? Today's evolutionists do not, like yesterday's anthropometricists, include demeaning comments and rough treatment in their studies.

The forest dwellers continue to charm, as when the Egyptians first called them "Dancers of God," though more and more *muzungus* wander for one reason or another into their lives—anthropologists, geneticists, ecologists, writers. With respect to appearance, however, they are sometimes markedly different than when they were brought ceremoniously up the Nile to dance for the pharaoh. Peter Matthiessen, on a recent trip through central Africa, saw one hunter in a "black remnant of an Apple Computer T-shirt" and another in a "kid's gray sweatshirt that reads PITTSBURGH STEELERS."

Other things are not so different. Asked who was cultivating a form of potato found in the bush, one hunter answered, "He Himself [meaning the forest] grew it." And, "In an overgrown camp by the Bougpa spring, an hour north of Lelo, are big marijuana plants ready for harvest. A hunter walks over, plucks some sticky leaves and smiles, murmuring "bangi."

Ota Benga's body lies in an unmarked grave in the town of Lynchburg.

A NOTE ON SOURCES

Phillips Verner Bradford was the most valuable resource in the research for Ota's story; his knowledge of his grandfather's character and his access to the far-flung Verner clan were both indispensable. Special appreciation must also go to Chauncey Spencer and Hunter Hayes for their recollections of Ota Benga.

The following is a selective listing of written material that was useful in the preparation of this book.

Those interested in pursuing S. P. Verner further are referred to his book, *Pioneering in Central Africa* (Richmond: Presbyterian Committee, 1903), his many articles—notably "The Adventures of an Explorer in Africa: How the Batwa Pygmies Were Brought to the St. Louis Fair" (*Harper's Weekly*, 10/22/1904, pp. 1618–1620), and "The White Man's Zone in Africa" (*World's Work*, 1/07, pp. 8227–8236)—and the large collection of unpublished material at the University of South

Carolina. We made ample use, as well, of Gordon Gibson's monograph, *Samuel Phillips Verner in the Kasai* (unpublished), and of two pieces by Jack Crawford—*Pioneer African Missionary: Samuel Phillips Verner* (*Journal of Presbyterian History 60*, Spring 1982, pp 42–57), and *Samuel Phillips Verner: Presbyterian Missionary in the Congo, 1895–1899: Racial Attitudes of the Lone White in an All-Black Mission* (unpublished). It is probably unnecessary to add that an understanding of S. P. Verner would be enhanced by a reading of *Robinson Crusoe*.

Slave-trade and slave-traders are documented in Leda Farrant's *Tippu-Tip and the East African Slave Trade* (New York: St. Martin's Press, 1975), Cyrus Townsend Brady's *Commerce and Conquest in East Africa* (Salem: The Riverside Press, 1950), Basil Davidson's *Black Mother* (Boston/Toronto: Little Brown and Company, 1961), George F. Kay's *The Shameful Trade* (London: Frederick Muller Ltd, 1967), and Alfred Swann's *Fighting the Slave-Hunters in Central Africa* (Chicago: AFRO-AM Press, 1969.)

Belgian rule is discussed in L. H. Gann's and Peter Duignan's *The Rulers of Belgian Africa 1884–1914* (Princeton: Princeton University Press, 1979), and Arthur Keith's *The Belgian Congo and The Berlin Act* (New York: Negro Universities Press, 1979). Mark Twain's *King Leopold's Soliloquy* (Boston: 1905), Arthur Conan Doyle's *The Crime of the Congo* (New York: Doubleday, Page & Company, 1909) and Edmund Morel's *Red Rubber* (New York: Negro Universities Press, 1969) were key expressions of the movement for Congo reform. Henry Wellington Wack's *The Story of the Congo Free State* (New York & London: G. P. Putnam's Sons, 1905) is an example of the material put out by Leopold's apologists.

For a biography of Leopold, see Barbara Emerson's *Leopold II of the Belgians, King of Colonialism* (New York: St. Martin's Press, 1979). Of the several good biographies of Henry Morton Stanley, we turned most often to Richard Hall's *Stanley* (London: St. James Place, 1974). For an intriguing fictionalized account of Bula Mutadi, see Lennart Hagerfors' *The Whales In Lake Tanganyika* (New York: Grove Press, 1989). For Joseph Conrad, not only *Heart of Darkness* but also *An Outpost of Progress* and the essay "Geography and Some Explorers" bear on the African portions of our story.

Stanley Shaloff's *Reform in Leopold's Congo* (Richmond:

John Knox Press, 1970) is the best history of the struggle between the Presbyterian missionaries and King Leopold, tracking Verner's peculiar role in the controversy. William Henry
Sheppard's Pioneers in Congo (Louisville: Pentecostal Publishing Company, 1902) is useful for the same period, as are
Sheppard's articles, among them "An African's Work for Africa" (Missionary Review of the World XIX, 10/06, pp 770–
774), and "Light in Darkest Africa" (Southern Workman, 4/05,
pp 218–227).

Pygmies continue to make memorable cameo appearances
in works by travelers to central Africa. See, for example, Alex
Shoumatoff's In Southern Light: Trekking through Zaire and
the Amazon (New York: Simon & Schuster, 1986). Jean-Pierre
Hallet's Pygmy Kitabu (New York: Random House, 1973),
Kevin Duffy's Children of the Forest (New York: Dodd, Mead
& Company, 1984), Ann Putnam's and Allan Keller's Madami:
My Eight Years of Adventure With The Pigmies (New Jersey:
Prentice Hall, 1954), and Timothy Severin's The Horizon Book
of Vanishing Primitive Man (New York: American Heritage
Publishing Co, 1973) contributed to our understanding of
pygmy culture. It does no insult to these works to single out
Colin Turnbull's loving, lucid, and informative The Forest
People (New York: Simon & Schuster, 1962) for special praise.

There are no better correctives to the recurrent racist mis-
uses of Darwinism than the works of Stephen Jay Gould, particularly Ever Since Darwin (New York: W. W. Norton &
Company, 1979) and the Mismeasure of Man (New York:
W. W. Norton & Company, 1981). See his essay "The Hottentot
Venus" from the The Flamingo's Smile (New York: W. W.
Norton & Company, 1983) for a succinct rendering of the phe-
nomenon of people on display. We recommend Leslie Fied-
ler's Freaks (New York: Simon and Schuster, 1978) for a
psychological perspective, Robert Bogdan's Freak Show—Pre-
senting Human Oddities for Amusement and Profit (Chicago:
University of Chicago Press, 1988) for a sociological view. For
a full-length study of a Kalahari Bushman who became one of
America's most popular freaks, see Laurens van der Post's A
Mantis Carol (London: Hogarth Press, 1975).

As their centrality to twentieth-century culture is more
widely appreciated the literature pertaining to World's Fairs
continues to grow. The Missouri Historical Society in St. Louis
is a repository for information about the St. Louis Fair, con-

taining official records, journals, unpublished manuscripts, and transcripts of conversations with ex-fairgoers. See also the 10 volume *Louisiana and the Fair: An Exposition of the World, Its People and Their Achievements* edited by J. W. Buel (Saint Louis: Worlds' Progress Publishing Company, 1904), and Mark Bennitt's *Louisiana Purchase Exhibition* (St. Louis: Universal Exposition Publishing Company, 1905).

Richard Drinnon's *Facing West: The Metaphysics of Indian-Hating and Empire-Building* (Minneapolis: University of Minnesota Press, 1980) places the Anthropology Department of the St. Louis Fair in the context of American expansionism. Robert Rydell's *All the World's a Fair: Visions of Empire of American International Expositions, 1876–1916* (Chicago: University of Chicago Press, 1984) deals with each significant American fair from the Philadelphia Exposition to the first world war. See also John Allwood's *The Great Exhibitions* (London: Studio Vista, 1977), John Findling's *Historical Dictionary of World's Fairs* (New York: Greenwood Press, 1990), Paul Greenhalgh's *Ephemeral Vistas: The Expositions Universelles, Great Exhibitions and World's Fairs, 1851–1939* (Manchester, U.K.: Manchester University Press, 1988), Neil Harris' *Cultural Excursions: Marketing Appetites and Cultural Tastes in Modern America* (Chicago: University of Chicago Press, 1990), and Kenneth W. Luckhurst's *The Story of Exhibitions* (London: Studio, 1951).

John S. Haller's *Outcasts from Evolution: Scientific Attitudes of Racial Inferiority, 1859–1900* (New York: McGraw-Hill, 1975) studies the passion for measurement that culminated in the Anthropology Department at St. Louis. Stanley Karnow's *In Our Image: America's Empire in the Philippines* (New York: Random House, 1989) provides background to the display of Filipinos. For a biography of Geronimo, see Angie Debo's *Geronimo* (Norman: University of Oklahoma Press, 1976).

Darwin's influence on the display of human beings was profound, but no more so than that of P. T. Barnum. For studies of Barnum's life and work see Neil Harris' *HUMBUG: The Art Of P. T. Barnum* (Boston/Toronto: Little, Brown & Company, 1973), A. H. Saxon's *P. T. BARNUM: The Legend and the Man* (New York: Columbia University Press, 1989), and *Barnum's Own Story: The Autobiography of P. T. Barnum* (Gloucester: Peter Smith, 1972).

Among many works on the conjunction of jazz and carnival in New Orleans, we recommend Jack Buerkle's and Danny Barker's *Bourbon Street Black: The New Orleans Black Jazzman* (New York: Oxford University Press, 1973), William Ivy Hair's *Carnival of Fury: Robert Charles and the New Orleans Race Riot of 1900* (Baton Rouge: Louisiana State University Press, 1976), Sam Kinser's *Carnival, American Style: Mardi Gras at New Orleans and Mobile* (Chicago: University of Chicago Press, 1990), and Martin Williams' *Jazz Masters of New Orleans* (New York: The MacMillan Company, 1976). Michael Ventura's "Hear That Long Snake Moan" from his *Shadow Dancing in the USA* (Los Angeles: Jeremy P. Tarcher, Inc., 1985) is a unique study of how the music, and what the author calls the metaphysics, of the ex-slaves transformed the world of their ex-masters.

Those who choose to approach turn-of-the-century New York City via Coney Island will find the following of use: John Kasson's *Amusing the Million* (New York: Hill & Wang, 1978), Gary Kyriazi's *The Great American Amusement Parks* (Secaucus: Citadel Press, 1976), and Richard Snow's *Coney Island, A Postcard Journey to the City of Fire* (New York: Brightwaters Press, 1984). See also Ric Burns' "Greetings From Coney Island" (*New York Times*, 5/17/91, p C1).

The story of the American Museum of Natural History is to be found in Geoffrey Hellman's *Bankers, Bones & Beetles* (New York: Garden City, 1968), and Douglas J. Preston's *Dinosaurs In The Attic: An Excursion into the American Museum of Natural History* (New York: St. Martin's Press, 1986). For the Bronx Zoo, William Bridges' *Gathering of Animals: An Unconventional History of the New York Zoological Society* (New York: Harper and Row, 1974), the standard account, is complemented by the more critical view of Helen Horowitz in "Animal and Man in the New York Zoological Park" (*New York History 56*: 1975, pp 426–55). For an example of the sort of racist thinking common at the museum and zoo during Ota's day, see Madison Grant's *The Passing of the Great Race* (New York: C. Scribner's Sons, 1923) with its introduction by Fairfield Osborn.

Our understanding of the Howard Colored Orphan Asylum owes a great deal to Carleton Mabee's "Charity in Travail: Two Orphan Asylums for Blacks" (*New York History LV*, Jan. 1974, pp 55–77). Our account of New York City's anti-draft riots drew on Adrian Cook's *The Armies of the Streets: The New York City Draft Riots of 1863* (Lexington: The University Press of Kentucky, 1974). Joan Elizabeth Harris' *The Progressive Era in Smithtown, New York: A Study of Five Charitable Institutions* (unpublished) was our guide to what awaited Ota Benga on Long Island.

Lee J. Greene's *Time's Unfading Garden: Anne Spencer's Life and Poetry* (Baton Rouge: Louisiana State University Press, 1977), B. W. Arnold's "Concerning the Negroes of the City of Lynchburg, Virginia" (*Southern History Association Publications*, x, 1906, pp 19–30), and the oral testimony mentioned above gave us access to some of the people and materials out of which Ota Benga fashioned his life in the South.

APPENDIX

St. Louis Exposition Letters

Text of Letters between Verner and McGee and Newspaper Articles from St. Louis in 1903–1904.

The following letters between Samuel Phillips Verner and William J. McGee are transcribed from originals at the South Caroliniana Library at the University of South Carolina, Columbia, SC. These letters show the detailed arrangements made by McGee to obtain the Africans for the ethnological exhibit at the World's Fair.

WORLD'S FAIR, ST. LOUIS

1904

LOUISIANA PURCHASE EXPOSITION

DEPARTMENT OF ANTHROPOLOGY

St. Louis, U.S.A.
October 21, 1902
[sic: 1903]

Mr. S. P. Verner,
    Present,
Dear Sir:
    Your plans and estimates for obtaining a group of African Pygmies and neighboring natives are in my hands and have been found satisfactory as a basis for the contemplated expedition in the interests of this Exposition.
    By authority of the Director of Exhibits, I beg to tender you the leadership and control of the African Pygmy Expedition, subject to the following general conditions and the special conditions incorporated in your plan and estimates:
    1. You are to secure the voluntary attendance at this Exposition of twelve Pygmies and about six neighboring natives from the Baluba territory in the vicinity of Kasai River; the group to include, so nearly as may be, six members of the Batwa Pygmy tribe, six of the Tueki people, and one or more Red Africans—if practicable, King Ndombe of the Bikenge.
    2. You are to assume full responsibility for the health, comfort, and safety of these natives from the time of leaving their homes until their arrival on the Exposition grounds, and are to hold yourself in readiness to continue the custody and responsibility until the natives are returned to their homes after the close of the Exposition.
    3. After you have received requisite credentials from the Exposition authorities, you are to secure the approbation and enlist the support of His Majesty, King Leopold of Belgium, and his Colonial Government in Africa, to such extent as to insure the success of the expedition.
    4. You are to so time movements as to permit installing the group on the Exposition grounds by May 1, 1904, delays by shipwreck or other catastrophe excepted.
    5. In accordance with the regulations of this Department, you will, by the acceptance of this commission, relieve the Louisiana Purchase Exposition Company and all other officers and attaches of the Exposition of financial and other responsibility for accidental or other injuries to or death of any member or members of the expedition or the group of natives; this Department undertaking, however, to furnish all reasonable facilities for securing the health and comfort of the natives during the time of their stay on the Exposition grounds.
    6. To defray all cost of the expedition up to the arrival of the native group on the Exposition grounds, there is allotted the sum of $5,500.00, which is designed to be expended in accordance with your plans and estimates; of this allotment, $1,000.00 in cash and transportation orders, and a letter of credit of $3,000.00, will be placed in your hands before you embark, and you will be authorized to purchase and ship necessary goods to the amount of $1,500.00 on vouchers to be paid by the Exposition. In addition to this initial allotment, you are advised that an additional allotment of $3,000.00 will be made to cover the cost of returning the natives to their homes after the close of the Exposition.
    7. In accordance with your estimates, the sum of $500.00 out of the initial allotment is assigned as full compensation for your services from the time of embarking on the expedition to that of arrival on the Exposition grounds; but it is understood that if by the exercise of economy without injury to the expedition you will be able to reduce the cost of delivering the African natives on the grounds below the cost of $5,500.00, half of the amount so saved will be presented to you as an honorarium.

If you agree to the foregoing stipulations, and accept the leadership of the expedition under them, please signify the same in writing; when requisite credentials, etc., will be conveyed to you.

> Yours with respect,
> [signed]   W. J. McGee
> Chief.

October 22, 1903

Sir:

By authority of the Louisiana Purchase Exposition Company, you are hereby commissioned as a Special Agent of this Department, and authorized to organize and conduct an expedition into the interior of Africa for the purpose of obtaining anthropological material and offering certain natives the opportunity of attending the Exposition in person.

I have the honor to be,

> Yours with respect,
> [signed]   W.J. McGee
> Chief

> Mr. Samuel Phillips Verner
> Stillman Institute
> Tuskaloosa, Alabama

Dr. W.J. McGee
Chief   Mr Dear Dr. McGee:

The first pygmy has been secured! He was obtained from a village in which he was held captive having been taken prisoner at a remote point in the great Kantsia forest twelve days march from any white settlement. Although still two hundred miles from our final destination, I thought it well to secure him at once, even if we get all we wish from Ndombe. This pygmy belongs to the same ethnic group as the Batwa, but probably his people are characterized by some local differentiations, which will emerge upon further study. As I wish to have this ready for any steamer I cannot enlarge upon his characteristics now, but will add to this if I have time. But he is one of them beyond any peradventure.

[Note: This "first pygmy" is Ota Benga.]

> Thanking you for your encouraging letter, I am
> My Dear Dr., with the warmest regards,
> Truly yours,
> S. P. Verner

April 1, 1904

My dear Mr. Verner:

It is a pleasure to acknowledge the receipt of your letter of February 18, which came in this morning, and to congratulate you on the eminent success of your expedition up to the date of your writing. You will be interested to know that the draft of which advices were previously sent, has just arrived and that the small formalities attending its payment in accordance with local banking customs had attention yesterday.

The more I have reflected on the distances and other difficulties you have had to overcome, the more I have been impressed with the clearness of your foresight and the soundness of your plans. As I have already written, it would be impossible for me to give you trustworthy guidance as to the details of your movements, even if I could be sure that my writing would reach you in time to be of service. Accordingly, I can only say that, while it would be desirable to have the Pygmies here on the first day of May, it would be incomparably better to have them later than not at all. Nor am I in the least apprehensive as to the success of your mission, despite, perhaps a few weeks delay; for your final possible obstacle cannot be more serious than those you have already surmounted.

Noting your reference to possible obstacles on the part of African missionaries, I mention that within the last week a group of missionaries, including Mr. Morrison of the Kasai region, have appealed to Secretary Hay and afterward to President Roosevelt to take action respecting alleged cruelties to natives by Belgian officials; while the Belgian Minister in

Washington has met the allegations by statements that, to say the least, reflect no credit on the complainants.

No one will be more interested than you to know that Professor Starr arrived yesterday at Vancouver with his Ainu party and is now on his way to these grounds; and that day before yesterday the Patagonian group arrived at Liverpool and are now at sea on the way to New York. You will be no less interested to learn that the Filipino exhibit is coming forward according to plans; three hundred natives (including Igorrotes and Negrito pygmies) arrived Monday, while four hundred more are in San Francisco awaiting improvement in weather. Of course, all such items will be stale unless, perchance, you are delayed and this catches you in the depth of the Dark Continent; but in that case even a stale item will be better than none.

Now, my dear Mr. Verner, I hope you will not be disappointed at the dearth of constructive suggestions in this and other letters. As you are now placed, you are a law unto yourself; and I have implicit confidence in the competence of the court. As on last writing, I make but a single plea—*get the Pygmies.*

Inquiries are made of me constantly as to your progress,—naturally enough, since your expedition has all the elements of the picturesque. Some who do not know you seem doubtful as to the success of your expedition; but those who have seen you are satisfied when I say—*he will bring the Pygmies.*

Believe me to remain,

Most cordially yours,

[signed] W. J. McGee

Chief

Mr. S. P. Verner,

Special Agent Louisiana Purchase Exposition

c/o H. P. Hawkins,

Luebo,

Kasai District,

Congo Free State,

Africa

Text of Newspaper Articles on Ota Benga in St. Louis

The following newspaper articles and headlines, pertaining to Ota Benga and other Africans at the Louisiana Purchase Exposition, are transcribed and excerpted from various newspapers, mainly from St. Louis, beginning on November 16, 1903. While not exhaustive, the authors believe that these articles and excerpts are representative of the treatment given to Ota Benga's story by the press. Some articles are included, in part, to convey some idea about the overall atmosphere of the anthropological exhibits. They are presented in chronological order.

New York Times, November 16, 1903:

[Similar articles appeared in the St. Louis papers and in newspapers all over the country.]

To Exhibit Man at The St. Louis Fair

DR. McGEE GATHERING TYPES AND FREAKS FROM EVERY LAND.

HE EXPLAINS THE PLANS OF THE DEPARTMENT OF ANTHROPOLOGY, OF WHICH HE IS THE HEAD.

W. G. [sic] McGee,—who is at the head of the Department of Anthropology of the St. Louis Exposition, has been in New York during the week past for a meeting of the American Ethnological Society, and while here discussed in outline the plans which he and his assistants are working out for the arrangement and coordination to the vast exhibits that come under his direction.

The lot of Dr. McGee is not altogether a happy one just at the present time, for he is trying to work out a scheme for the Department of Anthropology which will conform to the readjustment of appropriation and space allotment determined upon by the managers of the fair not long ago.

An idea of the magnitude of this task may be obtained from the statement that the original intention was to have the whole exposition in a developmental way grouped around the division of anthropology in a manner which would make that the greatest exhibition of its kind ever attempted. By subsequent changes, however, the appropriation was cut enormously and the space allotment reduced 20 per cent, so that Mr. McGee is now at work "trying to save something out of the wreck," as he expressed the case.

None the less the description which he gave of the plans for the six sections devoted to ethnology is indicative of no small undertaking. Beside those sections that devoted to the Philippines is to all intents and purposes ethnological in character. It will comprise forty acres of land in the southwestern part of the grounds, and the intention for it is that it shall be illustrative of the life of the islands, their people, and racial characteristics. Like the Philippine exhibit, the Alaskan exhibit will be primarily ethnological, and the fullest co-operation is planned between the respective managers of these departments and the ethnological department.

Of the six sections strictly pertaining to the ethnological department proper, the first will illustrate the outdoor family groups from different parts of the world. As many of the uncivilized and semi-civilized people will be here represented as there can be obtained individuals. An expedition is now on its way to Africa with a view to bringing here a group of pigmies of the Congo region.

Up to the present time all the efforts of scientists have resulted only in bringing out of Africa isolated individuals, or at best two or three of these pigmies at a time. Now the attempt is being made to obtain a considerable number, comprising several families, so that a true South African village establishment may be set up on the fair grounds.

In strange contrast to these pigmies will be the savages from Patagonia, to obtain whom an expedition is now in the field. These Patagonians with the South African pigmies will represent the extremes of physical development.

In the same group will be the representatives of the aborigine peoples of North America. In providing for these it has been the intention so far as possible to have the several exhibits illustrative of different branches of Indian industry. Thus there will be a party of workers with beads and porcupine quills: others engaged in the dressing of skins, and still others in basketry and pottery. Particularly instructive will be the copper and silver workers, fashioning their product with implements of stone of the most primitive nature.

The second group will present an Indian school, illustrative of the latest efforts for the education of the red man. One hundred pupils are to be loaned for this purpose by the Government, including an Indian band.

The third group in the department of anthropology will comprise a number of special exhibits, archaeological in character and covering a wide range of territory. Among the Mexican exhibits will be a partial restoration of the ancient City of Mitla and a great number of individual specimens illustrating modes of life and customs of the early peoples. These latter are to be arranged in four divisions, so as to be suggestive of, first, the discovery of the use of fire; second, the development of the knife; third, the use of the wheel, and fourth the working of metals.

By association, the reason for which does not appear at first, the Department of History is to be included in that of anthropology, and will constitute group 4. This will be shaped particularly as bearing on the history of the Louisiana Purchase and will offer collections of records and original documents of extreme value. In addition there will be general historical exhibits having to do with the Nation at large.

The fifth and sixth groups of the Department of Anthropology will be those of anthropometry and psycopometry, for which there will be good opportunity of development as the different tribes of men are gathered for group 1 and for the Philippine and Alaskan exhibits. For the present little can be done in these last two mentioned groups, which must necessarily wait upon the completion of the others to a large extent. Extensive sets of measurements are to be taken, and tests made of all the tribes available, and it is expected that important data will be collected to serve as the basis of subsequent anthropological study.

St. Louis Republic, Sunday, March 6, 1904:
[An illustrated half-page article]

World's Fair Department of Anthropology:

PORTIONS OF ANCIENT CITIES ARE TO BE REPRESENTED AND UNWRITTEN HISTORY REVEALED.

TREASURES OF ANTIQUITY WILL BE SO ARRANGED AS TO SHOW THE BEARING MAN'S PAST ACHIEVEMENTS HAVE UPON CONTEMPORARY PROGRESS.

Lowest Development

The three, the Ainus, the Pigmies and the Patagonians will represent the lowest degree of human development. But many other strange races are included as typical of stages of aboriginal progress by study of the white man's civilization.

Chief Ndombe himself will come, ruler of the bright copper colored tribe of the Congo region, the aristocrat of Central Africa, and it is thought to be settled that he will bring with him leading men of the tribes under him, the Baluba, the Biomba, the Banumfula, the Bashielele, the Bachoke, the Balundi. His own men are called the Bakwampesh.

Then we will see the American Indian in his lowest and his highest stages. Especially noteworthy are: The Cocopas of the lower Colorado, a tribe still cultivating aboriginal crops by aboriginal methods and who will demonstrate their agriculture proficiency upon the grounds; the Seri Indians of Tiburon Island, Northwestern Mexico, probably the most gigantic men extant and among whom culture is so low that they are just entering the Stone Age.

Of United States tribes will be found one or two Pueblo groups occupying structures modeled after portions of their native pueblos. Plains tribes, with their tipis, shields and other insignia are arranged as to express social organization; basket makers from Northern California and Central Arizona; blanket weavers, potters, skin dressers, bead workers, copper shapers, arrow makers and other native artisans pursuing their craft according to the ways of their ancestors in pre-Columbian times.

Several groups will cluster about notable figures. Chief Joseph of the Nez Perce tribe, one of the ablest leaders ever coming from American soil, the Apache chief, Geronimo, with his band, who withstood the United States Army for years, the stately Kiowa chief, Quanah Parker ... [the short remainder of this article was cut off in the source. The beginning section was deleted as well].

St. Louis Post-Dispatch, Friday, April 1, 1904:

10,000 Strange People For Fair

THE WORLD'S FAIR PIKE WILL SOON BE THE MOST COSMOPOLITAN SPOT ON FACE OF THE EARTH.

Whole Ship Loads en Route

FARTHERMOST CORNERS OF THE EARTH ARE TO BE REPRESENTED BY NATIVES IN THEIR CHARACTERISTIC SPLENDOR.

St. Louis landlords will soon be called upon to house 10,000 people from every quarter of the globe. Telegrams received by the various departments of the World's Fair indicate that caravans and shiploads of black, red, white and yellow men women and children with camels, donkeys, elephants, reindeers, Esquimaux dogs and other livestock are now on their way to St. Louis. Except in a few instances their quarters at the Fair will not be ready until the opening day.

The vanguard of this army was the native Filipinos who have reached St. Louis, 235 in number. Ten Esquimaux have arrived from Greenland. Another band of Esquimaux from the Behring Straits will arrive in two weeks. A band of Ainus from northern Japan will arrive soon.

750 Indians in Pike Congress

In Italy J. M. Carragian has gathered Italians who are waiting orders to start for St. Louis. They will be in ancient Rome. A band of gypsies with Spanish dancing girls is ready in Spain to begin work in the streets of "Gay Seville."

For the Indian Congress on the Pike 750 Indians will assemble before April 30, and Morris Tobin is now in Arizona gathering 130 Zuni and Mochi Indians for the Cliff Dwellers. In the states of the far South old negroes and negro "mammies" are engaged to furnish life in the "Old Plantation."

Dispatches received by Prof. McGee, chief of anthropology, say that the Patagonian giants have left Liverpool for New York. Others soon to follow are the pygmies from South Africa, the red negroes from Central Africa and representatives of many Indian tribes of Central and South America.

The Philippine Commission is preparing for the reception of 700 more natives now on their way.

St. Louis Post-Dispatch, Monday, April 18, 1904:

EXPOSITION ENVOY PYGMIES' VICTIM?

FAIR OFFICIALS HAVE NOT HEARD FOR TWO MONTHS FROM EXPLORER SENT TO AFRICAN WILDS.

TRIBE USES DEADLY ARROWS

PERILOUS UNDERTAKING OF ANTHROPOLOGICAL DEPARTMENT APPROVED BY BELGIAN COLONIAL GOVERNMENT.

Officials in the Anthropological Department of the World's Fair are greatly worried over the fate of Rev. S. T. [sic] Verner who was commissioned by the department to visit the interior of the Congo Free State and secure a number of members of a savage tribe of pygmies, discovered by Henry M. Stanley, and thus far hostile to every attempt made at visiting their villages.

Rev. Mr. Verner is head of a school for negroes at Tuskaloosa, Ala. and because he had previously visited Africa and was familiar with native dialects, he was selected for the dangerous mission. The Congo Free State is under the rule of Belgium and it was necessary for the minister to visit that country in order to secure governmental approval of his undertaking.

He left St. Louis in December, taking with him two native Congo boys whom he had brought to the United States on a previous trip, and whom he had educated. The last word received from his was written on board the steamship City of Antwerp and was dated Feb. 2, 1904. The City of Antwerp reached Leopoldville, Congo Free State two days afterwards and the letter was mailed there.

Mr. Verner expected to spend a month in the interior taking with him a large party from Leopoldville in order to make the journey through the jungle. He had notified the World's Fair authorities that he would send a cablegram as soon as he returned to the coast, notifying them of the success or failure of his mission, and of the number of pygmies he had secured.

It took his letter six weeks to reach St. Louis, but if the mission was successful, a cablegram would have been received a month ago.

In his last letter Mr. Varner [sic] said that he had met with every encouragement from the Belgian government, but had been discouraged by missionaries familiar with the hazards of his mission, who feared for his life.

The pigmies he wished to obtain are among the most primitive people in the world. They wear no clothing and use bows with poisoned arrows for weapons. They live in thatched huts in trees, and are more at home in the trees than on the ground.

The officials in the Anthropological department fear Mr. Varner's [sic] party was ambuscaded before it reached a pigmy village or had no opportunity to make its mission known.

St. Louis Republic, Thursday, May 5, 1904:

VERNER ESCAPES BEING EATEN BY CANNIBALS

MAN WHO WENT IN QUEST OF AFRICAN PYGMIES CABLES EXPOSITION COMPANY.

The South African pigmies are coming to the Fair. A definite statement to this effect was made yesterday, upon the receipt by Dr. W. J. McGee of the Department of Anthropology of a cablegram from the Reverend Samuel P. Verner, special agent of the department. The cablegram was dated Brazzaville, May 24. It announced that the pygmies would be here. Very little is known about this race of people. Their size does not exceed that of an ordinary 12-year-old boy. They live in the secluded forests along the Congo, and it is stated that no member of the race has ever visited the Western Hemisphere.

Shyness is their chief characteristic, which accounts, in part, for the fact that they are the least known of all aboriginal tribes. The expedition which went in quest of these savages, under the personal direction of the Reverend Mr. Verner, departed last November on what was considered the most dangerous and delicate mission of any party sent out by the Exposition.

Mr. Verner's plan is to bring a party of eighteen pygmies, including one aged patriarch, one patriarch's wife, one young married couple, one boy, one girl, two infants, four red Africans, four adults, including a priest and priestess and two other natives showing different ethnic types. It is expected that the little people will bring with them the material for four . . .[remainder of clipping is missing from the source].

St. Louis Post-Dispatch, June 8, 1904:

"GERONIMO ONLY A PILL MIXER"

ICONOCLAST SHATTERS TRADITIONS WHICH CLUSTER ABOUT DREADED LEADER OF APACHE BRAVES.

STANDS WITHOUT HITCHING

OTHER INDIANS ENVY HIM ATTENTION AND MANAGERS OF SCHOOL CALL HIM LAZY.

Geronimo was never a great warrior, according to Superintendent S. M. McCowan of the Indian school at the World's Fair.

Instead he was and is the big medicine man of the Apaches, Mr. McCowan explains.

"Natchez was the fighting chief of the Apaches," declares the superintendent, "and while Geronimo was no doubt a brave man and shared in the fighting, he nevertheless did not lead the Indians as Natchez did.

"The newspapers and other Indian historians have made a fighting hero out of the old fellow, however. I suppose he killed his share of people. His reputation is that he would slay a white woman as readily as a white man.

"But in many battles Geronimo was in the background mixing medicine, while Natchez was doing the fighting."

Geronimo is now an artist and a financier.

He amuses himself in the Indian building by painting his name on cards and selling the cards to admiring visitors.

The old Medicine Man does not look nearly so warlike as many other Indians about the reservation. There is a little of the heroic about him. He dresses not only very plainly, but, to quote a visitor, "rather sloppily."

Ten Cents His Price for Card.

He wears weather-stained coat and trousers, an old slouch hat and a negligee shirt. He does not answer questions in English, indicating by gestures that he does not understand the language of the paleface. He is not paid for answering questions. He paints his name in good English letters, however, at 10 cents per card.

Geronimo is not a hero among the Indians or the managers of the Indian school. The former are jealous of the attention the old man receives; the latter say he is lazy.

One official, with the recollection of the white victims of Geronimo still fresh, says he is being treated too well in being exhibited.

All these comments, however, do not worry Geronimo.

He looks at the visitors as curiously as they look at him, and grins approvingly when they smile at him. He shakes hands with all comers who extend their hands first.

Geronimo is now more than 70 years old. For several years he has lived on the government reservation at Fort Sill, I. T.'He arrived in St. Louis from Fort Sill Monday night.

Mr. McCowan says he will secure an Apache interpreter, through whom visitors to the Indian school may talk readily to "Jerry," as the attaches of the school have christened the notorious red man.

St. Louis Post-Dispatch, June 26, 1904:
An illustrated full page article.

African Pygmies For the World's Fair

AMAZING DWARFS OF THE CONGO VALLEY TO BE SEEN IN ST. LOUIS. SOME RED, SOME BLACK. THEY ANTEDATE THE NEGRO IN EQUATORIAL AFRICA. FEARLESS MIDGETS WHO BOLDLY ATTACK ELEPHANTS WITH TINY LANCES, BOWS AND ARROWS.

STANLEY, SCHWEINFURTH AND PAUL DU CHAILLU ENCOUNTERED THEM IN REMOTE AFRICAN FORESTS.

THEY HAVE FIGURED IN STORY AND LEGEND SINCE THE DAYS OF ANCIENT EGYPT.

NOW FOR THE FIRST TIME THEY WILL SET FOOT ON THE WESTERN HEMISPHERE—SOME FACTS ABOUT THEM.

From the secluded forests of the Congo region in Equatorial Africa an American clergyman, the Rev. Samuel P. Verner is bringing to the World's Fair a company of African pygmies, the smallest members of the human race.

Red pygmies and black, the dwarf tribesmen, concerning whom less is known than of any other people on the face of the earth, they come to St. Louis the first of their kind who ever visited the Western Hemisphere. It is only after surmounting tremendous difficulties that they are to be brought to the World's Fair.

For months after Mr. Verner disappeared in the unknown heart of Africa, nothing was heard from him.

But he cables from a little African port that he has been successful and is on the way to the World's Fair with a number of pygmies. A patriarch of the tribe, accompanied by his dwarf wife, a young married couple, one boy, one girl, two infants, four red pygmies and other ethnic representatives of the world's strangest people, constitute the party. They will bring with them the materials with which to construct their native huts and are to occupy quarters south of the Indian building.

Here are some queer facts about the African pygmies:

They come from the Congo country in equatorial Africa.

They live in forests.

They are extremely shy.

No member of their tribe has ever before visited the Western Hemisphere.

They eat the flesh of wild animals killed with poisoned arrows.

They were discovered almost simultaneously by Schweinfurth and by Stanley, one of whose lieutenants captured a queen of the tribe.

They are known under the several tribal names of Akoa, Batwa, Wamubuttu and Akka.

The average height of the men is that of a 12 year-old white boy.

Their existence was known of by the ancient Egyptians.

Their tribal name of Akka is recorded on an ancient Egyptian monument.

They are mentioned by Homer.

Their skin is of a dull brown tint.

Their abnormally large heads are mounted on weak and thin necks.

They have an exaggerated development of the abdomen.

Their unusual abdominal development is caused by the enlargement of the left lobes of the liver and spleen. This has necessitated the forward projection of the lower portion of the spinal column. Hence a remarkable curve of the spine resembling the letter S in shape.

Their hair is wooly and very short.

They have a snout-like projection of the jaw, and a deep indentation at the base of the nose.

They are extremely cunning and dextrous.

They are renowned for courage in war with tribes of greater stature.

They are cruel, finding delight in torturing animals.

Some of them have skins the color of half-baked red clay brick.

They are believed to exist in great numbers in the unexplored central heart of Africa, Stanley's reports supporting this belief.

They hunt elephants and are fearless in attacking them.

They are the smallest members of the human race.

Their men hate hair upon their chin and upper lip.

Their hands are marked by extreme delicacy of shape.

They are very agile, leaping about like grasshoppers.

Their senses are almost abnormally acute.

They are an older race than the Papuans and true Negroes.

Their legs are short and curved inward.

Their hair forms little sooty black balls on their heads.

Each of their tribes has its own chief or king.

Their various tribes are grouped as Negrillos by anthropologists.

Their folklore is rich in fables about animals.

They wear loin-cloths of bark and caps adorned with parrot feathers.

Their bodies are exceptionally hairy.

Members of the Akka tribe are so hairy that they seem to be covered with a sort of felt, or fur, which is nearly half an inch long. It is grayish in color and gives them an elfish appearance.

Those of the pygmies who have skins of reddish tint are thought to be of the purest pygmy blood. The darker tribes are classed as hybrids between the red pygmies and the Negroes.

Stanley estimates their height as ranging from 3 feet to 4 feet 6 inches and the average weight of an adult at 90 pounds.

They live in low huts, shaped like an oval cut lengthways. These huts are arranged in a circle, with that of the chief in the center. About 100 yards in advance of their camps is a sentry hut, occupied by two pygmies who levy toll on all passing caravans.

Their chief occupation is hunting.

They capture monkeys in traps suspended from vines.

Their arrows and lances are charged with deadly poison made from snake-fangs, the crushed bodies of ants and a species of strychnos root.

Their only vegetable food consists of bananas, sweet potatoes and casava, which they purchase or steal from their neighbors.

A pygmy has been known to eat 60 bananas at one meal, in addition to other food, and then ask for more.

They are reported to practice cannibalism.

They are intelligent, cheerful, quick-witted and eloquent.

Their women are described as "nut-brown little maids," pretty and pleasing, with very lustrous eyes.

If caught young they are said to make excellent servants.

They are remarkable mimics.

Their method of dancing is to strut round in a circle, with their legs quite stiff, beating time with bows and arrows.

They bury their dead without ceremony.

They have no religion, no records or traditions of the past, practice no fetish rites, and are without tribal superstitions.

The palms of their hands are nearly white.

The dwarf Bushmen of the Zambesi valley are of their family blood.

Those who live near the sea dwell in sheltered positions along the coast and subsist on fish or anything edible thrown up by the waves.

Their huts are made of flexible sticks covered with leaves.

They capture fish by poisoning rivers with the powdered fruit of a palm, which stupefies the fish until they float on the surface and are easily collected.

One of their modes of burial is to place the corpse in the interior of a hollow tree, filling up the hole with branches and leaves mixed with earth. Another is to divert a running stream, bury the body in a hole and then turn back the rivulet to its former course, covering the grave.

They keep no domestic animals.

One of the pygmy tribes known as the Obougos was encountered in the French Congo region by Paul du Chaillu.

They live in small scattered communities of from ten to twenty people and resemble Bushmen.

They are nomadic, following the migrations of game.

They have no knowledge of handicraft or agriculture.

They are dependent upon neighboring tribes for their weapons, cooking pots and water vessels, which they purchase with meat.

Although they have no religion of their own, they live in real dread of the medicine-man of adjacent Negro tribes, due, probably, to the fact that the rites of their neighbors are accompanied by human sacrifices.

Explorer Schweinfurth encountered the pygmy tribes of Akka in the northeast region of the Congo basin. This is the tribe discovered by Stanley farther to the south and west in the valley of the Ituri river.

The most northerly of the pygmy tribes have lost many of their tribal characteristics by intermarriage with Negroes.

They decapitate their enemies slain in battle.

Schweinfurth describes the delight of one of the Akka pygmies in playing with the head of a dead enemy and crying out derisively "Bakinda nova! Kakinda he ha koto!" (Where is Bakinda? Bakinda is in the pot!)

The Batwa tribe of pygmies boasts of the greatest racial purity.

They have long heads, long narrow faces and little red eyes, set close together, like those of ferrets.

The Wambuttu tribe, neighbors of the Batwa, have round faces, gazelle-like eyes and rich yellow-ivory complexions.

A Wambuttu woman described by Stanley measured 33 inches in height and was beautifully formed. Stanley writes that she seemed to enjoy admiration.

The red pygmies are less hairy than the black.

One of their methods of killing elephants is with poisoned barbs fastened to heavy blocks of wood suspended along an elephant trail; when a passing elephant breaks the cord by which the barb is suspended the poisoned weapon falls on the elephant's back.

Stanley reports the case of a man who died within one minute after having been wounded with a pygmy's poisoned arrow.

The color of the skin of the Akka pygmies deepens in summer and pales in winter.

A pygmy servant employed by Schweinfurth was so confirmed in the habit of leaping like a grasshopper that he could never carry a plate without spilling more or less of its contents.

They are fond of playing and their antics are childish.

They were at one time thought to be more nearly related to the ape than to the human race.

It is believed that the pygmies occupied a large part of Africa previous to the Negroes.

Their arms are long and thin.

They seem to be controlled by an impulse that makes them find a delight in wickedness.

They capture small animals by noose traps placed along the trail.

They are believed to be descendants of the "little men" reported to Herodotus by the pilgrims of Gyrene [sic].

African ivory dealers who have fought against the pygmies concede that they are brave enemies.

The Akka pygmies are said to number nine distinct tribes, each with its own chief or king.

They are pigeontoed.

Their women have small hands and feet.

They hunt the elephant with very short bows or with short lances hardly longer than themselves.

It is said that pygmies living after the manner of taller men have been known to lose their abnormal abdominal development, and regain the normal shape of the vertebral column.

[Note: The Africans from the Congo arrived at the World's Fair sometime between June 27 and July 1, 1904. The following articles appeared after their arrival:]

St. Louis Post-Dispatch, July 2, 1904:

PYGMIES DEMAND A MONKEY DIET

GENTLEMEN FROM SOUTH AFRICA AT THE FAIR LIKELY TO PROVE TROUBLESOME IN MATTER OF FOOD.

Yet another distracting problem is before the Exposition authorities. It is purposed [sic: proposed] to allow the recent arrived Central African pigmies to eat, drink and have their being in circumstances identical, as for [sic: far] as possible, with what they are accustomed to in their native wilds.

But John Kandola [sic], a native missionary who brought the little men over from the Congo Free State, says that they are in the habit of eating monkeys.

Can the management supply their larder with Simian savories and monkey a la mode? But worse than this, and more difficult to obtain, it is learned from Kandola that one or two of these harmless-looking gentlemen are fond of dieting upon human flesh. Perhaps they will be persuaded to cut out these two items of diet and subsist on nuts and potatoes. They have taken so naturally to civilized costume and to the use of tobacco, that one may expect them to accommodate the management in the matter of food. They are by no means ignorant of the value of money. "Artiba," the cannibal, had his photo taken today and held his hand out for recompense. He received a five-cent piece with a very poor grace and wanted more. He produced a very smart, civilized-looking purse and hid away his wage with his other wealth. He had nearly half a dollar already. Then he lit his cigarette and inhaled in huge breaths with the greatest delight, babbling volubly in the Baluba language.

The little men will have troubles of their own too. They are to be set to work at once to build huts for themselves after their fashion, but it appears these unchivalrous gentlemen are in the habit of having all the work done for them by their devoted wives. They have brought none of their women folk with them and will have to dig and delve and cook their food by their own efforts. It may be found necessary to take away any sort of shelter to induce them to work at all.

[Note: "Artiba" mentioned above is Ota Benga]

St. Louis Post-Dispatch, July, 1904:

PYGMY DANCE STARTS PANIC IN FAIR PLAZA

SEEING UNCLAD AFRICANS ADVANCING TOWARD HER, BRANDISHING THEIR SPEARS, WOMAN SCREAMS AND CROWD FOLLOWS HER IN TERROR.

The scream of a woman frightened at the realism of a dance by eight unclad African pygmies at the end of the anthropological performance on the Plaza St. Louis at the Fair last night, started a panic that brought the chief feature of midsummer carnival day at the Fair to a tumultuous end.

Brandishing their spears, bows and arrows and murderous-looking knives, shouting blood-curdling cries and dashing towards the crowd as if to cut their way through the 75,000 people closely packed abut the limits of the plaza, the pygmies so terrified a woman that she involuntarily cried out. Another woman equally frightened, screamed and in a moment the crowd breaking through the lines of Jefferson guards, swarmed into the plaza towards the pygmies, who appeared as much frightened as the women had been.

The hurried arrival of a detail of soldiers from the First Illinois regiment gave the pygmies, Indians, and other members of the anthropological exhibit on the plaza a chance to scurry to their quarters near the Administration building. Order among the crowd was then restored.

The panic came at the close of the hottest day of the year at the Fair, and with the largest crowd assembled there at any time since the Fourth of July, packed about the Plaza St.

Louis, where the first anthropological exhibit since the exposition opening was scheduled to take place.

Indians, Patagonians and Ainus preceded the pygmies on the program.

Chief Geronimo led the procession of Indians, and following him were White Horse, chief of the Iowas, and Jalahai, chief of the Sioux.

After the pygmies came the Pawnees, Apaches, Patagonians and Ainus and British Columbian Indians.

Each tribe danced or illustrated some regular feature of their native life.

The crowd of the day and evening was estimated at 125,000, the largest since the Fourth of July.

St. Louis Post-Dispatch, July 19, 1904:

ENRAGED PYGMIES ATTACK VISITOR

H. S. GIBBONS OF DURANGO COLO., PHOTOGRAPHED THEM, BUT GAVE NO TIPS.

HE WAS PURSUED AND BEATEN

MONEY WOULD HAVE BEEN AN EFFECTIVE WEAPON, BUT HE WOULDN'T USE IT.

The African pygmies of the Fair took to the warpath late yesterday because a visitor took a photograph of one of them and would not indemnify them to the extent that they deemed meet.

They gave the photographer a scare that he will remember after all his other experiences at the Fair have been forgotten. They attacked him and were handling him roughly and were attempting to take everything he had away from him when white men rescued him.

The photographer was H. S. Gibbons of Durango, Colo. He approached the wire fence in closing the pygmy kraal and focused a pocket folding kodak on Latuno of the Baluba tribe, one of the big Africans brought over with the pygmies.

Latuno tried to get behind a post, but Gibbons snapped him. With a yell of rage Latuno scaled the wire fence and catching hold a jagged stone rushed at Gibbons, demanding money. Gibbons gave him a nickel but that did not appease him. He [tried to grab] Gibbon's kodak. Gibbons held on to the kodak and the [fight ensued] for its possession. A large crowd quickly surrounded them. Latuna reigned and chattered incessantly. Each attempt of Gibbons to complain in a language which the black men could not understand brought the fulmination of wrath.

Money the Only Effective Weapon

It was plain that nothing but money or a fight would meet the African's idea of what the occasion called for. Soon the other black men were getting excited and one in charge of them did not attempt to control them. Gibbons was advised to raise his bid for peace but instead he wrested the kodak from the grasp of Latuno and tried to get away. Latuno, still carrying the big stone barred the way and tried to get his hands into Gibbons pocket. Gibbons broke away from him and took refuge in the trading post across the road. Latuno followed him in and all the other Africans ran chattering across and with Latuno surrounded Gibbons. They began to snatch at what he carried and what he wore. He pushed one of them away and they fell upon him and began to beat him.

The trading post was filled with men, women and children, and there was a good deal of excitement and alarm.

Several white men rushed to the assistance of Gibbons. He was pulled out of the way into a corner and the Africans were cuffed and kicked out of the building. Yelling with rage, they made a rush and tried to get back into the building, but were stopped by a wall of white men.

[Note: When Verner and the Africans arrived in New Orleans, Verner was stricken by an attack of the malarial fever and was transported unconscious from the steamship, on a stretcher, to a local sanitarium for treatment and recovery. The Africans were escorted to

St. Louis by John Kondola, their countryman and interpreter, and Mr. Dorsey of the Exposition Company. It was not until Aug. 5, 1904, that Verner was able to rejoin the Africans at the St. Louis Exposition.]

St. Louis Republic, Saturday, August 6, 1904:

PYGMIES SHIVER OVER CAMP FIRE

"GIVE US BLANKETS," IS THEIR GREETING TO MISSIONARY WHO BROUGHT THEM OUT OF AFRICA.

SAY IT'S COLD IN ST. LOUIS

DISCARD PALM LEAF SUITS FOR WARMER CLOTHING—DECLARE AMERICANS TREAT THEM AS THEY WOULD MONKEYS.

"Give us blankets; we are suffering from the cold weather in St. Louis."

The foregoing sentence, uttered in the Batwa pygmy language, was the greeting to the Reverend S. P. Verner yesterday morning from his first visit to their camp on the World's Fair grounds.

This if the first time Mr. Verner has seen his little black charges, whom he brought out of the African jungles, since they arrived in this country, for Mr. Verner, who was suffering from jungle fever, was taken to a New Orleans hospital on his landing, some time ago, and just returned to St. Louis.

When Mr. Verner visited the camp yesterday he found the little pygmies hiding together over a camp fire. They were shivering from the cold. When they espied Mr. Verner they rushed to him and the three of the little pygmies embraced him. "We are glad you have come," said Latuna, the spokesman of the party, "for we are suffering from the cold."

Mr. Verner looked at them and voiced his disappointment. Instead of the nice little palm leaf suits which he had expected to find them wearing, they were clothed in incongruous coats and jackets.

Mr. Verner pacified them by promising them a good cozy house to live in, where they could have a fire to keep them warm all the time. At present they are living in a tent.

The pygmies confided to Mr. Verner that they had accepted the kindness of their neighbors on Indian Hill, who had been good enough to lend them some blankets to keep them from freezing.

"The temperature in the country they come from," said Mr. Verner, "averages about 115 in the shade."

The pygmies also complained to Mr. Verner of the rudeness of the American people. Latuna said that the people did nothing but lean on the fence and ask questions, which they could not understand. "When a white man comes to our country," complained Latuna, "we give them presents, sometimes of sheep, goats or birds, and divide our elephant meat with them. The Americans treat us as they do our pet monkey. They laugh at us and poke their umbrellas into our faces. They do the same to our monkey."

Unidentified St. Louis Newspaper:

PYGMIES ATTEND IN KHAKI UNIFORM

LITTLE BLACK MEN OF CONGO DON WHITE MAN'S ATTIRE, AND LOSE THEIR INDIVIDUALITY.

Cold weather has bereft the pygmies of the Congo, now encamped at the World's Fair, of their principal charm. Each and every one of them has had his bare individuality buried in a khaki uniform, and they go about the purlieus of the Exposition without exciting any more interest from the visitor than a denizen of the quarters on lower "Mawgan" street.

The uniforms are of brown khaki, suggesting to the facetious and African version of a "Buster Brown" costume. Even the Prince, the heir-apparent to the throne of the Latubats, has his dusky limbs swathed in khaki.

With the polarized winds of autumn and their assumption of the white man's attire much of the old-time snap and nerve of the vivacious little Africans has disappeared, and they wander about the west end of the grounds in a disconsolate way, as though longing for the freedom of their gunnysack skirts and the ostrich plumes which constituted their native attire.

St. Louis Post-Dispatch, Aug. 6, 1904:

CANNIBALS WILL SING AND DANCE

On Children's Day at the World's Fair, Monday, Aug. 8, all children will be admitted free, accompanied by an adult. The principal people of the nations of the world will sing and dance on a stage in the Plaza St. Louis, 6:30 to 8:30 p.m.

St. Louis Post-Dispatch, Aug. 13, 1904:
[On the sports page, with the baseball scores for the St. Louis Browns.]

BARBARIANS MEET IN ATHLETIC GAMES

PYGMIES IN MUD FIGHT, PELTED EACH OTHER UNTIL ONE SIDE WAS PUT TO ROUT.

CROW INDIAN WON MILE RUN

NEGRITOS CAPTURED POLE-CLIMBING EVENT AND PATAGONIANS BEAT SYRIANS IN TUG-OF-WAR.

Thirteen different tribes were represent in the second Anthropological athletic meet at the Stadium Friday afternoon. All the contestants performed in their native costumes, which was a happy idea, as some of the events were especially adapted to certain styles of dress.

This was particularly true of the mud fight of the pygmies, which furnished the most amusing feature of the meet. Six pygmies, three on a side, were armed with several heaps of nice, soft sticky clay and at the starter's signal, each side began to pelt the other, keeping this up until one side was put to rout.

The little men fought hard until one of them was put out of commission, being almost blinded by the ammunition. It was then three against two and the weaker side was soon vanquished.

Probably the most interesting event from the athletic standpoint, was the mile run in which the following tribes were represented: Ainus, Kaffirs, Sioux, Pawnee, Crow, Maricabo, Cocopa Indians, Syrians, the Batatela tribe from the Congo and the Patagonians. Black White Bear, the Crow Indian, won the event, running the distance in 5 minutes and 38 seconds. Yousouf Hana, a Syrian, came in second and a Kaffir, Latrouw by name, got third money.

The pole climbing event was captured by the Negritos. They shinned up the fifty-foot pole in the fastest time, making the ascent in 20 and 2–5 seconds.

The tug of war between the Patagonians and the Syrians, three men on a side, was won by the former. Chief Guichico, aged 70 years also a Patagonian, won the baseball-throwing contest.

Geronimo, the old Apache chief, was on the field but took no part in the sports. He leaned silently against the track-rail looking on but gave no other sign that he was at all interested.

Doctor McGee, who had charge of the meet, said that he was well pleased with the results and that a similar meet probably will be held the latter part of the month.

The summary:

100 yard dash—George Menz, Sioux Indian, first; Mundude, Lanau Moro, second; Frank Moore, Pawnee Indian, third. Time 11 3–5 s.

Throwing the javelin for accuracy, target distance 25 feet—Timon, Lanau Moro, first; Shamba, pygmy, second; Kontoroy, Ainu, third.

120 yard low hurdle—Leon Poitra, Chippewa, first; George Menz, Sioux, second; Mundude, Lanau Moro, third. Time, 18 3–5 s.

Climbing 50-foot pole speed contest—Basilio, Negrito, first; Bushow, pygmy, second; Sayas, Negrito, third. Time 20 2–5s.

Running high jump—George Menz, Sioux, first; Black White Bear, Crow, second; Leon Poitra, Chippewa, third. Height, 4 ft. 7 in.

Archery contest, target distance 42 yards—Skuke, Cocopa, first, 3 points; Basilio, Negrito, and Bengia, Ainu, tied for second, 2 points each.

One-fourth mile run—George Menz, Sioux, first; Simon Marx, Sioux, second; Yousouf Hana, Syrian, third. Time 60 3–5 s.

Tug-of-war between Patagonians and Syrians, three men in each team—Won by Patagonians.

Throwing baseball for accuracy—Chief Guichico, aged 70 years, Patagonian, first; Frank Moore, Pawnee, second.

Kicking baseball for distance, by Cocopa Indians—Kipuck, first; Jerry, second; Jack, third, distance 90 ft.

One mile run—Black White Bear, Crow, first; Yousouf Hana, Syrian, second, Latrouw, Kaffir, third. Time 5m 38s.

St. Louis Republic, Aug. 14, 1904:

TRYING ORDEAL FOR SAVAGES

SCIENTISTS WILL BEGIN A SPECIAL STUDY OF WORLD'S FAIR TRIBES SEPTEMBER 1.

St. Louis Post-Dispatch, Aug. 16, 1904:

PYGMIES ORGANIZE A MILITARY COMPANY

A new military company has been organized at the World's Fair.

After watching the marching and evening drills at the Indian school, the Pygmies have appeared as a military organization, Capt. Latuna commanding.

The company reports for guard mount, armed with sticks varying from two to four feet in length with Capt. Latuna wearing a lath in his belt for a sword which he waves in the air at every command.

All during the unerring routines of the Indians the dusky guard goes through military maneuvers in obedience to orders from their captain, each man interprets and carries out the command to suit his own fancy, marching and countermarching in all directions.

All through the drill the company keeps perfect time to the music of the Indian band and in spite of the fact that they are marching in any and every direction, at a certain command they turn and form two perfect lines, march up to their captain, halt, and remain standing like statues until another command is given, when they resume their drill.

Not once during the entire drill did they interfere with the Indians except to keep them convulsed with laughter.

St. Louis Republic, Aug. 20, 1904:

Driven From Huts By Rainstorm

PYGMIES AND AINUS SEEK SHELTER FOR NIGHT IN INDIAN SCHOOL.

Resembles Noah's Ark.

SAVAGES INSIST ON TAKING PETS FROM JUNGLE HOMES WITH THEM TO ESCAPE TERRORS OF LIGHTNING.

St. Louis Post-Dispatch, Sunday, Sept. 4, 1904:
An illustrated two full page article in the Magazine Section.

An Untold Chapter of My Adventures While Hunting Pygmies in Africa

[BY] SAMUEL P. VERNER

[with illustrations as follows: A full face drawing of Verner by "Conrey," captioned "Samuel P. Verner"; A drawing of Verner meeting with natives in Africa, captioned "VERNER ARBITRATING A TRIBAL WAR IN AN AFRICAN JUNGLE."; a photograph of several African natives at the Exposition with no specific caption; an exaggerated drawing of Ota Benga showing protruding fang-like pointed teeth with the caption "NOTICE THE PYGMY CANNIBAL'S TEETH. EACH FILED DOWN TO SHAPE OF V"]

Rev. Samuel P. Verner Tells the Story of Difficulties
Encountered in Securing for the World's Fair the
Most Startling Ethnological Exhibit Ever Seen in
Civilization—Arbitrated a Tribal War in one Instance
and Bought a Cannibal Prisoner-Slave in
Another—The Loneliness of Filed-Teeth Otabenga,
Devourer of Human Flesh.

Have you seen Otabenga's teeth!
They're worth the 5 cents he charges for showing them to visitors on anthropology hill out at the World's Fair.
Otabenga is a cannibal, the only genuine African cannibal in America today. He's also the only human chattel. He belongs to the Exposition company. Step right up. There's no charge except to see his teeth. He has the reputation of being a man eater and has an exhibition the identical molars and incisors with which it was done.
His teeth are as sharp as those of any wild animal. They are pointed like the teeth of a saw. They have been filed that way.
Otabenga himself looks playful and harmless enough. He is gentle and graceful, and the first impulse of the visitor is to pet him and exclaim: "Poor little fellow; he looks so sad and lonely."
But look at his teeth!
Perhaps he's lonesome because he is deprived of his native food. Otabenga is pitiable, however, though he is to be feared and shuddered at.
Can you put yourself in his place for a brief period, say just between meals? Pity the fierce cannibal! He has a sad history. He is here alone in the world, quite alone, nearly nine thousand miles from those who can speak the only dialect he knows or enjoys a repast with him. He is heartsick because he has no one to chatter with. He is from a river bank far distant from the jungles of his fellow pygmies at the Fair, and not one of the

latter knows his tongue. He is lonely because he has learned but few words of the other pygmies' language. He picked those up while en route across the Atlantic or since reaching St. Louis.

And because he is a cannibal, the black lilliputians brought with him out of Africa look down on him. He is not in their set. And Otabenga is bowed with shame because he, too, realizes that man-eating is an old fogy idea. His people are behind the times in darkest Africa.

To determine what part the World's Fair specimen had taken in the actual eating of human flesh seems as hard as the problem of his age, yet certain it is that he is of a man-eating tribe who file their teeth to a point for the purpose of tearing human flesh. These very people are, within the last ten years, however, making denial that they are cannibals, conscious of the degradation and ashamed of a practice which more advanced savages look down upon. They are becoming ashamed of cannibalism just as civilized people discard and become shamed of certain old customs of a less repulsive nature.

Poor little Otabenga—most to be pitied, most to be feared! He is a Chirichiri. That's the name of his tribe, a name suggestive of the chattering tongue of his monkey-like people. He is a dwarfy, black specimen of sad-eyed humanity, 4 feet 9 inches tall and somewhere between 17 and 25 years old. That's as near as anyone can come at a guess. Nobody knows his age.

When he first reached St. Louis early in July Otabenga was asked his name. He understood what was wanted, but his questioners couldn't understand his reply, for thereafter they called him Autobank. To the reporters Autobank appealed as the nearest probable interpretation of the cannibal pygmy's chattering. The name was straightened out only upon the arrival later of Rev. Samuel P. Verner, the Presbyterian missionary who brought the pygmies of darkest Africa to the great World's Fair.

Otabenga's story as told to the Sunday Post-Dispatch by Rev. Verner is truly a pathetic one.

Otabenga was a slave, held captive by another tribe, till Rev. Verner bought him in a Congo slave market at a cost of $5. The price was not paid in cash, but in bright calico and such trinkets as appealed to the taste of his warlike captor, the giant Baschile. The little cannibal had his choice of remaining in captivity a slave of coming out of it to the World's Fair. He gladly accepted the trip across the unknown seas, though it meant that he must go thousands of miles farther and stay long away from his native shimbec under the bamboo tree.

Rev. Verner, delegated by the Louisiana Purchase Exposition Co. for the purpose on account of his previous years of experience down in the equatorian jungles, steamed up the Congo river from Matadi last spring on a pygmy hunt. He knew of the Batwa tribe at Wismann Falls near the headwaters of the Kasai, the largest southern tributary to the Congo river, and while traveling the thousand miles or so up those streams with his 15 native porters on board the 35 ton boat, Ville d'Anvers, he stopped at the village of the Baschile to inquire about the Chirichiri, which tribe, he knew, live some 75 miles inland. That distance through the torrid African jungle was to him equal to the distance from St. Louis to New York, and Rev. Verner was overjoyed to learn that there had been a tribal war and that one captive was held a hostage on the river bank. It was Otabenga.

Negotiations for his purchase were opened and a bargain was readily struck. Five dollars in goods was the price, and some of the Baschile who knew his tongue explained the situation tot he little slave. He was to go with the white man to escape captivity. Rev. Verner took the necessary steps at the nearest government post to have Otabenga officially [recognized when?] he is in St. Louis as a ¿. The Congo Free State government was assured that all the pygmies would be returned to their homes after the Fair.

The seven other Ethiopians brought out of Africa by S. P. Verner were secured by a single coup several hundred miles up river, but that coup was no or less than the arbitration of a tribal war, accompanied by the exercise of the shrewdest diplomacy. At Wismann, the cargo of the Ville d'Anvers was discharged in the jungle and Rev. Verner walked 20 miles to the village Ndombe, where he had formerly been stationed as missionary, only to find King Ndombe at war with his cousin, King Belinge of the village of Belinge, over a woman whom one of Belinge's lieutenants had stolen. The native chieftains are all eager to [?] the white welcome to their country, and by assuring Ndombe that by continual warfare he would get a reputation as a fighter and delay the white invasion. Rev. Verner succeeded in bringing the two chiefs together for a peace conference. Belinge came over under assurances of a safe escort in Ndombe's realm, and they [?] and deliberated until Ndombe finally gave up the stolen woman on the ground that she had really eloped, and the war was declared over. The pygmy people who were parasites on the Ndombe and Belinge tribes, now came out of hiding and Rev. Verner was able to negotiate with them for the first time. It was only by settling the war that he made this possible. The women, however, remained in hiding, for fear of being stolen, and only men and boys were courted for the World's Fair. The four Batwa pygmies who readily agreed to come were:

Name	Height	Age[*]	
Shamba	4 feet 9 inches	[28]	
Bushubba	4 feet 6 inches	[16]	[sic: Bomushubba was his name]
Lumo	4 feet	[20]	
Mushwaba	4 feet 8 inches	[20]	[sic: Malengo was his name]

[*The ages indicated in this article were depicted in a range of estimate, such as "16 to 19", but the numbers are obscured in the source from which this was transcribed. The bracketed ages and corrected names are from the final exposition report published in 1912.]

Ndombe's prime minister and son wanted to come to America, but were dissuaded by their lord and King, and instead there came from that larger tribe, Latuna, nephew of the prime minister, aged 18 years and Lumbango, nephew of Ndombe, aged 15 years. Two other [African natives] who helped to make up the expedition are Kalamma, a Baluba tribesman, aged 24 years, and Kondola a Batelea, who had been in America four years and who [?] to assist Rev. Verner in that undertaking. He is now their interpreter at the Fair. [remainder of article is obscured.]

St. Louis Post-Dispatch, December, 4, 1904:

Gifts to Royal Pair Cost $2.50

PRESIDENT FRANCIS MAKES HAPPY THE HEARTS OF WORLD'S FAIR PYGMIES FOR $8.35.

Barrel of Salt For King

AND OTHER PRESENTS OF SIMILAR VALUE ARE GIVEN LITTLE AFRICANS BEFORE DEPARTURE.

PRESIDENT FRANCIS' GIFTS TO THE PYGMIES

Cask of salt for King Ndombe	$2.00
"Pearl" necklace for Ndombe's queen	.50
Watch fobs for nine pygmies	4.50
Spending money, St. Louis to Africa 15 cents each, nine pygmies	1.35
Total	$8.35

President Francis of the World's Fair spent $8.35 for gifts for the Pygmies who have been in St. Louis this summer and for their king and queen who remained in Africa. When they called on him in his office before departing, he made a little speech of presentation.

The Pygmies are going home tomorrow. Their visit to the Exposition president last night was of a farewell nature. Dr. W. J. McGee, chief of the department of anthropology, accompanied them to President Francis' office.

"You have been with us all summer and we have enjoyed your presence," said President Francis as he faced Prince Latuna, the ranking Pygmy. "You have added to the success of this Exposition."

When the interpreter translated this the nine pygmies grinned and bowed low. If given half a chance, they would have danced.

"Now I want you to take home to your king and queen some remembrances of your trip and also some little articles for yourselves. Present to King Ndombe a cask of salt which has been prepared for you."

Salt is the costliest article in the land of the Pygmies, and therefore a gift of great value. The cask cost $2.

"To the queen please present this necklace of pearls, which we trust she will wear."

The "necklace of pearls" cost 50 cents and there were enough pearls to go around the waist of a Patagonian giantess.

"For each of you there is in this package a watch fob. If you don't need it for your watch use it for something else."

The nine fobs cost 50 cents each.

"And now," concluded the President, "you are going on a long journey. From here you will go down the Mississippi to New Orleans. Then you will cross the gulf of Havana. Thence you will steam to Portugal and from there reach your home in Africa. You will have occasion to spend money and I am glad to provide you with some."

Thereupon the president graciously presented each Pygmy with three 5-cent coins.

The bowed once more very low and at a signal from Dr. McGee backed from the room loaded down with their riches.

The Ainus, who are now the only persons left in the Anthropological section of the World's Fair, will leave for their homes Tuesday. C. P. Hulbert, secretary to Dr. McGee, will accompany them to Vancouver.

Text of Newspaper Articles on Ota Benga in New York

The following articles and excerpts of articles, pertaining to Ota Benga, are transcribed from various New York newspapers beginning on Sept. 9, 1906. While not exhaustive, the authors believe that these articles are representative of the treatment given to the Ota Benga's story by the press. They are presented in chronological order.

New York Times, Sunday, Sept. 9, 1906:

BUSHMAN SHARES A CAGE WITH BRONX PARK APES

SOME LAUGH OVER HIS ANTICS, BUT MANY ARE NOT PLEASED

KEEPER FREES HIM AT TIMES

THEN, WITH BOW AND ARROW, THE PYGMY FROM THE CONGO TAKES TO THE WOODS

There was an exhibition at the Zoological Park, in the Bronx, yesterday which had for many of the visitors something more than a provocation to laughter. There were laughs enough in it too, but there was something about it which made the serious minded grave. Even those who laughed the most turned away with an expression on their faces such as one sees after a play with a sad ending or a book in which the hero or heroine is poorly rewarded.

"Something about it that I don't like," was the way one man put it.

The exhibition was that of a human being in a monkey cage. The human being happened to be a Bushman, one of a race that scientists do not rate high in the human scale, but to the average non-scientific person in the crowd of sightseers there was something about the display that was unpleasant.

The human being caged was the little black man, Ota Benga, whom Prof. S. P. Verner, the explorer, recently brought to this country from the jungles of Central Africa. Prof. Verner lately handed him over to the New York Zoological Society for care and keeping. When he was permitted yesterday to get out of his cage, a keeper constantly kept his eyes on him. Benga appears to like his keeper too. It is probably a good thing that Benga doesn't think very deeply. If he did it isn't likely that he was very proud of himself when he woke in the morning and found himself under the same roof with the orangoutangs and monkeys, for that is where he really is.

The news that the pygmy would be on exhibition augmented the Saturday afternoon crowd at the Zoological Park yesterday, which becomes somewhat smaller as the Summer wanes. The monkey—or rather the primate—house is in the centre of Director Hornaday's animal family.

New York Times, Monday, Sept. 10, 1906:

MAN AND MONKEY SHOW DISAPPROVED BY CLERGY

THE REV. DR. MACARTHUR THINKS THE EXHIBITION DEGRADING

COLORED MINISTERS TO ACT

THE PYGMY HAS AN ORANG-OUTANG AS A COMPANION NOW AND THEIR ANTICS DELIGHT THE BRONX CROWDS

Several thousand persons took the Subway, the elevated, and the surface cars to the New York Zoological Park, in the Bronx, yesterday, and there watched Ota Benga, the Bushman, who has been put by the management on exhibition there in the monkey cage. The Bushman didn't seem to mind it, and the sight plainly pleased the crowd. Few expressed audible objection to the sight of a human being in a cage with monkeys as companions, and there could be no doubt that to the majority the joint man-and-monkey exhibition was the most interesting sight in Bronx Park.

All the same, a storm over the exhibition was preparing last night. News of what the managers of the Zoological Park were permitting reached the Rev. Dr. R.S. MacArthur of Calvary Baptist Church last night, and he announced his intention of communicating with the negro clergymen in the city and starting an agitation to have the show stopped.

"The person responsible for this exhibition degrades himself as much as he does the African," said Dr. MacArthur. "Instead of making a beast of this little fellow, he should be put in school for the development of such powers as God gave to him. It is too bad that there is not some society like that for the Prevention of Cruelty to Children. We send our missionaries to Africa to Christianize the people, and then we bring one here to brutalize him.

"Our Christian missionary societies must take this matter up at once. I shall communicate with Dr. Gilbert of the Mount Olivet Baptist Church and other pastors of colored congregations, that we may work together in this matter. They will have my active assistance."

Colored Ministers Will Protest

Dr. Gilbert said he had already decided that the exhibition was an outrage and that he and other pastors would join with Dr. MacArthur in seeing to it that the Bushman was released from the monkey cage and put elsewhere.

Any suspicion that the exhibition was the result of error was contradicted by yesterday's developments. Benga was removed from the chimpanzees' cage to the crescent shaped construction in the southwestern end of the Primate House, and on the cage was posted this sign:

> The African Pigmy, "Ota Benga." Age 23 years. Height, 4 feet 11 inches. Weight, 103 pounds. Brought from the Kasai River, Congo Free State, South Central Africa by Dr. Samuel P. Verner, Exhibited each afternoon during September.

To increase the picturesqueness of the exhibition, moreover, an orang-outang named Dohong, which has been widely described as showing almost human intelligence was put in the cage with the Bushman and with them the parrot which Dr. Verner brought from Africa with Benga.

The Bushman and the orang-outang frolicked together most of the afternoon. The two were frequently locked in each other's arms, and the crowd was delighted.

There was always a crowd before the cage, most of the time roaring with laughter, and from almost every corner of the garden could be heard the question:

"Where is the Pygmy?"

And the answer was, "In the monkey house."

Perhaps as a concession to the fact that it was Sunday, a pair of canvas shoes had been given too the Bushman to wear. He was barefooted on Saturday. He seemed to like the shoes very much. Over and over again the crowd laughed at him as he sat in mute admiration of them on his stool in the monkey cage. But he didn't mind that. He has grown used to the crowd laughing, has discovered that they laugh at everything he does. If he wonders why he does not show it.

New York Globe, Monday, Sept. 10, 1906:

LIVELY ROW OVER A PYGMY

A mighty fuss has been raised over the African pigmy, Ota Benga, who is being exhibited in the Bronx Zoological Park. Ota himself does not comprehend the trouble, for he has so far grasped the meaning of only 100 English words. But the Rev. R. S. MacArthur of the Calvary Baptist Church and William T. Hornaday, director of the park have shot strong words at each other.

"Instead of making a beast of this little fellow," said Dr. MacArthur, "he should be put in school for the development of such powers as God gave to him. It is too bad that there is not some society like that for the Prevention of Cruelty to Children. We send our missionaries to Africa to Christianize the people, and then we bring a native here to brutalize him."

"This is most ridiculous thing I have ever heard of," said M. Hornaday. "If the Rev. MacArthur or any other clergyman should get up any movement against this boy he will make his race look ridiculous.

"As for the boy being exhibited in a cage, it was done simply for the convenience of the thousands of people who wanted to see him. We have no platform that we could place him on, and this big open air cage was the best place we could find to put him where everybody could see him.

"Why, we are taking excellent care of the little fellow and he is a great favorite with everybody connected with the zoo. He has one of the best rooms in the primate house."

[New York] *Evening Post,* Monday, Sept. 10, 1906:

A Pygmy Among the Primates

ONE OF THE "BANTAMS" OF THE AFRICAN RACE AT THE ZOOLOGICAL PARK—HIS DIVERSIONS—TWENTY-THREE, AND TWICE MARRIED—TO RETURN TO AFRICA LATER.

A genuine African pygmy, Ota Benga, is at the Primates' House, in the Zoological Park, working with the chimpanzee and the orang. His height is 4 feet 11 inches: he is about twenty-three years old, and has been married twice. His first wife was stolen by a tribe of unneighborly savages, and his second wife died from the bit of a poisonous snake.

Ota Benga is a well-developed little man, with a good head, bright eyes, and a pleasing countenance. He has already become quite "chummy" with the keeper of the Monkey House, Engelhome, and has picked up near a hundred English words, which he weaves with his own scanty native vocabulary of barely 300 distinct words, with a queer sort of pigeon English not unlike that heard on the Pacific Coast. Keeper Engelhome has learned a number of the little man's words, and thus the two are able to communicate to a certain extent on such simple subjects. While the dwarf is extraordinarily good tempered, he strongly objects to being made the object of curious examination by everyone, as was shown by an incident yesterday afternoon, when a visitor was watching him weave a hammock out of a ball of twine. His room is situated at the end of the Primates' House, and a door on one side into the outer yard has an upper pane of glass. While the pygmy was busily working at the network of twine a number of children watched him. For a time he worked in silence, a broad grin, which seldom leaves his face, gaping his mouth and showing the rows of sharply filed teeth. Suddenly he turned his head, the smile contracted into a snarl, and he leaped to his feet with a chatter of indistinguishable English and Bachichi, and pulled the curtain down. "He says they are making fun of him," explained the keeper.

Ota Benga, or "Bi" (which means friend in his own language), as he is commonly called, is possessed of a great deal of childish vanity and pride. While he thinks a great deal of his two best friends, Samuel P. Verner, the American explorer who brought him here, and the keeper, Englehome, he considers himself every bit as good, in fact, a trifle better. As for women—well he has no use for them. To him they are menials, not worth noticing. Mr. Verner has had a great deal of trouble in teaching him how to raise his hat and be polite to women, and he still views them with a half-concealed contempt that is comical.

His principal duty in the monkey house is to look after the residents there, especially a little chimpanzee. Mr. Verner has loaned him to the Zoo, and the keepers say he has a great influence with the beasts—even with the larger kind, including the orang-outang with whom he plays as though one of them, rolling around the floor of the cages in wild wrestling matches and chattering to them in his own guttural tongue, which they seem to understand. At any rate, they obey him when he speaks to them much better than they obey the regular keepers. Notwithstanding his influence with monkeys, he is unable to understand the white man's ability to handle different kinds of animals and reptiles, particularly the latter, and in the true spirit of his race, sets it down to witchcraft. To the same cause he ascribes all the wonders of the Zoo, and is firmly convinced that his white friends are the best witch doctors he ever saw . . .

The tribe to which the little man belongs is known as the Bachichi, a word which means "bushman." The Bachichi are true pygmies, but they are not "dwarfs." They are the bantams of the African race. They are found in scattered communities in many portions of the great equatorial forest, and have been met and described under various names by DuChaille, Stanley, Schweinfurth, Wells, and other explorers.

Ota Benga is black—though not what is called "coal black"—beardless, and well formed. As has been said he has a short English vocabulary, but it is not Mr. Verner's purpose to educate him beyond the necessities of his own sphere. In a short time he will be back again with his own people. Just how long he will remain at the Zoological Park no one can say.

New York Times, Tuesday, Sept. 11, 1906:

NEGRO MINISTERS ACT TO FREE THE PYGMY

WILL ASK THE MAYOR TO HAVE HIM TAKEN FROM MONKEY CAGE

COMMITTEE VISITS THE ZOO

PUBLIC EXHIBITIONS OF THE DWARF DISCONTINUED, BUT WILL BE RESUMED, MR. HORNADAY SAYS.

A committee of the Colored Baptist Ministers' Conference will call on the Mayor today on behalf of Ota Benga, the African pygmy, who is being exhibited with the monkeys at the Bronx Zoological Park. The ministers will ask the Mayor to save the little African for what they term "the degrading exhibition" of a human being in a cage disporting himself with apes. If the Mayor declines to assist them they propose to hold an indignation meeting . . .

Some one explained that Benga was kept in the monkey house because Mr. Verner, who brought him over here, said he had no other place to put him. To this Supt. Gordon, speaking for the committee said:

"The trouble seems to be that Dr. Verner did not apply to the proper persons. We have 225 children in the institution to which I belong—some of them pretty large children. We will take this little African and be pleased to have him. We will vouch for it that he will be well taken care of, and we will be responsible for him. If this does not suit, I will take him personally into my home and be responsible for him to the fullest extent.

"We are frank enough to say we do not like this exhibition of one of our race with the monkeys. Our race, we think, is depressed enough without exhibiting one of us with the apes. We think we are worthy of being considered human beings, with souls. . . ."

Dr. Hornaday, he said, had suggested to him that he should allow Benga to stay at the Zoological park so that he might show visitors how they did things in Africa. Dr. Verner said that he had not been at the park on Sunday. He went on to say:

"If Ota Benga is in a cage, he is only there to look after the animals. If there is a notice on the cage, it is only put there to avoid answering the many questions that are asked about him. He is absolutely free. The only restriction that is put upon him is to prevent him from getting away from the keepers. This is done for his own safety."

"Benga will stay at the Zoological Gardens for the present. Care will be taken not to give exhibitions on Sundays and not to hurt any one's feelings. There is no financial benefit accruing to me, or to the Park for the boy's stay there. The public is the only beneficiary.

"In answer to Dr. MacArthur, I desire to say a great part of my work in Africa is of a humanitarian character. I brought the pygmy here to show that he is an intelligent being, and that the zoological and psychological gap between the pygmies and the apes constitutes a cataclysm. The 'missing link' will never be found alive."

Director Hornaday said he proposes to continue the exhibitions until the Executive Committee of the Zoological Society orders him to stop. "I would like to say," he added, "that I do not wish to offend my colored brothers' feelings or the feelings of any one for that matter. I am giving the exhibitions purely as an ethnological exhibit. It is my duty to interest the visitors to the park, and what I have done in exhibiting Benga is in pursuance of this.

"I am a believer in the Darwinian theory." Mr. Hornaday continued, "but I hope my colored brethren will not take the absurd position that I am giving the exhibition to show the close analogy of the African savage to the apes. Benga is in the primate house because that was the most comfortable place we could find for him."

New York Times, Tuesday, Sept. 11, 1906:

Topics of the Times

SEND HIM BACK TO THE WOODS.

Not feeling particularly vehement excitement ourselves over the exhibition of an African "pygmy" in the Primate House of the Zoological Park, we do not quite understand all the emotion which others are expressing in the matter. Still, the show is not exactly a pleasant one, and we do wonder that the Director did not foresee and avoid the scoldings now aimed in his direction. Ota Benga, according to our information, is a normal specimen of his race or tribe, with a brain as much developed as are those of its other members. Whether they are held to be illustrations of arrested development, and really closer to the anthropoid apes than the other African savages, or whether they are viewed as the degenerate descendants of ordinary negroes, they are of equal interest to the student of ethnology, and can be studied with profit. The display now making, however, does not lend itself well to scientific purposes, but only gratifies an idle curiosity and a rather brutal sense of humor, and can therefore be criticised with reason.

The object of it, no doubt, is to attract a crowd to the park and to increase the patronage of those holding "privileges" there—an object in itself innocent enough, but in this instance attained in a tactless way. Dr. Verner's purpose in lending his little protégé is presumably that which leads the menagerie to make similar loans of lions and other beasts—the purpose of getting free keep for them until a more convenient season comes around.

As for Benga himself, he is probably enjoying himself as well as he could anywhere in his country, and it is absurd to make moan over the imagined humiliation and degradation he is suffering. The pigmies are a fairly efficient people in their native forests with enough intelligence to be successful hunters and to secrete themselves from hostile—that is, other—tribes, but they are very low in the human scale, and the suggestion that Benga should be in a school instead of a cage ignores the high probability that school would be a place of torture to him and one from which he could draw no advantage whatever. The idea that men are all much alike except as they have had or lacked opportunities for getting an education out of books is now far out of date. With training carefully adapted to his mental limitations, this pigmy could doubtless be taught many things of use too him as a tolerated member of a civilized community, but there is no chance he could learn anything in an ordinary school. It must be remembered that he is not a child, but an adult, long past the receptive age. The best place for him is probably his native forest. His life is likely to be short and unhappy out of it, however tenderly he may be treated.

New York Daily Tribune, Tuesday, Sept. 11, 1906:

Negro Clergy Protest

DISPLEASED AT EXHIBITION OF BUSHMAN IN MONKEY HOUSE.

The [New York] Evening Post, Tuesday, Sept. 11, 1906:

No Aid From M'Clellen

Mayor "Too Busy" to See Committee of Colored Men

THEY VISITED TO PROTEST AGAINST THE PUBLIC EXHIBITION OF A NEGRO DWARF IN THE MONKEY HOUSE AT THE ZOOLOGICAL PARK—THE DELEGATION TOLD BY A SUBORDINATE TO COMPLAIN TO THE NEW YORK ZOOLOGICAL SOCIETY.

The committee appointed by the negroes of the city to protest to Mayor McClennan about the exhibition in the primate house of the New York Zoological Society in Bronx Park of Ota Benga, an African dwarf, called at the city Hall to-day, but the mayor referred them to the New York Zoological Society. One of the committee, the Rev. J. H. Gordon, superintendent of the Howard Orphan Asylum in Brooklyn, declared, while waiting to see that Mayor:

"If Mayor McClennan won't see us it certainly won't do him any good."

The mayor excused himself from seeing the delegation on the plea that he was too busy. He had his secretary write the following note: "The mayor directs me to acknowledge your letter of this date, and to say in reply that the conduct of the Bronx Zoological Park rests with the New York Zoological Society. His Honor suggests that you bring your complaint to the attention of the society."

New York Times, Wednesday, Sept. 12, 1906:

THE MAYOR WON'T HELP TO FREE CAGED PYGMY

HE REFERS NEGRO MINISTERS TO THE ZOOLOGICAL SOCIETY

CROWD ANNOYS THE DWARF

FAILING TO GET ACTION FROM OTHER SOURCES THE COMMITTEE WILL ASK THE COURTS TO INTERFERE.

After having been refused an interview by the Mayor, the committee of colored Baptist ministers which wants to have Ota Benga, the African pygmy, relieved from what they regard as the degradation of appearing in a monkey cage at the Bronx Zoological Park, consulted a lawyer yesterday with a view to obtaining the dwarf's release by legal means. Supt. J. H. Gordon of the Howard Colored Orphan Asylum in Brooklyn, who is Chairman of the committee, said that the committee's chief desire was to prevent Ota Benga's appearance with the apes. They were also anxious to have the pygmy entrusted to their care, he said, to show that he could be educated. The committee later in the day visited Madison Grant, Secretary of the Zoological Society, in the hope of getting through him the custody of the dwarf . . .

New York Globe, Wednesday, Sept. 12, 1906:

THE CAGED PYGMY

Editor of the Globe:

Sir—I lived in the south several years, and consequently am not overfond of the negro, but believe him human. I think it a shame that the authorities of this great city should allow such a sight as that witnessed at the Bronx Park—a negro boy on exhibition in a monkey cage. If the park is so barren of interest as to necessitate such a degrading spectacle to attract the people I think the best thing to do would be to close the gates.

This whole pygmy business needs investigation. The facts are the Rev. Mr. Verner brought over eight or ten negro boys from Africa at government expense as an exhibit at the St. Louis Fair.

I was told by both English and Boer officials who were familiar with the different tribes that they were not pygmies, but merely members of a tribe of small negroes.

Mr. Fillis of the Boer War concession said that the reverend promoter could not have got into the pygmy country in the time given to the enterprise.

Another formerly scout and interpreter in the British Army said that he in thousands of miles of travel in the interior, had never seen a pygmy, and that one had never been captured alive; that the Rev. Verner's claims were absurd. These so-called pygmies were larger than the Igorrotes.

A.E.R.

New York, Sept. 12

New York American, Wednesday, Sept. 12, 1906:

M'CLELLAN SNUBS COLORED MINISTERS

CURTLY REFUSES TO RECEIVE PROTEST AGAINST EXHIBITION OF MAN IN APE CAGE.

On the pleas of "too busy" and "no jurisdiction," the "Mayor" yesterday refused to see the committee of negro clergymen, who called upon him to request that the exhibitions of the African pigmy in the monkey cage at the Bronx Zoo be stopped.

After a long wait, the Rev. J. H. Gordon, chairman of the committee, was handed a note in reply to one which he had sent into the "Mayor" in which that dignitary, through his secretary, declared that the conduct of the Zoological Park rested entirely with the New York Zoological Society.

Mr. Gordon then sent in a letter of introduction from the Rev. R. S. MacArthur of the Calvary Baptist Church. The letter explained the nature of the exhibition, in which Ota Benga, an African pigmy, has been shown in the monkey cage, and protested against its continuance. The "Mayor" begged to be excused on the ground that he was "too busy."

The members of the committee, which was appointed by the General Baptist Conference, were highly indignant. They next called on Madison Grant, secretary of the Zoological Society, but no promise that the exhibitions would be discontinued could be obtained.

Later the committee secured legal advice from Wilford W. Smith, of No. 150 Nassau street.

If further appeals fail, suit may be instituted at once against the Zoo authorities.

New York Times, Thursday, Sept. 13, 1906:

OTA BENGA HAVING A FINE TIME

A VISITOR AT THE ZOO FINDS NO REASON FOR PROTESTS ABOUT THE PYGMY.

To the Editor of the New York Times:

I saw the pigmy on exhibition, and must frankly state that the storm of indignation which some well-meaning clergymen are trying to raise around it is absurd. The unprejudiced observer cannot possibly get the impression that there is in the exhibition any element implying the slightest reflection upon human nature or the colored race. It is far from suggesting—as these good clergymen did so hastily suggest—that the presence of a chimpanzee with the African is intended to "show" a close relation or remote parentage between a human and an animal being. Physically and otherwise this African is not a representative of the lowest savage.

The clergymen's error arises from the unreflected use of a word—the word "cage." The pygmy is in a cage. This so-called cage is a vast room, a sort of balcony in the open air, where the numerous visitors may observe the African guest while breathing the fresh air. Dressed like a New Yorker, he is there, and goes out of the cage once in a while and comes back, swings himself, counts his money, plays with the chimpanzee, fixes his arrow, all the time good-humored, cheerful, happy, manifesting not the slightest consciousness of being in an undesirable situation. His childlike ways and broken English are very pleasing, and the visitors find him the best of good fellows.

It is a pity that Dr. Hornaday does not introduce the system of short lectures or talks in connections with such exhibitions. This would emphasize the scientific character of the service, enhance immeasurably the usefulness of the Zoological Park to our public in general, and help our clergymen to familiarize themselves with the scientific point of view so absolutely foreign to many of them.

M.S. Gabriel, M.D.
New York, Sept. 12, 1906

New York Times, Sept. 12, 13, or 14, 1906:

TOPICS OF THE TIMES

THE PIGMY IS NOT THE POINT.

Mr. Hornaday [Director of the Zoological Society] seems to have been little disturbed by the indignant comments which his exhibition of an African homunculus [sic] in rather close association with his big monkeys has excited, but the chances are that he will soon find it judicious to heed them and close this part of his show. The question whether there is any real and intrinsic harm in thus grouping the pigmy with animals held by so many to be nearly related to us all is not the one at issue. As to that, the Director has as good right to an opinion as anybody else, but if what he is doing offends certain members of the clergy for one reason, and a considerable number of our lay citizens for another, he, as the head of what is in effect a public institution, is under some obligation to abate the offense.

And apparently it does. To be sure, the expressions of horror and rage are sometimes laboriously emitted, and they are justified by eloquence which deals little with fact and much with fancy, but there is some sincerity in it all, and we do not know of any measurable benefits to science that will accrue from the continued display of Ota Benga as the playmate of an orang-outang. Not a few people are coming to look sourly on menageries, anyhow, and to wonder if they are worth while. Those who believe in them, therefore, should be particularly careful to respect the public's sensibilities, and to heed its opinions and even its prejudices.

It is amusing to note that one reverend colored brother objects to this curious exhibition on the ground that it is an impious effort to lend credibility to Darwin's dreadful theories. To find that there are still alive those who do not accept the greatest of generalizations as a matter of course is now almost as startling as it was in our grandfather's day to find any respectable person who did. The reverend colored brother should be told that evolution, in one form or another, is now taught in the text books of all the schools, and that it is no more debatable than the multiplication table.

New York Times, Sunday, Sept. 16, 1906: Photo section:

(A FULL FRONTAL PORTRAIT OF OTA BENGA IN SKIRT, BAREFOOT AND SHIRTLESS WITH A LARGE CLUB-LIKE STICK STANDING IN FRONT OF A TREE HOLDING A CHIMPANZEE) THE CAPTION UNDER THE PHOTOGRAPH:

Ota Benga

The African pigmy, and the monkey, which have been on exhibition in Bronx Park.
(Photo by Courtesy of N.Y. Zoological Society.)

New York Daily Tribune, Sunday, Sept. 16, 1906:

ESCAPED THE GRIDIRON

PYGMY MAN SAVED FROM CANNIBALS VISITS NEW YORK.

The exhibition of an African pygmy in the same cage with an orang-outang at the New York Zoological Park last week stirred up considerable criticism. Some persons declared it was an attempt on the part of Director Hornaday to demonstrate a close relationship between negroes and monkeys. Dr. Hornaday denied this. "If the little fellow is in a cage," said Dr. Hornaday, "it is because he is most comfortable there, and because we are at a loss to know what else to do with him. He is in no sense a prisoner, except that no one would say it was wise to allow him to wander around the city without some one having and eye on him. Talk of his being the so-called 'missing link' is an absurdity, for he has much more sense than many a white man I have met. If there is a sign on the cage it is only because without it some one would be kept busy all day long answering questions."

Meanwhile the subject of all the discussion, Ota Benga by name, seems to be exceedingly happy. He spends a great deal of his time at weaving materials which are given him into baskets and nets, in which he is most skillful. His particular chum is Dohong, an orang-outang of prepossessing countenance and no race prejudice. [Photograph of Ota Benga: a full frontal portrait of Ota Benga in skirt, barefoot and shirtless with a large club-like stick standing in front of a tree holding a Chimpanzee. The photograph is the same as appeared in the New York Times on the same day (see above) but with sides cropped to fit it into a column. The Caption under the photograph read:]

OTA BENGA, AFRICAN PYGMY

Considerable criticism was aroused last week
when Ota was placed on exhibition at the New
York Zoological Park in a cage with an orang-
outang.

Ota Benga was brought to this country by Samuel P. Verner, an African explorer and collector, who found him in 1904 on one of the southern tributaries of the Congo, a captive in the hands of a tribe of cannibals. It seems that this tribe had invited Mr. Verner to a feast, and in order to whet his appetite showed him Ota Benga—shining and fat, and in the very pink of condition for roasting. From motives of humanity Mr. Verner offered to purchase him. The tribe expressed surprise. Would not a thin man do? Why take Ota Benga (whose plumpness bore witness to the good treatment he had received) from the very mouths of his loving friends? But Mr. Verner would not listen, and the upshot of it was that Ota Benga escaped the fire to visit New York.

Although he is less than five feet tall and less than twenty-three years old, Ota has been twice married and twice left a widower. His first wife excited the hunger of the rest of the tribe, and one day when Ota returned from hunting he learned that she has passed quietly away just before luncheon and that there was not so much as a sparerib for him. The loss of his second wife was occasioned by her stepping on the head of a poisonous snake.

He is devoted to Mr. Verner, but his English vocabulary is limited to about 100 words.

New York World, Sunday, Sept. 16, 1906:

OTA BENGA SAYS CIVILIZATION IS ALL WITCHCRAFT

ON EXHIBITION AT THE NEW YORK ZOOLOGICAL PARK, IN BRONX, HE RULES MONKEY HOUSE BY JUNGLE DREAD

WANTS TO GO HOME TO BUY HIM A WIFE

AFRICAN PIGMY ASSERTS NEW YORK IS NOT WONDERFUL AND THAT WE ARE ALL MADMEN

New York Journal, Monday, Sept. 17, 1906:

THE BLACK PIGMY IN THE MONKEY CAGE

AN EXHIBITION IN BAD TASTE, OFFENSIVE TO HONEST MEN, AND UNWORTHY OF NEW YORK CITY'S GOVERNMENT.

The gentlemen in charge of the Zoological Garden in the Bronx have again illustrated the foolishness of allowing semi-official busybodies to manage public affairs.

These men—with good intentions probably, but without thought and intelligence have been exhibiting in a cage of monkeys, a small human dwarf from Africa.

Their idea, probably, was to inculcate some profound lesson in evolution.

As a matter of fact, the only result achieved has been to hold up to scorn the African race, which deserves at least sympathy and kindness from the whites of this country, after all the brutality it has suffered here . . .

It is shameful and disgusting that the misfortune, the physical deficiency, of a human being, created by the same Force that put us all here and endowed with the same feelings and the same soul, should be locked in a cage with monkeys and be made a public mockery.

It is an absolutely shameful disgrace to every man in any way connected with it, and this newspaper indorses most earnestly the action of clergymen and other of the Afro-American race in protesting so vigorously against it.

New York Sun, Monday, Sept. 17, 1906:

ZOO HAS A PYGMY TOO MANY

DOES ANYBODY WANT THIS ORPHAN BOARDER?

HE DOES NOT BITE, HE DOES NOT VOTE, HIS MANNERS, THOUGH VARIOUS, ARE MILD—PROF. VERNER, AFRICAN TRAVELLER, WHY DON'T YOU COME AND GET HIM?

"Wanted—a benevolent, middle aged person that would like to adopt an intelligent Congo pygmy; mild mannered, clean; does not bite. Apply at once to—"

Director Hornaday of the New York Zoological Park out in the Bronx suddenly bit his pipestem hard and leapt from his chair. His pen fell from his fingers and the advertisement lay blotted and unfinished before him.

For a bound of a gurgle of delight Ota Benga jumped through the door of Director Hornaday's office and began to hang his grass rope hammock from the end of the curtain pole over to the knob on the director's filing cabinet. With a final hitch of the rope around the top of Director Hornaday's chair the Zoo's fine specimen of the African tree dweller kicked off his shoes, ripped off his pink and blue shirt and climbed into his hammock. He allowed one eye to peer unwinkingly through the meshes of the hammock at the director.

The reporter who had been standing behind the railing waiting for Director Hornaday to finish the writing of his advertisement and grant him an interview reached for his hat and laid a hand on the door knob.

"Oh, that's all right." interjected the director hastily, "We are getting used to this sort of thing. Just step inside and sit down over there by Benga and I will tell you my troubles."

The reporter preferred to stand.

"If you can find a certain Prof. Verner, African traveller and lecturer, for me," said Director Hornaday as he leaned back and ran his fingers through his hair, "I will bless you for all time to come. Now, this Prof. Verner left this untamed ebony bunch of bother on our hands a few weeks ago with the assurance that he would be a drawing card for the zoo. Anyway, he said he would come back and get him in a week or so and—"

"Boola boola-boola-boola," crooned Ota Benga softly in a delicate bass as he swung himself to and fro over the head of the director. He playfully stuck out one bare toe and propelled his hammock by getting an occasional leverage with that member on the mirror over the director's glass case of stuffed birds.

"As I say, he promised to come back and get this pygmy creature and take him away back to Congo or Timbuctu—the further away the better. And he hasn't come. And we don't know where to find him. And we are just about ready to take to the psychopathic ward."

The director's voice trailed away in a sigh of resignation. A deep voiced roar, drawing nearer every minute, sounded from outside the administration building.

"Where's the wild man? Did you see the wild man sneak this way? Hey, tell us where the wild man is!" The noise of the jumbled voices without grew deafening, and suddenly a face appeared at the window of the director's office, then another and another, and a great cry went up when one of the scouts, with face against the pane and hand shading eyes, announced that the wild man was swinging in his hammock over Director Hornaday's head.

"There's the crowd again," said the director, "Always the crowd; in the monkey house, through the lion house, under the trees by the wolf den—always hunting, hunting this African person."

"Rata-ta trat-ta-trat-ta-trat," murmured Ota Benga, gently swinging to and fro, unperturbed by the voice of the mob without.

Mr. Hornaday motioned for the pygmy to come down. He did, laying a threatening finger on an important button meanwhile.

"No, no! don't take 'em off," said the distracted director. "Put 'em on. (You see he's always wanting to take off his clothes when he gets excited.) Put 'em all on again and get out!"

The director hurried Benga into his shirt and shoes and hustled him out a back door in the woodshed. The crowd, believing that the pygmy had taken to the trees, ran shouting down the path toward the reptile house. Mr. Hornaday sighed.

"Here we are feeding and clothing this . . . [remainder of clipping torn and lost]

The North American, Sept. 17 or 18, 1906:

CIVILIZATION

A little episode at the Bronx Park yesterday contained the story of civilization in microcosm.

Ota Benga, the African pigmy, who is not here of his own volition, but has been thrown to the monkeys by external forces for the amusement of the most enlightened and advanced of races, was surrounded by a crowd of the inquisitive while he was wandering through the park. They pressed so close and were so importunate that his anger was aroused. This, of course, a big, strong crowd of stalwart Anglo-Saxons could not tolerate. They gave chase, and the pygmy, with a courage which his betters might have admired, shot an arrow, striking one of his pursuers in the face.

It was always so. For ages man has acted in just this way. We entice the backward race into our well secured back yard and tease it with straws or knives or laws. We become a nation of sociologists, look at the curious object's teeth, feel his muscle, prick his skin. We try to make him swallow a constitution, and wonder whether he can sit up straight when it gets lodged at a painful angle in his abdominal region. And if he is peevish or irritable—if he is so lost to virtue as to show signs of anger—our indignation begins to move us, and belike is soon lashed into a fury. And if he lets fly an arrow, there's an end of it. We say he has committed suicide, for we like euphemisms.

New York Times, Tuesday, Sept. 18, 1906:

AFRICAN PYGMY'S FATE IS STILL UNDECIDED

DIRECTOR HORNADAY OF THE BRONX PARK THROWS UP HIS HANDS

ASYLUM DOESN'T TAKE HIM

BENGA MEANWHILE LAUGHS AND PLAYS WITH A BALL AND MOUTH ORGAN AT THE SAME TIME.

"Enough! enough!" said Director William T. Hornaday yesterday, after he reached his office in the Zoological Park in the Bronx. "I have had enough of Ota Benga, the African pygmy. Ring up the Brooklyn Howard Colored Orphan Asylum. Tell them that they can get busy tinkering with his intellect. I'm through with him here."

This outburst came after the keepers had had their say and after they had told the Director of their troubles on Sunday. There were 40,000 visitors to the park on Sunday. Nearly every man woman and child of this crowd made for the monkey house to see the star attraction in the park—the wild man from Africa. They chased him about the grounds all day, howling, jeering, and yelling. Some of them poked him in the ribs, other tripped him up, all laughed at him. Then, when the keepers had caught him once again, they asked him how he liked America.

Benga has answered this question often lately, and like this:

"Me no like America: me like St. Louis."

New York Times, Wednesday, Sept. 19, 1906:

PYGMY TO BE KEPT HERE

COLORED MINISTERS WANT TO TAKE HIM WHEN GUARDIAN COMES

Ota Benga, the African pygmy, is to stay at the Zoological Park a few days longer. This was decided at a conference between Director and the committee of Baptist clergymen appointed by the Colored Baptist Ministers' Conference, to save Ota Benga from appearing on exhibition in a monkey cage, and if possible, also to get the custody of him.

The length of time he is still to remain an inmate of the primate house in the park is dependent on Dr. Verner's return from North Carolina. As soon as he returns he, Director Hornaday, and the Rev. James H. Gordon, the Chairman of the committee, will have another conference. The colored clergymen will then try through Mr. Gordon to get possession of Benga, so that they may send him to Lynchburg, Va., to be educated.

There is a hitch at present on the matter of signing an agreement. Director Hornaday, who is willing to give up the custody of Benga, is not willing to give him into the hands of the colored clergymen without an agreement that he will be delivered to Dr. Verner again when he wants him. That was the understanding which Director Hornaday had with Dr. Verner when the latter allowed him to go to the Zoological Garden.

Benga had a new guardian yesterday, a tall colored man. This colored man took no chances with the crowds. He kept Benga on the move most of the time, leading him into secluded wooded spots in the park, and waving the crowd back as he entered.

New York Times, Wednesday, Sept. 19, 1906:

OTA BENGA

From his native land of darkness,
  To the country of the free
In the interest of science
  And of broad humanity,
Brought wee little Ota Benga,
  Dwarfed, benighted, without guile,
Scarcely more than ape or monkey,
  Yet a man the while!

So, to tutor and enlighten—
  Fit him for a nobler sphere—
Show him ways of truth and knowledge,
  Teach the freedom we have here
In this land of foremost progress—
  In this Wisdom's ripest age—
We have placed him in high honor,
  In a monkey's cage!

'Mid companions we provide him,
  Apes, gorillas, chimpanzees,
He's content! Wherefore decry them
  When he seems at ease?
So he chatters and he jabbers
  In his jargon, asking naught
But for "Money—money—money!"
  Just as we have taught!

                              M. E. BUHLER

New York Times, Sunday, Sept. 23, 1906: [Editorial]:

BENGA

If the race of African Bushmen ever grows into a history, with its running roots of tradition and legend, the representative of their tribe now here and a thorn in the side of Mr. Hornaday, keeper of the Bronx Park animals, who never pretended to be a curator of pygmies, will come to the front and occupy a shining place in the story. He will be put forward as having gone forth with only his bow and arrows for weapons to do battle single handed with mighty nations; and there is no doubt that in the recital he will allowed to come off victorious, his enemies in number as the leaves of the forest flying before him as they before the autumnal gale. Since Benga, the little Bushman champion, with the aid of a string of colored Baptist ministers, got out of the monkey house, where the associations were beneath him, and obtained the freedom of the park to ramble around in, he has been in no end of scrapes, the last one calling a mob around him which he kept at bay with his bow and arrows till he had made good his retreat and taken up again a temporary refuge in the monkey house. The red-headed man struck with one of the pigmy arrows will no doubt have a shining place in the legend, his flaming finial growing in time into a halo against which the whole drama, transfigured and sublimated, will float like a sun-kindled mirage in the desert. Although Benga has shown himself in many ways to be no end of a nuisance, he may turn up a trump in the legendary scheme outlined for him, so that instead of resenting his shaft the red-headed man ought to exult in its puncture as qualifying him for a future place in what may turn out to be a particularly interesting mythology.

New York Daily Tribune, Wednesday, Sept. 26, 1906:

BENGA TRIES TO KILL

PYGMY SLASHES AT KEEPER WHO OBJECTED TO HIS GARB.

Ota Benga, the pygmy at the New York Zoological Gardens, the Bronx, made a desperate attempt to kill one of the keepers yesterday afternoon with a knife, and had to be overpowered before he was driven into his cage. Benga was in good spirits yesterday and allowed the children and other visitors to tease him as much as they pleased.

Several keepers came along and added to the sport by turning a hose upon him. He enjoyed this, and grew so boisterous that he finally took off nearly all of his clothing. The keepers hadn't bargained for this. Benga was advised to put them on again. He became furious and rushed into his cage. A minute later he was out again with a big knife used to cut his food. He ran at one of the keepers and tried to slash him, but the others pressed in, took the knife away and hustled him into his cage.

New York Times, Saturday, Sept. 29, 1906:

COLORED ORPHAN HOME GETS THE PYGMY

HE HAS A ROOM TO HIMSELF AND MAY SMOKE IF HE LIKES.

TO BE EDUCATED IF POSSIBLE

WHEN HE RETURNS TO THE CONGO HE MAY THEN HELP TO CIVILIZE HIS PEOPLE

Ota Benga has left the New York Zoological Park, in the Bronx, and has been installed in the Howard Colored Orphan Asylum, Dean Street and Troy Avenue, Brooklyn. There it is hoped that by association with the colored children and their instructors the pygmy may be civilised, so that when he goes back home he will be able to teach his people.

The teachers in the orphan asylum realize that they have a difficult problem, but they are hopeful of Ota Benga. He is in an institution where the inmates are children. Not larger than they, he is a man. The children are under thorough discipline, but Ota Benga, although he is as gentle as a child, is impatient of restraint.

Dr. J. H. Gordon, who is in charge of the orphan asylum, said last night: "Prof. Charles [sic] P. Verner brought the pigmy here this afternoon. He looks like a rather dwarfed colored boy of unusual amiability and curiosity. Dr. Verner said to him in his native tongue that he had taken him to the only place in the white man's country where they would welcome him for his own sake. His face lighted up and he asked the professor to tell us that he was pleased to be with black people and free from the witchcraft of the white man.

"Now our plan is this: We are going to treat him as a visitor. We have given him, a room to himself, where he can smoke if he chooses. We have not placed him with the children in their dormitories and he eats with the cooks in the kitchen. He has already made good friends with them. He has learned a surprising amount of English, and we believe he will soon understand not only most of what is said to him, but will be able to express himself. This will be the beginning of his education.

"We put a pencil in his hand, writing his name, as you would with a child. Then we pronounced his name, pointing to the writing. He repeated his name and tried to imitate the writing. That is a beginning.

"Prof. Verner has not surrendered his charge to us because he is under pledge to take him home. He brought the little man to us at our suggestion, and we are quite convinced that he has done all he could for the pigmy and that his treatment in the Zoological Park where he was put in the monkey cage, was not intended to degrade him, but rather to supply him with amusement until the professor could come back from a trip South. He is to be taken out for walks by the attendants and by me. We hope to arouse his ambition and to make him feel that he at least ought to know as much as the children."

Prof. Verner, who brought the little black man to this country from Africa, went yesterday to the Zoological Park, where he sought Director William T. Hornaday and asked for his pigmy. Mr. Hornaday was quite willing to surrender him.

Prof. Verner was much interested in the statement of John F. Vane-Tempest, who insisted that Ota Benga was not a pigmy, but a Hottentot. Mr. Vane-Tempest's belief that he had talked with Ota Benga in the language of the Hottentots struck Prof. Verner as perhaps of great scientific interest. He was of the opinion however, that Mr. Vane-Tempest was mistaken in his belief that he had made the little African understand him.

Ota Benga was allowed to say good-bye to the attendants, to some of whom he had become attached. He gave his arrows to them as souvenirs and the bow to the chief keeper.

New York Times, Sunday, Sept. 30, 1906:

HOPE FOR OTA BENGA; IF LITTLE, HE'S NO FOOL

AND HAS GOOD REASON FOR STAYING IN THE WHITE MAN'S LAND.

WON'T BE AN ENTREE HERE

BUT HIS CHIEF IN AFRICA MAY DIE SOON AND THE CUSTOM IS TO HAVE A CANNIBAL FEAST.

Inquiries made yesterday by a New York Times reporter regarding the health and progress of Ota Benga at the Howard Colored Orphan Asylum at Dean Street and Troy Avenue, Brooklyn, resulted in the discovery that the pigmy of the checkered career is confronted by a greater problem than was at first supposed.

Ota Benga, it was thought, had always a loophole of escape from the Zoological Park and exhibitions and asylums. That loophole was a return to his native land. But it now appears that Ota Benga would rather go anywhere than back to the tall palms. He has a suspicion that he would be made very welcome there: in fact, he thinks that the cannibal tribe to which he belongs has the pot already on the fire for him.

When he went back from the St. Louis Exposition with Prof. Charles [sic] P. Verner he found that he had no relatives left. He found, too, that the tribal chief was getting on in years, and that when he died there would be a few persons eaten to rest his soul. Dr. J. H. Gordon, who is in charge of the orphan asylum where Ota Benga now resides, says he understands that this cannibal custom is observed for the propitiation of the spirits that rule the destinies of Ota Benga's people. Ota, who ought to know, swears that he stands a good chance, of being one of the propitiations.

He admits that he does not like the white man's magic, and is not particularly enamored of a country where cars move without the aid of a yoke of oxen, but, on the whole, he opines, it is rather better than a country where a citizen may become an éntree without his consent.

Aside from that, however, Ota Benga is apparently delighted with the Colored Orphan Asylum. He prefers it to the Zoo. He is getting a new suit of clothes to-day and already received a dollar watch. He can shake hands and say "How de do!" in accents so startlingly positive that one is tempted to make a further remark.

New York Daily Tribune, Wednesday, Oct. 3, 1906:

OTA BENGA AT HIPPODROME

PYGMY MEETS HIS OLD FRIEND, THE BABY ELEPHANT, GIVING OUT PROGRAMMES.

Ota Benga, the African pygmy who was brought to this country by Dr. Samuel P. Verner, and who until recently was exhibited in a cage at the New York Zoological Gardens, took his first step toward civilization yesterday afternoon, when he saw the performance at the Hippodrome. He was escorted by Dr. J. H. Gordon, superintendent of the Howard Colored Orphan Asylum, of Brooklyn, where Ota is at present endeavoring to learn his alphabet and the virtues and vices of the United States.

Ota had his first automobile ride in going to the Hippodrome, and, while he was all smiles over that experience, it was nothing compared to his delight when he entered the lobby and saw the baby elephant distributing programmes. The audience was filing in for the matinee when Benga arrived. The moment he recognized his fellow countryman, the baby elephant, he gave three shrill shrieks and fairly danced for joy. Then rushing forward but keeping at a respectful distance, he muttered a great variety of unintelligible sounds that could only be translated as words of pleasure.

Benga was seated in a prominent box, and gazed in awe and wonder at "A Society Circus," and kept muttering and grunting throughout the performance. The dancing particularly pleased him. Dr. Verner, who joined the party said:

"The pygmies are great dancers in Africa, and I am not surprised that Ota found his feet going in ragtime when the chorus sang several of the numbers. Benga could easily give an exhibition of native dancing that would be very interesting."

After the performance the pygmy was taken on a tour of inspection through the Hippodrome, visiting the animal cages, the trained bears, the ostrich and every other feature of the big establishment.

New York Daily Tribune, Wednesday, Oct. 3, 1906:

A WORD FOR OTA BENGA

MR. VERNER ASKS NEW YORK NOT TO SPOIL HIS FRIEND, THE BUSHMAN.

To the Editor of The Tribune.

Sir: Permit me to correct an error in your issue of this morning. I was not at the Hippodrome with Dr. Gordon and Ota Benga at all. While I appreciate the courtesy of the management in giving the little African some pleasure, such as it was, really I have no time for the "Circus Society" or "Society Circus," whatever it may be.

I take this opportunity to ask the intelligent and serious part of the public not to believe most of the tales told about Ota Benga and myself and our doings. We were simply two friends, travelling together, until, for some inexplicable reason, New York's scientists and preachers began wrangling over him, and the peaceful tenor of our way was so ruthlessly disturbed.

If he survives scientific investigation, reportorial examination and eleemosynary education, perhaps he may rejoin me on our further travels, and be happy in the sunshine of the

Kasailand. At present, however, I can only disavow responsibility alike for the wonderful tales about him, as well as for the correctness of the notions advanced as to what is best for him.

I saved him from the pot and he saved me from the poisoned darts, and we have been good friends for a long time. I beg New York not to spoil him.

S. P. VERNER
New York, Oct. 8, 1906.

New York Daily Globe, Sunday, Oct. 16, 1906:

OTA BENGA NOW A REAL COLORED GENTLEMAN

LITTLE AFRICAN PYGMY BEING TAUGHT WAYS OF CIVILIZATION AT HOWARD COLORED ORPHAN ASYLUM.

"A, B, C! Boola—boola! Boola—boola." These are some of the strange sounds which have been issuing of late from the classroom of the Howard Colored Orphan Asylum, at the corner of Dean street and Troy avenue, Brooklyn. It sounds like "monkey talk," but it isn't. Indeed, the sound comes from no less a personage than Ota Benga, the African pygmy. Ota is now learning his A-B-C's. So far he has only got down to the letter C. After that he talks "monkey talk." "Boola" in monkey language means "skidoo".

Ota has changed very much since he shared the monkey cage at the Bronx Zoological Gardens, although little more than a month as passed since he was rescued from the companionship of a chimpanzee by a delegation of ministers, who placed him in charge of Superintendent Gordon at the orphan asylum, where the whole staff is now engaged in the very difficult task of making a "gentleman" out of the little black fellow.

Instead of breechclout [sic], Ota now wears real clothes and he is very proud of them. Whenever a visitor calls at the asylum Ota insists upon showing off his new clothes. They are "hand-me-downs" of gray worsted, consisting of trousers, sack coat, and waistcoat. When they were first given to Ota to put on he insisted upon wearing the coat and vest, but frowned upon the trousers until he was shown the mechanism of a nice pair of red and white suspenders. Now he wears the trousers for the sake of the suspenders.

Real Colored Gentleman

He has a watch, too, with a nickel-plated chain, and wears a gray cap. Besides all these trappings of civilization, he wears shoes and stockings and a shirt with a collar. The collar choked him at first, and the shoes pinched his feet, but now—well, he's tickled to death to be a real colored gentleman.

He has good table manners, according to the superintendent. Of course, now and then he tries to eat his soup with a fork. He says he can carry so much more on his knife than on his fork, and he wonders why the matron frowns whenever he uses his knife instead of his fork.

Every morning at 9 o'clock sharp Ota is in his seat in the classroom with several hundred other little colored waifs, and for a while he seems to be contended but when he takes a notion to leave the room he does so without formality. The other pupils must raise their hand and snap their fingers in true old-country school style before being allowed to leave the class. Not so with Ota. He just gets up when he feels like it and out he goes, sometimes to assist one of the porters with his duties, or to go down to the high wooden fence and peep through the wide cracks at the passers by at whom, alas! he frequently makes faces.

Likes His Own Signature

Ota can spell his name now, and write with the assistance of his teacher, although he tries to drink the ink between sessions. He howls with glee whenever he writes his name or finishes repeating the letters of the alphabet, and . . . [missing text] . . . suddenly surprised the reporter by jumping from the stool and going to the door. He stood there for a moment and showed his teeth in good-by. Then, as he passed out, he traced two numbers upon the door with his fingers. They looked all the world like "23".

Ota, they say, has a most ravenous appetite. The present cold snap did not faze him in the slightest. In fact, he rather likes it, because he complains that his civilized clothes are too warm, especially around the collar. He seems not to be susceptible to catching cold.

He's Still a Heathen

Since his release from the monkey cage at the Zoo his rescuers have been paying quite a little attention to his spiritual welfare. But Ota is a heathen pure and simple, and the superintendent says it is very hard to hold his attention long enough to teach him anything. Like Topsy, he seems content with his lot and believes that he "just growed," and never had mother or father.

He goes to Sunday school with the other inmates of the institution, but he does not seem as yet to have grasped the meaning of the singing. Now and then he will sing at the top of his voice in his own tongue the song which his people sang while gathered around some nicely cooked missionary who had been sizzling on the fire for several hours, and who was all ready to be eaten.

Ota was once himself slated to be the chief viand at the cannibalistic feast, but was rescued by Dr. Verner. It was in 1904 that he was found on one of the southern tributaries of the Congo by Verner, the African explorer, who saved the boy's life by paying a price in calico and beads.

At that time Ota was the son of a chief of a pigmy tribe, and he had been twice married, although only 23. His first wife was eaten by the cannibals, and his second wife died from the sting of a viper. He is now only four feet eleven inches in height and weighs about ninety pounds.

Wants To Go Home

He seems to have become perfectly reconciled to being just like any American boy now, and single at that. But he wants to return to his native state. Speak of Africa, and there will come an indescribable longing in the jet-blacked eyes and a sort of droning like the sigh of an alien in a strange land. He wants to go back to his native state, and, above all, he wishes to return to any country where it is not the style to wear "pants."

Ota, by the way, is only housed temporarily at the institution. Later on he will be sent to a school in the South, where his education will be completed.

[ALMOST TEN YEARS LATER]

New York Times, Sunday, July 16, 1916:

OTA BENGA, PYGMY TIRED OF AMERICA

THE STRANGE LITTLE AFRICAN FINALLY ENDED LIFE AT LYNCHBURG, VA.

ONCE AT THE BRONX ZOO

HIS AMERICAN SPONSOR FOUND HIM SHREWD AND COURAGEOUS—WANTED TO BE EDUCATED.

Ota Benga, the first of the African pygmies to consent to leave his native wilds and the first who ever elected to remain in this country, committed suicide recently at Lynchburg, Va. During his stay in this city he was employed in the Zoological Park in the Bronx. He fed the anthropoid apes. It was this employment that gave rise to the unfounded report that he was being held in the park as one of the exhibits in the monkey cage. The story, though denied, persisted, and Ota became the centre of a discussion in which the public became interested.

Samuel P. Verner, who brought Ota here in 1906, has retold the story of the coming to the United States of his protégé, and paid a tribute to the African as a man of native courage and resource. Ota Benga was from a settlement remote from that of the other pygmies who came here to go to the St. Louis Exposition. They came from the town of King Ndombe at

Wismann Falls on the Kasai. All of them except Ota were later returned to their homes and were content to stay there. Of the arrival of Ota, Mr. Verner said:

"When our steamship called at the confluence of the Kasai, where Commandant Loos of the Belgian Army was stationed, he told me of a strange little man in his settlement, who had been found by his soldiers as a captive slave in the hands of the cannibal Baschiele, when he had gone on an expedition to stop one of the tribe's periodical raids into the interior. The Baschiele nearly always ate their captives, but Ota Benga was rescued and returned to the settlement. Very little could be learned from him regarding his tribe, for his language was different from that of other pygmies. Being an old-timer and knowing the pygmies at Ndombe, I managed to find out from him some facts which were later enlarged upon when Ota could speak a little English. It appears that his tribe was known as the Badi. In contrast with the pygmies at Ndombe, who were of the Batwa tribe. His language differed from theirs to a considerable extent though there was a great deal in common.

"When I asked him whether he would like to go to America with me, he said he would stay with me for a while in the Kasai country and see how he liked it, provided I would agree to let him remain behind should he so decide before we were due to leave. On these conditions he agreed to go with me further up the river to Wismann Falls, where the Batwa lived.

"When the palavers about the group going to St. Louis were under way Ota Benga urged the natives to go, and it was largely because of his influence that the trip was arranged. I got back to Ndombe and offered to leave Ota at the Belgian station below, but he would not stay. His own country was remote and his people were at war with the Baschiele, who were between them and the white settlements. Ota said he wanted to go to America, and with some misgivings I permitted him to come along."

The African pygmy liked this country so well that when the other natives were returned to their own land from St. Louis he decided to remain behind, and absorb the civilization of the white man. Mr. Verner urged him to go back to Africa, but he would not. He said he had left Africa because he did not want to be a slave, and preferred to die in America rather than endure the confinement at which his spirit rebelled. Ota also became ambitious for an education, and after he left the Zoological Park in the Bronx, through the good offices of a New Jersey Baptist association, he was admitted to a Southern school for negroes. After leaving school Ota Benga went into a colored home near where he received his education, and earned his livelihood by working in a tobacco factory. Finally the burden of the white man's civilization became too great for him to bear, and he sent a bullet through his heart.

"I never believed that the sort of education which seems to be the standard today was suited to him, nor did I encourage that educational experiment." said Mr. Verner. "At the same time I was not willing to combat his chance along that line, especially since his other friends sincerely believed it wise. Even had he gone back to Africa he might have fared no better.

"His country is now torn by war made by the white men among themselves, a war far more terrible than any of the pygmies ever waged. Between the impossible conditions of Ota Benga's own land and those which he could not surmount in ours, the homeless pygmy found no abiding place. Can we wonder that he gave up his little life as an unsolvable problem?

"I never understood his mental attitude but he was one of the most determined little fellows that ever breathed. Possibly he was trying to prove all the time that he was not a pygmy, as that term even in Africa always conveys the idea of inferiority. I never addressed him as one. To me he was very human, a brave, shrewd little man who preferred to match himself against civilization rather than be a slave to the Bachiele."

INDEX

277